August 2000

WAKEFIELD PRESS

# McLAREN VALE: SEA & VINES

23-50

- 2

Barbara Santich is a writer and cultural historian whose work has been published all over the world. Her most recent book, *Looking for Flavour*, was judged best soft cover book in the 1997 Australian Food Writers' Awards.

CW01095609

*Looking for Flavour, 1996*
*Apples to Zampone, 1996*
*The Original Mediterranean Cuisine, 1995*
*What the Doctors Ordered, 1995*

# McLAREN VALE

# SEA & VINES

BARBARA SANTICH

Photographs by Christo Reid

Wakefield
Press

WAKEFIELD PRESS
Box 2266 Kent Town
South Australia 5071

First published 1998
Reprinted 1999

Cover and text designed by Liz Nicholson, Design Bite, Adelaide
Typeset by Clinton Ellicott, MoBros, Adelaide
Printed and bound by Hyde Park Press, Adelaide


National Library of Australia
Cataloguing-in-publication entry

Santich, Barbara.
McLaren Vale: sea & vines.

Bibliography.
Includes index.
ISBN 1 86254 437 9.

1. McLaren Vale Region (S. Aust.) – History.  2. McLaren
Vale Region (S. Aust.) – Social life and customs.
3. McLaren Vale Region (S. Aust.) – Description and travel.
I. Title.

Promotion of this book has been assisted by the South Australian Government through Arts South Australia.

This project has been assisted by the Commonwealth Government through the Australia Council, its arts funding and advisory body.

# CONTENTS

## COLOUR ILLUSTRATIONS

# INTRODUCTION

Perhaps it is the coastline and beaches and clear, turquoise water that attract me to this area, that teasing flash of blue as I turn a corner or crest a hill. But I also love its Mediterranean qualities, the impossibly high summer sky, the parched brown summer landscape, the olives and vines and almond blossom.

This is a book about an area south of Adelaide, a mostly rural region between the Onkaparinga River and the Willunga hills which form Sellicks Hill Range. Circling round to the east and north to meet the river near Clarendon, these hills enclose the land as in a gentle maternal embrace.

I have chosen to call it the McLaren Vale region, the town of McLaren Vale being its geographic and commercial centre; furthermore, it coincides reasonably well with the area recently defined as the McLaren Vale Wine Region.

How could anyone not be moved by the beauty of this privileged pocket: the neat symmetry of vineyards, the sinuously meandering Onkaparinga, stands of stately red gums and boldly daubed cliffs? Constantly changing with the seasons, the landscape captivates and intrigues, whether the bold profile of winter-pruned vines or the whole vast panorama that opens itself to view from the heights of the hills.

The hills, for me, are the commanding feature. Each time I venture south, the first glimpse of these majestic and enigmatic hills, solid and stable and impregnable, inspires a sense of wonder. From a distance, it sometimes appears as though they have vaporised, their physicality magically absorbed into the sky. Later, as evening falls, they shyly allow themselves to be discovered, their mysterious folds and fissures gradually revealed before darkness overtakes.

But there is more to the region than its landscape, its coast and hills. A while ago, I began to immerse myself in its history, the stories of its early settlers, the planting of its orchards and vineyards. I became a silent spectator at the beach picnics and ploughing matches of the nineteenth century and toasted the new vintages at the Bushing Festival. Little by little my understanding of the region deepened, as did my respect for its inhabitants, past and present.

This book is the story of the McLaren Vale region, its fortunes and festivities, its inns and institutes, its wine, almonds, olives and fruits. *McLaren Vale: Sea & Vines* recounts the region's history and describes its present. It is an attempt to portray the cultural identity of the region, the way various generations have shaped its landscape and contributed to its culture through their buildings, celebrations, wines and foods.

I hope readers of this book share my experiences as they, too, come to know and appreciate the McLaren Vale region.


Barbara Santich, 1998

# END OF SUMMER, PORT WILLUNGA

It should be enough –
this one bale of hay,
rolled into a lozenge
of late-afternoon light –
its rightness
in the field
on the sea's verge.

It should be enough –
that single wave
slowly mounting
from the expanse of grey,
the sun torching
its leading edge –
But why does it cut
like a flensing knife?

Out there is a black dot.
It could be a seal,
or a swimmer,
or me,
thirty years ago.
Even if I swam out,
it would stay unreachable.

Behind the beach houses,
those dry hills,
the crinkled hide
of an impossible beast …
Just that colour
should be enough.

MIKE LADD

# CHAPTER
# THE LAND

At the crest of the hill above the Onkaparinga River, a summer vista presents itself: rolls of hay silhouetted against a blue sky and the sparkling waters of the Gulf St Vincent. All regions have images that belong to them exclusively, and this particular one is characteristic of the region extending from the Onkaparinga to the Sellicks Hill Range, and centred on McLaren Vale.

A little further down the South Road a vast expanse of vines begins, the vivid rows of regimented vineyards contrasting with the dessicated yellow of barley stubble. Completing the mosaic are dappled almond groves, grey-green olives and paddocks of pasture with occasional sheep, and then the sea, transparently turquoise. Beyond all this is the dramatic backdrop of hills, two-dimensional in midday's harsh glare, gentle and sensually curvaceous in the muted light of early morning or evening.

Around the end of March, with vintage under way, vineyard slopes exchange green for gold, with splashes of reddish bronze and deep claret. The first season-breaking rains of April or May cast a veil of green over the hills, which in misty winter take on a softer, more kindly face. Ploughed

# ONE

# AND

# ITS PEOPLE

paddocks expose rich textures of brown and black, and limed green poles marching across the landscape announce the conquest of vineyards. As winter progresses, yellow soursobs brighten the roadside, and soft white almond blossoms spread from the Willunga slopes almost to the sea.

Short-lived spring is tinted tender green and mauve as pastures and vines unfurl their foliage and Salvation Jane clothes whole hillsides, especially along Seaview Road above McLaren Vale. But with the first blast of summer the purple fades to brown, as does the green of the hills which, parched and bleached and massive, restate their role as a natural boundary.

This is man-made vista – or more specifically, a landscape created by immigrant white settlers over the past 150 or so years. Even the seemingly permanent features of hills, rivers and beaches have been modified by the impact of these colonists, through land clearing, water control and the intro-duction of imported flora and fauna. During the previous 6000 years or longer, Aborigines had shaped the land to their uses, at the same time defining it through their stories and their culture.

# THE STORY OF TJIRBRUKI

*This is a condensed version of the story as told to anthropologist Norman Tindale in 1934 by Milerum, who as a child had heard it at Yankalilla in the early 1880s. Tindale's spelling of the name, 'Tjirbruki', is apparently closer to the actual pronunciation, though today it is generally written as 'Tjilbruke'.*

One day some men of the Putpunga (meaning 'place in the south') group decided to hunt emus in an area to the north of their region, adjacent to the area of the Tandanja local group. They knew there would be plenty of emus as the emu was the totem of the Tandanja and not hunted. Taking part were Kulultuwi and his two half-brothers, Jurawi and Tetjawi, all nephews of Tjirbruki, a well respected member of the Putpunga group. Tjirbruki did not accompany them but travelled northwards along the coast, catching fish for his group to eat. On one of his brief excursions inland he found tracks of emus and hunters heading north, and the fresh tracks of a male bird which he decided would be his to hunt.

Tjirbruki pursued the emu as far as Witawili (Sellicks Beach), where he lost the trail. Meanwhile, the three nephews had killed and eaten one emu and were on their way back to Putpunga land when they came across fresh tracks and found an emu. Kulultuwi killed this bird, and they prepared an earth oven to cook it.

Attracted by the smoke, Tjirbruki arrived, annoyed that 'his' emu had been killed by another in contravention of the customary code; once one person had located an animal it was rightly his. He claimed Kulultuwi should have recognised his footprints. Kulultuwi apologised, saying he had not known the bird was his uncle's. Tjirbruki then continued on his journey.

The emu was cooked in a stone-lined pit, with water poured over the stones to make steam. Testing to see if the emu was cooked, Kulultuwi cut out the head, and was blinded by a sudden rush of steam from the beak. At this, his two half-brothers, who had been jealous of Kulultuwi's popular esteem in the community, speared and killed him on the pretext that he had

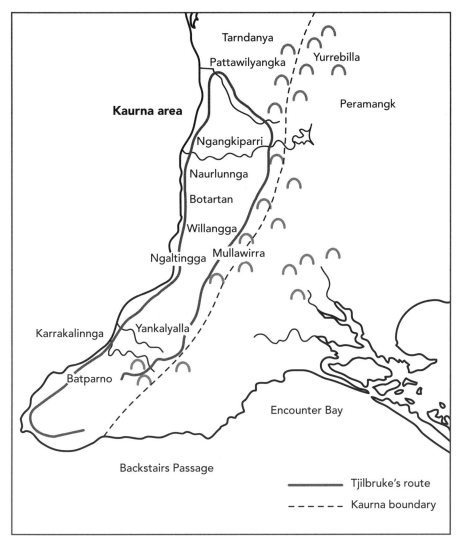

Tarndanya
Pattawilyangka
Yurrebilla

**Kaurna area**

Peramangk

Ngangkiparri

Naurlunnga

Botartan

Willangga

Ngaltingga   Mullawirra

Karrakalinnga   Yankalyalla

Batparno

Encounter Bay

Backstairs Passage

——————— Tjilbruke's route

– – – – – Kaurna boundary

Adelaide Plains before European settlement

broken the law in killing his uncle's emu. They took his body to Warriparinga (Sturt Creek) to be dried and smoked, in the traditional preparation for burial. To explain his absence they then spread a story that Kulultuwi, fearing his uncle's anger, had left on a hunt.

Tjirbruki went looking for Kulultuwi. He suspected that his nephew was dead, and later found where the body had been. Having collected some good spears, he arrived back at his group's camp, where Jurawi and Tetjawi acknowledged Kulultuwi's death but blamed it on people from another tribal group. That night Tjirbruki lit a fire around the sleeping group and, as Jurawi and Tetjawi tried to flee, speared both of them. He took Kulultuwi's dried body to Tulukudank, a freshwater spring (at Kingston Park), and completed the drying process. He then set off south with the remains.

As he rested at Kareledum (Hallet Cove), Tjirbruki burst into tears thinking about his nephew, and a spring welled up on the spot. From this site Tjirbruki travelled south with his nephew's body, and at each of his resting places along the coast – Tainbaran (Port Noarlunga), Potartan (Red Ochre Cove), Ruwarun (Port Willunga), Witawili (Sellicks Beach), Karikalinga (Carrickalinga) and Konaratinga – Tjirbruki's tears created freshwater springs. He continued to Cape Jervis, then placed Kulultuwi's remains in a cave below the cliffs, just north of the Cape.

Tjirbruki followed the cave underground to emerge near Mount Hayfield; the yellow dust he shook off became a deposit of yellow ochre. He then turned towards the ocean and arrived at Lonkowar (Rosetta Head). Believing he no longer had reason to live as a man, he smeared himself with fat from a grey currawong, tied its feather to his arm and began to fly. As befits a creator of springs, he became a bird of the wetlands, either a glossy ibis or a blue crane. His spirit continues in these birds.

Along the coast south of Adelaide, seven rock monuments mark the seven important sites of the Tjilbruke Dreaming. The first site is at Kingston Park, where John Dowie's powerfully symbolic sculpture, representing Tjirbruki carrying the body of his nephew, was unveiled in 1972. This commemoration of Kaurna culture was instigated by the Tjilbruke Monuments Committee, later reconstituted as the Tjilbruke Track Committee which has since become the Kaurna Aboriginal Heritage Committee.

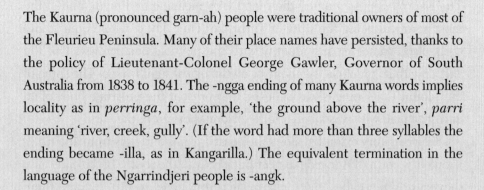

# KAURNA PLACE NAMES

The Kaurna (pronounced garn-ah) people were traditional owners of most of the Fleurieu Peninsula. Many of their place names have persisted, thanks to the policy of Lieutenant-Colonel George Gawler, Governor of South Australia from 1838 to 1841. The -ngga ending of many Kaurna words implies locality as in *perringa*, for example, 'the ground above the river', *parri* meaning 'river, creek, gully'. (If the word had more than three syllables the ending became -illa, as in Kangarilla.) The equivalent termination in the language of the Ngarrindjeri people is -angk.

Carrickalinga (karra-gadla-ngga) – 'place of red gum firewood'

Kangarilla – 'place where something was looked after'

Katunga (kata-ngga) – 'place of low thick scrub'

Mullawirra (east side of the Aldinga plain) – 'dry forest' (mulla means 'dry', wirra means 'forest, grove, bush')

Noarlunga (nurlo-ngga) – 'the place on the river bend' ('nurlo' means corner, or turn of a river)

Onkaparinga (ungke-perre-ngga) – 'place of the women's river'

Tartachilla (Tortachilla/Tatachilla) – 'red earth place'

Wangkondanangko (the Washpool, Aldinga ) – 'possum place' (wangko means a small possum)

Willunga (willa-ngga) – etymologically means 'place of dust'

Wongayerlo (Gulf St Vincent) – 'overwhelming water in the west' or 'place where the sun disappears'

Yankalilla – 'place of the fallen bits' (a reference to the story of Tjilbruke, who carried the dried body of his nephew from place to place along the southern coast)

# THE KAURNA PEOPLE

The Kaurna people imbued their land with meaning and myth, one of the most powerful being the story of Tjirbruke. They 'knew' their country, and their place names clearly identify with the physical characteristics of the site, or with its practical, symbolic or mythological significance. The spine of the Mount Lofty ranges was believed to represent the prostrate body of an ancestral man who was killed after attacking them from the east.

Their territory extended along the coastal plains and hills from about 130 kilometres north of Adelaide to near Rapid Bay in the south. In the early days they were often called the Onkaparinga Aborigines to differentiate them from the Encounter Bay Aborigines, with whom they appeared to be on reasonably friendly terms. Kangarilla seems to have been almost on the border of the two territories. The family groups of the area between Glenelg and McLaren Vale were called the Winnaynie; between McLaren Vale and Rapid Bay, the Putpunga.

Sand-bar at the mouth of the Onkaparinga (E.C. Frome)

The Kaurna had links with Aboriginal people further north, with whom they shared circumcision rites. On the the eastern side of the Mount Lofty Ranges lived the non-circumcising Peramangk people, whom the Kaurna seem to have feared and distrusted though they probably exchanged goods such as possum skin cloaks, quartz flakes and red ochre. While the Ramindjeri and Peramangk people knew how to start a fire using flint on iron pyrites, the Kaurna people relied on friction, rubbing together two sections of the flowering stem of the grasstree.

By all reports, the Kaurna were a relatively peaceful people, trading among themselves and also with neighbouring groups. Their land supplied them with adequate water and plentiful food. Before contact with Europeans they were probably quite numerous, but their numbers declined with the arrival of sealers and whalers who not only introduced smallpox and other diseases but also raided coastal camps and kidnapped Kaurna women. The last person of full Kaurna ancestry was Ivaritji, who died in 1929.

Like all Aborigines, the Kaurna people journeyed over their territory, following tracks well etched into their collective mentality and usually returning annually to specific places. The cycle typically reflected the seasonal abundance of certain foods, but it might also have been related to certain rituals. It seems that in the summer the Kaurna people gathered along the coast, taking advantage of the resources of the sea and estuaries, while still making occasional forays inland to collect additional plant foods. In autumn they retreated to the foothills where firewood was abundant, constructing shelters to escape the cold southerly blasts. They stayed there until the warmer weather had sufficiently dried the coastal swamps, by which time the fish were once again making their runs up the gulf.

Some camping sites were returned to year after year. According to Mary Maud Aldam (1872–1962), a descendant of one of the pioneer families of Willunga, the Beltunga gully behind Willunga:

*was the favourite camping place for the Natives, as many as 300 would arrive on their walkabout to or from the sea & would build their Wurlies of boughs or branches from the trees of the vicinity. When the fires were roaring at night the Corroboree was held. King John's tribe were a peaceable tribe who roamed the Willunga District from the Lakes to St Vincent's Gulf.*

King John was the name bestowed by colonists on Mullawirraburka, one of the first of the Kaurna people to come in contact with the new settlers. He was also known as 'Onkaparinga Jack', and acted as a sort of intermediary between the indigenous people and the whites, being appointed an honorary constable in 1837.

Ivaritji in possum skin cloak

Corroborees were also held at Toondilla on the flat banks of the Onkaparinga River, near the present Clarendon Oval. Different groups of Aborigines would assemble here before making the trek to Adelaide, via the coast, for the annual blanket issue. Initiated in 1840 in honour of Queen Victoria's birthday (24 May), this distribution of blankets and rations was an annual ritual until the late 1850s. Blankets and rations of tea, flour, sugar and tobacco were also distributed to Aborigines from police depots, including the one at Willunga.

Similar gatherings took place at other times, for the purposes of trading and arranging marriages (people were obliged to marry outside their homeland group). The red ochre from the cliffs near Maslin Beach was traded for mallee spear shafts from the groups of the Lower Murray, and for flint from Kingston, on the southern coast, while cured animal skins were traded with inland Aborigines.

# OCHRE POINT

Between Moana and Maslin Beaches are the dramatic cliffs of Ochre Point and the small inlet of Ochre Cove, one of the spots where Tjirbruki rested and wept, creating a spring.

Ochre was a valuable trading commodity for the Kaurna people, and was also important in certain rites. The palest, almost white ochre was used to coat the head during mourning, while red and yellow ochres seem to have been important in initiation ceremonies.

Just north of Ochre Point, near the mouth of Pedler Creek, are the remnants of the red-brown coloured sandhills of Moana, now protected as the Moana Sands Conservation Park. Stone hearths and middens – the inedible remains of meals enjoyed over 6000 years ago – have been discovered here, and also just behind Ochre Cove. Stone tools at the Moana site include small scrapers for working wood and microlithic knives. These were probably summer camps, summer being the migration season for mulloway; one Aboriginal informant reported that the older men used to watch from the clifftops for fish close to shore, and mulloway remnants were found in the middens. Aboriginal burial sites have also been found in the general area.

Around the turn of the century ochre was mined from the area and used to give natural colour to roofing tiles. From the 1920s sands in varying shades of red, pink and mustard have been quarried from the sand pits just behind Maslin Beach.

The intense and striking colours of these natural sands inspired German artist Nikolaus Lang to produce a series of 'masks' of the quarry face by laying treated fabric over the profile then peeling it off so that a thin layer of the actual sand strata adhered to the cloth. One of these works (from *Imaginary Configurations* no. 8, 1987) is on display in the Art Gallery of South Australia.

# LIVING OFF THE LAND

Essentially hunter-gatherers, the Kaurna nonetheless practised firestick farming, transforming what was once dense woodland into open grassland. Tjirbruki was known as a master of fire, his name meaning 'hidden fire'. From his ship in March 1802 Matthew Flinders reported seeing fires on the mainland. This controlled late-summer burning of the undergrowth, at a time when the annual grasses had dried off, served several purposes, the most immediate of which was the driving out of small marsupials and reptiles which were then easily caught. In addition the ashes fertilised the soil, and the new growth after the autumn rains attracted food, in the form of animals, back to the area.

The Kaurna people were unusual among mainland Aborigines in that they seem not to have used boomerangs, neither for hunting nor fighting. For men the principal tools, used for both war and hunting, were the spear and spear-thrower, club and the shield, made from either red gum or hardwood.

Spear fishing at Port Noarlunga, in E.C. Frome's watercolour *Old Whaling Hut*

Netting fish, *Coast scene near Rapid Bay, sunset* (J.W. Giles)

Spears were of two types; the fighting spear had barbs cut into the ends, while the hunting spear ended in a sharp point of tea-tree wood. The men threw their spears with the aid of small spear-throwers made from sheoak wood. They also had stone tools for making wooden and bone implements and for cutting flesh.

Spears were used for catching fish, especially large fish such as mulloway which could reach weights of 25 kilograms. Standing very still in the water, men would wait for the fish to come near and with one swift, accurate movement, stab them. In shallow waters fish traps, such as the semi-circular stone enclosure still in place on the coast south of Normanville, entrapped fish at low tide, making them easy to pick up.

Nets, some as long as 30 metres, were also used for fishing and hunting. When fish were spotted near shore, men would wade or swim out with their nets, enclose the school of fish and draw the catch on to the beach. Nets were made with animal tendons, or with bark or bulrush fibre, teased into strands then rolled into thin 2-ply strings that were knotted together, using a short stick or piece of bone as a needle. Fibre from the outside of bulrush stalks was spun into ropes and belts.

Large game such as kangaroo and emu were stalked – like Tjirbruki, the Kaurna were expert at recognising tracks – and cornered, then killed with spears and clubs. When nets were employed, these were set across the paths frequented by animals that were driven into the nets then speared and clubbed. The more wary emus were trapped at night. Swans, geese, ducks and other waterbirds were snared with a noose at the end of a long stick, or grabbed from beneath by an underwater swimmer and drowned. Burrowing animals were dug out with digging sticks (which were also used to extract possums from hollow tree trunks) or forced out of their hiding places by fire and smoke.

In accordance with the customary division of labour, men hunted and women gathered, collecting their foods and carrying them back to camp in net bags (though some would have been eaten on the spot). In terms of quantity and variety, the women's contribution – fruits, roots, nuts and seeds, together with eggs, shellfish, yabbies, frogs, lizards and other small animals – was more valuable, and probably more dependable. What they gathered varied with the seasons and the habitat, but with their intimate knowledge of the distinctive ecological environments, the Kaurna people made effective use of the full range of natural resources from coast and estuaries, gorges and swamps, hills and gullies.

From the coast came muntries or mantiri (*Kunzea pomifera*), sweet berries that could be gathered from the sand dunes in summer, and the fruits of the quandong (*Casuarina stricta*) and native cherry (*Exocarpus aphyllus*), all eaten raw. The young cones of the slender drooping sheoak (*Casuarina stricta*) suppressed thirst when sucked, and the leaves of the pigface (*Carpobrotus rossii*) could be chewed, raw, for their moisture or their salt content. Kangaroo bush (*Acacia armata*), which also grew in this environment, was valued for its medicinal properties. Lumps of gum on the lower parts of wattles were eaten raw as a sugar substitute, while wattle seeds were roasted and crushed. In the estuaries and swamps where reeds grew prolifically, the onion-sized bulrush roots were roasted then beaten between two stones while still hot, to make a flat cake; reed stems could be made into spears, the fibre into nets.

In winter and spring, the inland regions yielded a variety of roots and tubers – yams, wild carrots, wild potato, vetch roots and and the small, reddish, bitter-tasting bulbs of oxalis that the women would dig with their digging sticks and roast in hot coals. There was also the sweet, sticky berry of the mistletoe (*Amyema miquelii*), eaten raw in autumn and winter, and in summer the native cranberry (*Astroloma humifusum*). The blossoms of wild honeysuckle (*Banksia marginata*) were sucked for their sweetness or dropped into water to sweeten it, especially if it was unpalatable. Honey and a sweet sap were extracted from tussocks of yacca, also known as blackboy or grasstree (*Xanthorrhoea semiplana*), while the resin that exuded from the foot of the stalk and accumulated in very hard lumps at the foot of the tree was used to fasten sharp stones (and, later, broken glass) to the heads of spears. People chewed the young, tender leaves from the centre of the grasstree, taking care to remove only single leaves and not the growing heart.

The banks of rivers and streams were lined with majestic river red gums (*Eucalyptus camaldulensis*), their blue-grey trunks and hollow limbs homes for brush-tailed possums. Aboriginals ate the seed vessels of this tree after they had been soaked in water, but more delectable were the grubs which lived in holes in the trunks. Red gums were also a source of 'lerps', sweet scales of the psyllid insect adhering to the leaves, and of honey, native bees often making their hives in these trees.

Over one hundred campsites and middens have been found along the sandy coastline from Moana to Normanville. Excavations at the Moana sandhills have revealed small, shallow hearths, probably used to cook small food items over glowing embers or on top of a fine layer of sand. Kaurna people would have cooked cockles, pipis, abalone, crabs, small fish, freshwater yabbies, mussels and snails, and even snakes, lizards and other small animals in this fashion. There were also larger, deeper hearths that probably served as a kind of earth oven to cook larger animals, such as kangaroos and emus, as well as vegetables, effectively steam-roasting them. People would line the hole with stones, rounded pebbles of quartzite found in creek beds and on beaches,

Earth oven (G.F. Angas)

and light a large fire inside it; when the stones were hot enough, they would place the animal on top, cover it with grass and leaves, then place more hot stones on top, finishing with bark and earth. Hot stones might be placed inside the animal as well. Vegetables were cooked between layers of reeds or damp grass, and additional water would be poured in to generate more steam. A wisp of steam from the ground was a sign that the food was cooked.

Most animal foods required little preparation before cooking, unlike many vegetable products. The presence of grindstones, smooth pebbles used in the same way as a mortar and pestle, indicates that nuts and seeds – grass seeds, or the seeds of trees such as wattle and native box – were ground into a paste or flour to be mixed with water, the dough then baked in hot coals.

Food taboos applied to animal foods, these carrying more significance than plant foods. For example, people did not eat their totem animal. Dingoes and the forearm of kangaroos were reserved for fully initiated males, and young men undergoing initiation could not eat fish. Circumcision was associated with rain-making, and water with fish, therefore consumption of fish by a newly circumcised boy might bring rain, unwanted at a time of ceremonial activity. Young unmarried men were not permitted to eat fish or the meat of a female kangaroo, and possum meat was forbidden to women until after the birth of their second child. Grubs collected from the roots of plants could be eaten by everyone, but only adult men could eat grubs from the trunk and branches of a tree.

## THE NATURAL ENVIRONMENT

The landscape has been completely transformed over the last 150 years but the plant species that provided the original inhabitants with food, medicine and shelter, and that were later turned to good use by the newer arrivals, still flourish in isolated pockets and in the conservation reserves of the region. The Aldinga Scrub has preserved the original coastal vegetation, and Hardy's Scrub Conservation Park, Manning Flora and Fauna Reserve and the Douglas Scrub Complex, all in the Blewitt Springs area, present examples of virtually untouched bushland area. Hardy's Scrub, which covers an area of 155 hectares and is now part of the Onkaparinga River Recreation Park, occupies land once belonging to wine pioneer Thomas Hardy.

Manning Reserve represents the sclerophyll woodland of the foothills, dominated by autumn-flowering pink gums (*Eucalyptus fasciculosa*), their clusters of creamy blossoms a haven for bees, their branches sometimes supporting strings of native mistletoe. The understorey includes hakea, sheoak, wattles, tea-tree and yacca. Associated with pink gums on sandy ridges are messmate stringybarks (*E. obliqua*). These trees, also common on the higher parts of the Clarendon Range, could reach 12 metres in circumference and provided both bark and wood to the early settlers. Open woodland was characterised by grey box (*E. microcarpa*), blue gum (*E. leucoxlyon*), mallee box (*E. porosa*), sheoak and golden or broadleaf wattle (*Acacia pycnantha*).

The dramatically bare hills of the Sellicks Range may once have carried stringybarks, though their windswept summits were probably always bald. In the folds and gullies blue gum, pink gum and sheoaks possibly flourished before European settlement. E.H. Hallack refers to the clearing of timber from the hills that took place before 1892, and photographs taken around the turn of the century show stunted spindly gums scattered on hillsides now completely denuded. In recent years Landcare groups have been replanting gullies and sheltered slopes with indigenous flora, in part a restitution process but also for erosion prevention.

Among the many wattle varieties growing in this region, the broadleaf wattle, with its big golden clusters of flowers in spring, was highly valued by Europeans for its bark in the nineteenth century. The blackwood wattle (*Acacia melanoxylon*), on the other hand, provided timber admired for its wood-working qualities and its distinctive golden-brown sheen. Lesser known is the wirilda wattle (*A. retinoides*), which flowers in summer with small clusters of pale creamy blossoms. A hedge of these wattles has been planted at Wirilda Creek Winery, together with other flora native to the area.

Wildflowers were once prolific – native orchids, blue boronia – but today these are generally confined to the few reserves of natural bushland such as Hardy's Scrub, which in spring presents a spectacular wildflower display – shiny crimson flowers of the flame heath (*Astroloma conostephioides*), many different wattles and rare orchids.

# THE ALDINGA SCRUB

The Aldinga Scrub is the only substantial area of natural coastal bushland near Adelaide. It was declared a Conservation Park in 1985, under the control of the National Parks and Wildlife Service, after nearly 300 hectares of land were progressively purchased between 1965 and 1982. For Nancy Weisbrodt, who spent summer holidays in her family's shack at Aldinga Beach in the 1940s, the Aldinga Scrub was 'a special place':

The Aldinga Scrub

*Virgin bushland. In the Spring there were wildflowers everywhere and many kinds of orchids. I remember a large swamp in the middle of the Scrub. I came upon it one evening just as a flight of black swans was coming in to land on it. There were wild ducks, herons, cranes, all manner of swamp birds and in the evening a cacophony of frog songs could be quite deafening on the night air. Cape Barren geese would come to this place, too . . . The grassy paddocks with clumps of reeds and bracken were home to countless quail and the sky-larks could be heard every morning and evening. Hares, snakes, lizards, the whole area was teeming with wildlife.*

Many Aboriginal campsites and burial sites have been discovered in the Aldinga Scrub which, with its rich food resources and reliable water, could well have been a semi-permanent camp. In the nineteenth century wild ducks and geese and other water birds were in abundance. Mary Maud Aldam remembered wild geese regularly flying (in her words, in 'alphabetical formation') through Willunga to a lagoon at Sellick's Beach. Emus, possums and other marsupials were also attracted to the area, and the sea yielded a feast of fish and shellfish. Among the plant foods available to the Kaurna were muntries and quandongs, yams and the nutritious sporocarps of a silky-leaved aquatic fern, nardoo (*Marsilea drummondii*), which grows on the muddy edges of waterholes; once extracted from the hard capsules, the sporocarps can be ground into a kind of flour to be made into a dough with water and baked as a damper.

The two lagoons in the area, today known as the Washpool and Blue Lagoon, were both permanent waterholes, the latter originally up to five metres deep. Both contained fresh water, except when when seas broke over the protecting sand bar in winter storms and made the Washpool waters brackish (in early maps it is always shown as a saltwater lagoon). For the Kaurna people, the mud surrounding the lagoons, shrunken at the end of summer, had particular properties that made it ideal for curing animal pelts. This important annual activity earned Aldinga Scrub the Kaurna name of Wangkondanangko, or 'possum place'.

Kaurna people stretched out the skins and pegged them down on the ground, fur side up, then rubbed cold ash or dust over to absorb any fat that might exude in the drying process. When dry, they scraped the inner surface of each skin clean with slate scrapers; thicker, larger skins were made more flexible by shaving off the inner layers, while the surface of smaller skins was scored with a pointed tool. Small skins were sewn together into roughly square shapes the size of a small blanket, using bark fibre or animal sinew as thread and kangaroo bone or pointed stone to puncture the holes. They were valued possessions of the Kaurna Aborigines, who used them as both cloaks and rugs and also traded them with other Aboriginal groups.

# COLONISATION

Even before the arrival in 1836 of the *Buffalo*, bringing some of the colony's first settlers, the Kaurna people had encountered Europeans in the form of the sealers and whalers who worked the southern coasts. In 1802 French explorer Nicolas Baudin was investigating the lands and seas of southern Australia in *Le Géographe*, on 8 April 1802 unexpectedly meeting the English explorer Matthew Flinders, who was also charting the Australian coast. Flinders was inspired to name the spot Encounter Bay. The Fleurieu Peninsula is itself named after the Comte de Fleurieu, French Minister of Marine at the time.

In April 1831 Captain Collett Barker landed briefly on the coast near Port Noarlunga. In the wake of Charles Sturt's exploration of the River Murray the previous year, Barker had been instructed to survey the eastern coast of the Gulf St Vincent for any outlets from Lake Alexandrina. Travelling inland, he eventually came to Lake Alexandrina where, after swimming across the river mouth, he was speared by Aborigines and died. In 1933 a commemorative cairn to Captain Barker was erected above the crumbling white cliffs at Port Noarlunga, using smooth, honey-coloured stones collected from the Moana foreshore; the inscribed plaque was presented by members of the 'Gang Camp', members of the Norwood Cycling Club whose clubhouse was on the southern side of the river.

The Onkaparinga was again 'discovered' on 3 October, 1836, by Lieutenant Field, who was in charge of the *Rapid*. He reported it to Surveyor General Colonel William Light, who a week later sent someone to examine the entrance. According to James Hawker, who assisted John McLaren in surveying the region, the Onkaparinga River was initially called Field's River; he recollected having seen it marked as Field's River in the map drawn by Light. After Governor George Gawler's arrival in 1838, however, the name was changed to Onkaparinga.

The history of settlement in the earlier-established eastern colonies offered valuable lessons to colonists of South Australia, and the founding fathers preached an attitude of tolerance and respect towards the Aborigines. According to J.D. Woods, author of *The Native Tribes of South Australia* (1879), 'South Australian colonists happily cannot be accused of those dreadful crimes against the natives which disgrace the annals of the convict times in other colonies.' There were occasional murders of whites and consequent, sometimes excessive, retaliation, but not the bitter conflict and massacres that occurred elsewhere – though one possible explanation is that, within a short period, the Aboriginal population was so depleted, and so sparsely distributed, as to offer little resistance.

But while professing tolerance, the colonists could not help but apply passive pressure to the Kaurna people. When Europeans took possession of the soil, they deprived Aborigines of traditional foods. They fenced the land, preventing access; they shot wild game such as kangaroos and emus, driving them further away; their firearms scared away water birds; and the clearing of trees not only removed the possums' habitat but left little shelter for birds. By 1876 the Aboriginal population had been at least halved as indigenous peoples succumbed to introduced diseases and the disruption of their traditional lifestyle. The Select Committee appointed in 1860 to report on Aborigines seemed to believe that only 180 Aborigines were living in the Adelaide area, roughly from Mallala to Mount Compass, and east as far as Murray Bridge, though a later estimate by the Reverend G. Taplin in 1879 put total Aboriginal numbers for the whole of the settled districts, including the Lower Murray, at a minimum of 3500; at this time the white population of South Australia was approaching 220,000.

Some people acknowledged the opportunism of European claims. Dr William Wyatt, interim Protector of the Aborigines from 1837 to 1839, stressed that the authorities did not recognise (nor even try to ascertain) tribal boundaries and territorial rights. John Stephens, writing in his 'authentic and impartial history of South Australia' entitled *The Land of Promise* (1839), expressed fears that the authorities would take advantage of the Aborigines' nomadic habits to deprive them of certain rights, adding:

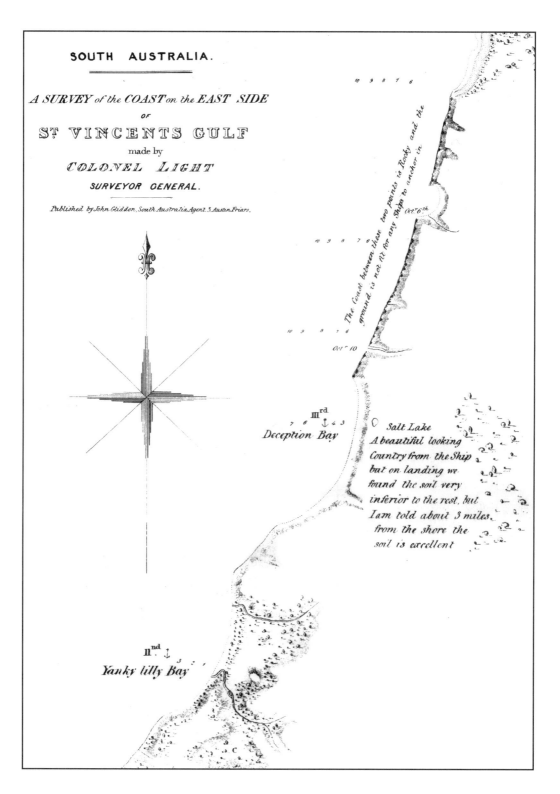

SOUTH AUSTRALIA.

*A SURVEY of the COAST on the EAST SIDE*

OF

ST VINCENTS GULF

made by

COLONEL LIGHT

SURVEYOR GENERAL.

Published by John Gliddon, South Australia Agent, 5. Austin Friars.

The Coast between these two points is Rocky and the ground is not fit for any Ships to anchor in

Oct 6th

Oct 10

III rd
Deception Bay

Salt Lake
A beautiful looking
Country from the Ship
but on landing we
found the soil very
inferior to the rest, but
I am told about 3 miles
from the shore the
soil is excellent

II nd
Yanky lilly Bay

*Although they have yet advanced no claim to any part of the soil appropri-ated by the colony, the colonists appear to have made very free use of the kangaroos, emus, &c., which, with Major Mitchell, and the commissioners, we regard as in all fair construction of natural rights, the undoubted property of the aborigines.*

Attempts to 'civilise' the Aborigines were meant kindly. The town plan for Willunga made provision for a reserve where Aborigines were allowed to camp near the creek. And certainly, many aspects of the European lifestyle were welcomed by Aborigines – though they took more eagerly to the foods than to the clothing. According to Mary Maud Aldam:

*The Natives ate She Oak Apples, Cranberries. Wild Peaches. Snakes, Cicadas etc and were very fond of flour, sugar, bacca when Settlers came to the Colony.*

Relations between Aborigines and settlers in the Fleurieu region seem generally to have been amicable. Many Aborigines became known to the farmers, and farmers were invited to corroborees. One of the early settlers of Kangarilla, Samuel Bottrill, is said to have learnt the Kaurna language. The tracking ability of Aborigines, which helped locate lost cattle and horses, and lost children in particular, was greatly appreciated. Aborigines were offered work on farms; in 1842 Charles Hewett employed thirteen Aborigines to help with the harvest. They were invaluable during the gold rush years, when many workers left the district. In 1852 they were paid one shilling per day, plus rations, to bring in the harvest.

From the beginning of the nineteenth century, however, the Kaurna were a threatened people. Even in 1839 they were outnumbered by the Ngarrindjeri people from around the lower Murray and Lake Alexandrina region. The process of resettlement on designated Aboriginal reserves, which began in 1850, further depleted their numbers. Kaurna traditions and culture are today kept alive by members of the Kaurna Aboriginal Community and Heritage Association and the Kaurna Aboriginal Heritage Committee.

# FIRST ENCOUNTERS

A description of one of the earliest encounters, within a few weeks of the first settlers landing, indicates that the 'foreigners' were more afraid of the natives than the other way around. John Bull, in his *Early Experiences of Life in South Australia*, reports that when horses went missing from the camp on the Sturt River, a small group including Nat Thomas, a sealer from Kangaroo Island and Hector, a kangaroo dog, set out to find them. Towards the end of the day they arrived at the banks of the Onkaparinga, where:

*smoke was seen to arise from a clump of honeysuckle trees, or Banksias, and a native camp was soon perceived ... Mr Allen and Alford were in great alarm on this their first sight of natives; and they exhibiting threatening actions, Nat also seemed disconcerted, and muttered, 'Full moon, come down to fish and hold a corroboree; they must be Onkaparinga and Encounter Bay blacks' ... Nat now explained ... that the black woman whom he had on the island belonged to one of these tribes, and he was aware that they were not pleased at her absence ...*

*At length eight warriors came forward with spears in their hands ... in single file, but in such an open manner that it was felt that they were not bent on mischief ... [The leader] stepped up to Mr Stuart, and first took from his head the cabbage-tree hat and touched up his hair, and then opened his waistcoat and shirt-front to examine his skin; then lifted up one of his feet and, like a vet, examined his boot. The others also had to submit to a similar examination ... They did not attempt anything until they discovered the sugar and salt pork; of the first they partook, also of the fat of the pork, which they devoured greedily. They were much frightened of Hector ... Having now satisfied their curiosity, one of them said, 'Cowie,' and led the party to one of their native wells, and then left them.*

*By the time the sun was getting low a bush tent was made ... Pots of tea having been made, as they were discussing their diminished provisions, two old women appeared, bearing on small sheets of bark a supply of fried fish, which was a most acceptable addition to their fare ...*

*All being tired an early coil was adopted, but before sleep closed their eyes musical sticks were beaten in time, and a blaze of fire shot up in the natives' camp, and a grand corroboree was commenced ... The men, as usual on such festivities, were adorned with white stripes on their faces and breasts, and down the arm and leg bones.*

The next day the search party gave the Aborigines, in return for their hospitality, some swans and ducks they had shot. Then they continued on to Horseshoe Bend, where they found signs of the missing horses, by this time well out of reach. The following day they returned to Adelaide:

*Many of the natives kept with them. On reaching the high land near what is now known as O'Halloran Hill, the* Buffalo *and other ships lying at anchor in Holdfast Bay were visible. The blacks who were in company expressed their astonishment by yells and dancing ... On the double party reaching the tents they were met by Governor Hindmarsh ... His excellency expressed himself shocked that Mr Stuart should have brought the naked black men amongst the tents of the numerous immigrants, and immediately called upon Mr Gilbert, the Government storekeeper, to supply the men with clothing ... The dressed-up black men displayed anything but comfort or content in their unaccustomed array, which on becoming apparent, the Governor, on advice, was considerate enough to order blankets to be exchanged for the unpopular garments, and the men soon retired greatly pleased with the blankets enveloping them, and rejoined their anxious and doubting families.*

# EUROPEAN INTERPRETATIONS

The same landscape known to the Kaurna people presented itself to the first Europeans. They saw it with different eyes, not so much for what it was but what it could become, appraising it in terms of its future and its economic potential.

In 1836 John (later Sir John) Morphett, having made two expeditions along Gulf St Vincent, reported: 'It is impossible to include the area of land on such an extent of coast under one designation; but I may say that by far the greater part is a rich light soil, wanting nothing but irrigation, during the four or five hottest months, to make it eminently productive all the year round.' He gave a glowing description of the Willunga Basin region, north of 'Yanky Lilly', where:

*the hills come down in a very bold manner to the sea, but soon recede again, leaving an undulating country for a few miles of a singular description. The different elevations have perfectly flat tops, are covered with a very nice herbage, and are much barer of trees than the hills we have hitherto seen [further south]. This portion of the coast terminates to the northward in a gentle slope, called by the natives 'Aldinghi Plains'. The upper part consists of the same sort of land as the hills, and would do admirably for sheep-runs in winter. The lower part is impregnated with salt, being beneath the level of the sea at spring-tides, and this imparts a brackish taste to the rains, which collect there during the winter months, and form a small lake ... The sloping grass-land in front, without a single tree for three or four miles square, of a beautifully bright green in winter and spring, and a golden colour during the hotter months, is surrounded by finely-wooded eminences, and by a bold range of hills beyond. To the north the country stretches for miles; it is of the richest character, and is so covered with so long and thick an herbage that it is quite laborious to walk through it. There are numerous woods, or what might be termed groves, of a very open description ... Here was a most luxuriant soil ... Sometimes the country is undulating; at others the view is bounded by boldly shaped hills ... It wants but water in its varieties of torrent, stream and lake, to make this part for many miles in extent the most beautiful that nature has created, or that art could improve. I have seen a greater number of kangaroos and emus here than in any spot along the coast.*

Exploring south from Adelaide in 1837, Colonel Light described the country around Hallett Cove as 'altogether adapted for grazing or agriculture'. Camping on the banks of the Onkaparinga a few days later he wrote:

*the country is not only beautifully picturesque, but rich in soil. I have seldom seen a place more inviting than this, and I have no doubt at some future time it will form a country town of considerable consequence.*

The following year Mr William Giles, the South Australian Company's agricultural expert, and manager of the Company from 1841 to 1861, travelled overland from Adelaide to Encounter Bay, visiting the Onkaparinga and Rapid Bay districts where he:

*found a beautiful black mould in the low grounds from two to three feet in depth, and on the hills the finest sheep runs. There is a singular feature in this country; namely, that on many of the high hills up to the very summit, we find a beautiful soil, fit for garden-ground.*

John Stephens, who in 1839 enticed would-be emigrants with a book entitled *The Land of Promise*, saw the pastoral potential of the region: 'this is beyond question a splendid sheep country,' he wrote. John Morphett agreed, remarking that 'the experience gained in the other Australian settlements shows [wool-growing] to be the most prudent plan ... [with] little or no risk'.

Being relatively lightly wooded, the land would have been easy to clear, and the natural pastures were very favourably assessed. Stephens described kangaroo grass as:

*the richest and most valuable grass known in Australia; and on it sheep fatten very rapidly. This species of grass appears in tufts from twelve to eighteen inches apart, and is superior to rye-grass, which it resembles. It is often as high as a man's breast.*

According to James Hawker, it was called kangaroo grass because it grew to such a height, though sometimes settlers called it 'native wheat'. He added:

*Colonists of the present day can have no idea of the wonderful length to which it grew in the rich valleys, where the pasture had never been disturbed except by an occasional bush fire.*

Beyond the economic possibilities, many early settlers appreciated the natural beauty of the environment while applying to it an English aesthetic. Mary Maud Aldam recalled with pleasure bush walks in the 1880s with schoolfriends:

*Mabel Hardy and Nellie Saunders and I spent a delightful day among the Bushland's natural flowers. Where lovely wildflowers ran riot, & how delighted we gathered them all; the lovely white and purple violets, the dainty Blue Bells, the red and yellow heath, the Scarlet Runner that went voyaging about close to Mother Earth. Honeysuckle and Broom. Quaint old Grasstrees, everywhere the Golden Wattle hung with gold ... The Hillside clothed with the dark bracken fern & in the Sylvan nooks and Gullies we'd gather the dainty maiden Hair Fern that grew in profusion, it was Nature's lovely Garden ... the yellow & white Everlasting too I must not forget were among the Great Bouquet we'd carry home those days.*

Not only did the colonists modify the landscape by deforesting, fencing, grazing, cultivating and mining but they also introduced new plants and animals; the soursob which at the end of winter colours roadsides bright yellow was originally brought in as a garden plant. They made different use of the land's resources, compared with the Kaurna. The bark of stringybark trees, which split easily from the trunk, served to construct huts or other temporary dwellings, while the wood was useful for fencing and paling. Houses were roofed with wooden shingles. Slabs from the huge red gums were used for enclosing gardens, or for post-and-rail fencing; red gum girders supported the first Clarendon bridge (1857) and red gum was also used for railway sleepers. In the late nineteenth century Manning Park winery had a press made of blue gum. Blackwood (from the blackwood wattle) was popular for cabinet work, panelling, gun stocks and furniture. Wattle bark was valued for its tanning properties.

The game eaten by the Kaurna people was also appreciated by the whites, whose firearms were efficient agents of destruction. The bustards or wild turkeys, said to be finest of the game birds, were soon virtually exterminated; the wild geese and black swans that inhabited lakes and rivers had become rare by the turn of the century. Kangaroo and emu populations were swiftly depleted. James Hawker, engaged to survey the area in 1838, was given leave 'for an afternoon when practicable to take two of my men and my dogs for a hunt' and managed to keep the camp well-supplied with kangaroo meat (which the men enjoyed, as long it was not served every day) and occasionally emu. He described the meat of the emu as rather coarse, but the liver palatable. One of the most popular dishes, he wrote, was the kangaroo steamer:

*being made of kangaroo meat, plenty of slices of fat salt pork, and flour for thickening, plenty of pepper, and, if procurable, some onion – the whole was stewed slowly over a bushfire, until it could be eaten with a spoon.*

Hawker also shot wild ducks along the Onkaparinga River. Pigeon, snipe, plovers and quail were said to be easy game and good eating as well. As recently as the 1950s quail abounded in paddocks of barley stubble in the region; according to Greg Trott of Wirra Wirra Vineyards, his grandfather used to shoot them to supply the governor's table.

While the pioneer settlers took to the area with enthusiasm and relish and, oblivious to the indigenous inhabitants, stamped on it their own brand of civilisation, at the hazy back of their minds seems to have been the Mediterranean ideal imagined by so many of the colony's leaders. Sir John Morphett wrote in 1836:

*The climate appears to me to bear such a resemblance to Syria, and other countries in the Mediterranean, that I have sanguine hopes we might raise such valuable products as wine, olive oil, figs, maize, flax, silk, rice, indigo, and tobacco.*

Quail Shooting party at Pirramimma, c. 1929.

# CHAPTER
# SETTLEMENT

South Australia was envisaged and established as a model, convict-free colony, founded on principles of democracy and freedom of religion. The South Australian Act, passed by the British parliament in 1834, set out the terms for land sales, the proceeds to be used solely to finance emigration of 'honest, sober, industrious' labourers, 'of sound mind and body'. These emigrants were to be young (over 15 but not more than 30 years of age) and carefully selected, their good character attested by an employer or clergyman. To attract men of capital, every £20 subscribed to the land fund earned free passage to one labourer. Between 1836 and 1840 over 12,000 men, women and children received free passages to South Australia, vastly outnumbering those who paid their own way. Over half of these emigrants were agricultural workers – farmers, well-diggers, shepherds, ploughmen.

Land regulations issued in 1835 set a price of £1 (20 shillings) per acre. This was soon reduced to 12 shillings, at which price the South Australian Company bought nearly one-quarter of the preliminary land orders, each entitling the purchaser to 80 acres of land in the country and one acre in the

# TWO

# AND

# AGRICULTURE

town. The South Australian Company, founded in 1836, thus became the biggest investor in the new colony. It offered tenants long leases at moderate rentals, with the option of purchasing the land freehold at any time during the period of the lease, at a price fixed at the time of setting the lease. A prospective tenant had to be presented with five portions of land from which one could be selected; if he was not satisfied with any he could, for a 'trifling expense', cancel the lease. By 1844 the Company had leased a total of 11,000 acres to 92 tenants, accepting wheat in payment of rent.

The survey of the land south of Adelaide began in 1838, and John McLaren completed the survey as far south as Sellicks Hill Range in 1840, partitioning the land into 80-acre sections. The survey method seems to have involved little more than laying a regular grid over the land, with minimal attention paid to natural features. Further, the minimum price of £1 per acre did not help distinguish between one section and another, which explains why it was important to inspect the land and assess its agricultural potential before making the final selection.

# FIRST FURROWS

In a letter to the South Australian Company dated 16 September 1839, land agents O'Halloran, Nixon & Co made clear their choice of land near the Onkaparinga River:

*... we will say first which we should select: Nos. 324 & 329, or 329 & 338 on the Eastern side; on the Western side for farming operations 328 & 337 or 337 & 339 or 339 and eastern portion of section 69. The soil of all these sections on the alluvial flat with the exception of the greater part of 69 is similar to that in the Horseshoe and that of the western part of all the sections on the western side of the Unkeparinga is of a hard brick clayey nature on which there is very little verdure.*

*Section 324: A first rate section in which many tons of hay can be annually made – beautiful site for a house: at the N.E. end of section a very high bank makes the road impracticable at present.*

*Section 329: A first rate section consisting of a beautiful rich alluvial flat on the Unkaparinga – the rampart lined with large gum or swamp oak – on the Northern side a gully runs in from the Eastward in which water can be procured at about 20 feet.*

*Section 338. The road along river for two hundred yards from the Southern termination of section is impracticable being perpendicular – thence to N.W. good – The Southern part of section rests on the Unkaparinga – it is precipitous along the bank for two hundred yards then gradually opens into a rich meadow flat in which are some large gum or swamp oak trees.*

*Section 339: S.E. a beautiful rich meadow flat; in the part nearest the river not a stone or tree to hurt the scythe – close to the bank from the high lands to the alluvial flat are large gum or swamp oak trees. S.W. a few gum, wattle, scanty herbage – the western part of section being a brick clay with rotten limestone. N.W. same as S.W. N.E. clear of all timber same as S.E. The part under the gum trees not much grass, the soil in alluvial flat same as in the Horseshoe – the road along the river is very good.*

Sections 324 and 329 were subsequently leased, the former to Samuel Clark who by August 1842 had eight acres of wheat, two acres of barley, one acre for his horse and two acres of garden. He fenced the section the following year, constructed a brick house, pig-sty, goat pen and fowl sheds, and sowed 26 acres to wheat and four acres to barley. Delaney & Co leased section 329 and within three years 11 acres had been cleared and sown to wheat, three acres to barley, maize and millet, and garden occupied another half acre. By 1844 the section had been enclosed with a 'substantial Kangaroo Fence', a wooden house had been built and 35 acres were under wheat.

John McLaren's survey of District C, 1840, showing Sections 324, 329, 338, 339

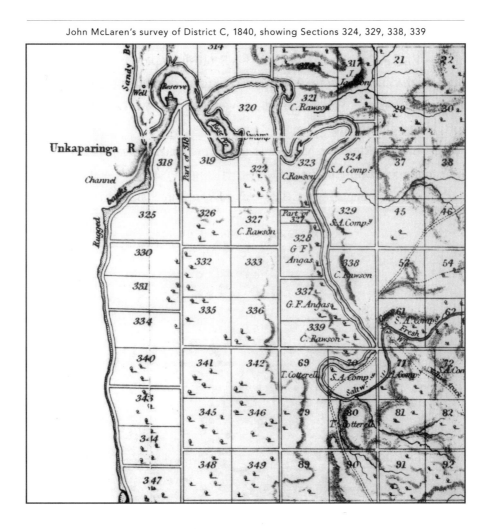

The changes in the landscape, over such a short span of time, were prodigious. The Willunga district, opened for selection in October 1839, was effectively domesticated within ten years. Described as level and fruitful, it had 'large tracts of wheat-land, whilst the hills are scattered over with cattle and sheep'.

In August 1840 the *Adelaide Chronicle* carried a report of 'the beautiful valley called McLaren Vale', situated a few miles beyond the Onkaparinga, where 'there are at present twelve settlers who possess stock to the amount of upwards of 2000 sheep and 200 head of cattle ... [and] about 70 acres under crop.' Among them was Lieutenant James McLeod, who purchased land in England and emigrated with his Scottish employees. He chose sections on the northern side of McLaren Plains, and towards the end of 1839 James Hawker wrote about spending evenings at the McLeod's 'very comfortable establishment'.

Just outside McLaren Vale, next to the present Dennis winery, a large ironstone rock commemorates the district's pioneers, led by William Colton and Charles Thomas Hewett. These two Devonshire farmers settled in the

A.C. Kelly's sketch of Morphett Vale, 1845

area a few months after McLeod, having arrived in Adelaide in December 1839 as assisted emigrants together with their families, employees, sheep, cattle and some machinery. They selected four sections of land belonging to the South Australian Company, and settled there in January 1840. By September of the same year they had sown eight acres of wheat and twelve of barley, and planted substantial vegetable gardens. They had also built houses for their families, huts for the men, outhouses, pig-sties, stock yards and pens. Blackfellows' Well nearby provided them with water, and until a church was built church services were held under a large gum tree in the vicinity.

In 1842 Colton gave a considered report on farming prospects in the area:

*'Corn [ie wheat], the great staff of life, grows well; but very little of the land hath as yet been managed as we have been accustomed to in Devonshire. The land hath not generally been half broken; we find, where the land is ploughed deep, and sown in season, the corn to grow long and strong, both in stalk and ear; yet it doth not corn as well as I have seen from some of the* BEST *land in England. But on the average, much better and more quantity than the general crops in Devon ... Oats have not, generally, done too well. Potatoes have been but partially good. I think we have but seldom broken the ground deep enough for the root ... With regard to cattle and sheep, no country can be better; we scarcely hear of a disorder in cattle.'*

In the early years success stories were not uncommon, though hard work was involved. Thomas Atkinson arrived in 1839, and within 12 months had 40 head of cattle, a dairy herd, several horses and an area of wheat. Some settlers were less fortunate. Edward Giles, who arrived on the same ship as the Colton and Hewett clans, leased part of section 69, on the bend of the Onkaparinga, from the South Australian Company in 1841. Three years later an unprecedented flood swept away his pigs and pig-sties, fencing and stockyards. The following year, threatened by a plague of caterpillars, he disconsolately informed the Company that: 'destruction of the crop is pretty certain'.

# REPORT TO
# SOUTH AUSTRALIAN COMPANY

From William Colton, Lower Oxenbury Farm, sections 136, 147,
9 September 1843:

(Colton's farm also went by the name of Daringa)

| | |
|---|---|
| *Wheat* | *53 acres* |
| *Oats* | *3 acres* |
| *Barley* | *1 acre* |
| *Garden stuff* | *1 acre* |

*Remainder grass pastrage.*

From Charles Thomas Hewett, Oxenberry Farm, sections 148, 135,
4 September 1843:

| | |
|---|---|
| *Wheat* | *39 acres* |
| *English barley* | *36 acres* |
| *Potatoes* | *1/2 acre* |
| *Maize* | *1 1/2 acres* |
| *Garden* | *3/4 – This I am planting to froot trees as I find hand labor is to much expence. I therefore plow in Pease Beans Cabbage etc in section* |
| *Pease* | *1/2 acre* |
| *Tobacco* | *1 1/2 acres* |
| *Sweeds* | *4 acres* |
| *Melons* | *2* |

*a little flax seed all I could get*

*Section 148 hath excellent surface water all the year for house and five Hundred cattle & sheep.*

*Section 135 Water in well, constant, 10 feet deep.*

*Dwelling House 50 ft by 20 ft Brick built slate cover'd*

*Barn 40 ft by 15 ft Brick built thatch cover'd*

*Brick sufficient to build another Barn before harvest and Laborers Cottage*

*One Hundred acres fenced*

# WHEAT-SICKNESS

In his *Working Man's Handbook to South Australia*, written in the late 1840s, George Wilkinson described the 'simplicity of farming operations' which required 'no study at an agricultural college to learn it, [nor] even any elaborate knowledge of the succession of crops'. To begin with, he wrote:

*the land is cleared, if necessary ... when the wet season has commenced, ploughing begins, and as many acres as are required are broken up: once ploughing is all the land generally gets. Seed is then sown broad-cast, and well scratched in by heavy harrows ... By the time the blade appears above the soil, the fencing should be completed, to prevent the cattle from intruding. That is all that is done until the grain has ripened and needs cutting.*

In the early years even such crude farming practices yielded good crops. In 1839 South Australia had 400 acres under crop; three years later 12,000 acres were sown. The invention in 1843 of John Ridley's stripper, a machine that reaped and threshed in one operation, made wheat farming an even more attractive proposition. Using a stripper, 125 acres could be reaped in a day, while manual labour could cut only one acre a day. In that year the South Australian harvest produced twice as much as people could eat, and the colony's first grain export was 260 bags of flour sent to Perth.

By 1846, 800,000 acres had been surveyed, 460,000 acres sold, and 35,000 acres were under wheat. South Australia was exporting around three-quarters of its wheat harvest, mainly to other colonies.

The McLaren Vale region shared in this prosperity. Between 1841 and 1844 the area cleared and cultivated expanded rapidly, the crop acreage increasing more than 30-fold. The District Council of Willunga had 6716 acres of land under cultivation by 1861, six times as much as in 1844. In 1863 almost 85 per cent of wheat in the Willunga District Council area was harvested by machine.

Construction of steam flour mills had begun in the 1840s, and soon there were mills at Aldinga (White's and Butterworth's); at McLaren Vale

(Leonard's and Mortlock's Mill, both later owned by Samuel White); at Willunga and at Noarlunga. Flat-bottomed barges transported flour and wheat from Noarlunga along the Onkaparinga, still tidal in this stretch, to ships at Port Noarlunga where a jetty was built in 1855. By 1861 a thriving export trade in both wheat and flour made Port Willunga, where the first jetty was completed in 1854, the second busiest port in the colony after Port Adelaide.

The Onkaparinga at Noarlunga, 1929; old flour mill on left

As early as 1858 the journal *Farm and Garden* warned that continuous wheat cropping exhausted the soil and suggested measures to prevent what became known as 'wheat sickness'. The problem was exacerbated by the loss of nutrients such as phosphate and nitrogen, leached out by rains which fell predominantly in the winter months. In the County of Adelaide the ten-year average wheat yield fell by 25 per cent from the 1860s to the 1870s, and by 1880 the area under wheat was only half what it had been ten years previously. In the McLaren Vale region wheat production never again reached the heights of the 1860s and in 1874 only four ships loaded cargo at the Port Willunga jetty, compared with an average of 31 vessels per year between 1861 and 1867. In any case, railways were a cheaper means of transport for agricultural produce and gave an advantage to northern regions (the extension of the northern line to Kapunda was completed in 1860, to Burra in 1870). Many farmers sold their land and migrated to the newly-opened farming lands north of Gawler and, in the 1890s, to the Victorian Wimmera.

The Willunga flour mill had a new lease of life in 1869 as a flax mill, but this phase of activity was brief and the mill itself was accidentally burnt down soon afterwards. It was many years before the cause of this fire was revealed – a couple of boys, hiding from parental eyes to smoke dried gum roots at the back of the mill, tossed away a butt that set alight a pile of teased flax, flames quickly spreading through the building.

Mortlock's mill, which operated into the 1870s, is now part of Hardys Tintara Winery, having been purchased by Thomas Hardy in 1878; the Dridan Fine Arts gallery occupies the lowest level where sacks of flour were stored. After years of neglect Leonard's mill was knocked down towards the end of the century, but its ironstone (after another life in a private dwelling) has since been incorporated into the new Chapel Hill winery.

White's Aldinga mill, the last to remain in service, shut down in the mid-1890s and was demolished in 1908. The three-storey Noarlunga mill, built of local bricks and Willunga slate, has been converted to residential units, after brief stints of chopping straw into chaff and crushing barytes during the life of the nearby mine. As E.H. Hallack reported in 1892: 'The flourmills, once humming hives of industry, are, in the southern districts proper, all closed or demolished. The jetties at Noarlunga, Willunga, Myponga, Yankalilla and Second Valley stand like the tombstones of a departed industry.'

# PLOUGHING MATCHES

The enthusiasm of the first farmers, and their pride in their achievements, led to the establishment in 1842 of the Willunga Farmers' Club, the first in the state. Six years later the district's first Ploughing Match was organised. 'Open to competitors from all parts of the Colony', it was held at Willunga in 1848, with classes for both bullock teams and horse teams, for champions (from other ploughing matches), for men and boys. The rules specified: 'The

furrows to be not less than nine inches by four and a half inches, and the quantity ploughed to be half an acre, and the work to be completed in four hours.' On this occasion the silver medal was presented to James Foreman at the subsequent dinner at the Bush Inn, Willunga.

Ploughing matches, a traditional feature of English country life, were designed to test the ploughman's skill and speed in ploughing a prescribed area of land with straight, even furrows. The tradition continued in the new colonies, the first South Australian contest taking place in 1843, about the same time as similar contests were initiated in the much older colony of New South Wales. The Willunga contest was the first in a country district in South Australia, but by 1856 there were fifteen local competitions in different regions of the state. Aldinga and McLaren Vale initiated their own local competitions in 1858.

The ploughing match became an annual festival and a holiday for the whole region. Games such as quoits and cricket and races were organised for

those not guiding the plough, and even 'a game of kiss-in-the-ring' at the McLaren Vale ploughing match of 1866 which, according to the *Chronicle*, attracted 'a considerable number of the fair sex'. It was always followed by a celebratory dinner (typically described as 'handsomely supplied' or 'an excellent repast' but, frustratingly, with no further elaboration) in one of the local inns.

# DIVERSIFICATION

Once the wheat fever had subsided, the Noarlunga–Willunga–Aldinga–McLaren Vale–Kangarilla area began to develop more as a mixed farming region, though even in the early days most farms combined farming with grazing. The combination of poor seasons, declining yields, lower grain prices and the economic depression of the 1880s stimulated farmers to consider other ways of using their land. At different times since, new and different land uses have been proposed for the district, and prevailing economic currents and relative expediencies have shaped a subtly changing balance of activities. The face the region shows today – mixed farming and grazing, with an increasing concentration of vineyards – has evolved gradually over the past 120 years. One of the few mixed farms remaining around McLaren Vale belongs to the Oliver family, who grow olives and summer stone fruits, cut hay and raise cattle and fat lambs.

After wheat, the first new crop to be encouraged was flax, then considered one of the best crops for exhausted soils. Thomas Smith Kell, one of the Willunga pioneers, pointed out in 1869 the profits to be made from flax. Having imported machinery, he initiated the Willunga Flax Company, which would purchase flax from growers, prepare it and export it. The processing plant took over the abandoned Willunga flour mill but was obliged to close in 1875 after only a few years of operation, the steeping water having polluted a nearby creek. (Once harvested, the flax plant undergoes a process of 'retting', through immersion in water, to allow the flax fibres to be separated.) One of the early managers of this mill was Thomas Dawson, father of Australian baritone Peter Dawson. Another burst of enthusiasm for flax occurred during the second world war but was equally short-lived.

While less land was cultivated, barley and oats began to be substituted for wheat, and hay, rather than grain, was the final product. Huge loads of hay were carted to Adelaide by horse teams which would take three days for the return journey. Gigantic bales of hay in the summer landscape indicate the continuing importance of haymaking in the district. At various times, potatoes

and field peas have been favoured but the main cereal crop now is barley, the region's good rainfall and mild spring weather ensuring good quality barley for the brewing industry. Even in the early years a small proportion of malting barley was grown, and in the days of local self-sufficiency there were breweries at McLaren Vale, Noarlunga and, for a time, Aldinga. Today only a small proportion of the South Australian harvest is taken by Adelaide brewers, the surplus exported to Asia and the Middle East.

In the days of early settlement, crop farming was increasingly combined with pastoral activities, especially sheep grazing. Livestock numbers had increased dramatically from 1839 when Evelyn Sturt, brother of explorer Charles Sturt, at that time Surveyor-General of South Australia, arrived in the Willunga area with nearly 5000 sheep and cattle he had driven overland from Bathurst in New South Wales. Sturt undertook a second cattle drove in 1841. Stock were also imported from England and Europe; David Colville, who arrived in 1840, brought with him 1500 sheep from Scotland. Sheep numbers in South Australia increased almost tenfold from 1838 to 1841.

Wool, which had made the fortunes of squatters in other Australian colonies, was also important in South Australia in the nineteenth century – in the 1890s the value of wool shipments easily exceeded the value of wheat exports. In the early decades of the twentieth century the development of the chilled meat trade to England, together with the introduction of superphosphate and pasture improvement, shifted the emphasis from wool to fat lambs, which in turn meant changes in the breeds seen in the region. Willunga was considered to have some of the best fat lamb country in the state.

The emphasis on livestock production was boosted by the establishment of the rail link to Adelaide in 1915. Stockyards, saleyards, and a selling ring were built close to the station at Willunga, and two or three sales were held each month. Willunga eventually became the largest selling centre in the Fleurieu Peninsula and supported five stock and station agents in the town. Sales continued for a time even after the railway closed in 1969, but eventually ceased. The old saleyards now resound to the hammer at the monthly Lions auctions.

# OSTRICH FARMING

At the end of the nineteenth century, when ostrich feathers were a handsome adornment to ladies hats, ostrich farming was advocated as a fortune-making industry for South Australia. One ostrich was said to yield feathers worth £5 each year, equivalent to the income from 100 sheep. In 1882 ostrich farming began on a small scale near Gawler, using ostriches from South Africa. By 1888 the South Australian Ostrich Company had been established, running over 500 birds at Port Augusta. Best quality feathers were shipped to London, 'common' ones made into feather dusters.

In 1915 ostriches from this farm stocked the Prior's Court Ostrich Farm near Noarlunga, where the exotic birds attracted much attention. Fred Low recorded in his diary for Sunday 10 October 1915: 'In the afternoon I put Dot in the little cart and Effie, Olive and Hilda went to see the Ostritches and then went down on the beach'. As fashions changed, however, the fall in prices made ostrich farming no longer economic, and the remaining birds were sold to a circus proprietor.

Ostriches have recently made a reappearance in the region. This time their meat and leather are the most important products, though the feathers still have a commercial use and the oil is valued as a massage oil. Some of the birds are descendants of the ostriches brought to South Australia

Prior's Court Ostrich Farm, c. 1915

over 100 years ago, but new stock has been imported from other states. The Consolidated Ostrich Corporation at Kangarilla runs several hundred of the thousand or more birds scattered throughout the region, but its main role is developing the market for ostrich products. The meat is said to taste like mild beef; the uniquely patterned leather is soft, strong and very, very expensive.

# COWS, PIGS AND POULTRY

As self-sufficient farmers in the English tradition, early settlers such as William Colton and Charles Hewett kept cows and pigs, skimming cream off the milk to make their own butter, feeding the rest to the pigs. In the 1920s, when Jack Connor Sparrow worked on McMurtrie's McLaren Vale farm, a typical farm still had five or six cows, as well as pigs and poultry. While Connor's main work was cereal farming, he also had to hand-milk the cows. The milk was separated on the farm and the skim milk fed to the pigs, or sometimes made into cheese. The cream was made into butter, either on farms or, later, in factories. In summer the cream would be lowered down into a well – and wells could be as deep as 20 metres – to keep it cool before churning.

Recollecting life around the turn of the century, Mary Maud Aldam wrote of:

*the dairy piled with golden butter, cheese, pans of cream, 2 things those early homes could boast – enormous logs in the huge fireplace & the trestle table groaning with abundance of food. Barrels of Salt Beef, the rafters of the kitchen hung with sides of Bacon. Pork Pies, Apple Pies, Tarts, every Kind of Cake. No Rations.*

Similarly, Mrs Ethel Martin (née Semmens), who grew up near Daringa, just east of McLaren Vale, recollected how her mother made fresh curd for cheese cakes:

*I must tell you what a wonderful cook my mother was ... the cheese cakes made one's mouth water to think about. She made a mixture from heated milk and while hot, buttermilk was poured into it, and after the liquid had been poured off a lovely white curd remained, to which was added spice, eggs, sugar, currants, lemon peel, and this was then put into tins lined with pastry and baked.*

Running a few cows was initially a domestic necessity, but as part of the diversification of the 1880s it began to be seen as a source of supplementary income. This change had repercussions on the hay industry, local demand for hay increasing at the same time as the Adelaide market declined. In 1890 the Southern Co-operative Produce Factory was established at Aldinga, near the former flour mill in White's Valley. It was a general cooperative whose principal interest was dairy farming, but it was also intended to purchase pork and cure ham and bacon, to purchase fruit and turn it into jams, and generally to market farm and garden produce. By 1892 it could treat nearly 5000 litres of milk per day. Farmers who delivered their milk were entitled to receive, free, one-third the quantity as skim milk, and surplus skim milk was piped to an adjacent piggery. Butter produced was sold locally, any surplus sent to Adelaide.

Landcross Farm, Noarlunga, late nineteenth century

## POT BUTTER

From Mrs Hughes of Willunga, in Bertha Prior's manuscript recipe book:

*2 lbs salt 1/4 lb sugar 1/4 lb saltpetre*
*Roll ingredients all together untill smooth use one oz of mixture to each*
*Pound Butter.*

Established soon after the Aldinga butter factory, and associated with it, was the McLaren Vale creamery, which separated the milk and sent on the cream for processing. There was also Kondoparinga butter factory, just east of Meadows, which sourced some of its milk from the Kangarilla area. Around the same time, however, the first hand-powered cream separators appeared, allowing milk to be separated on the farm. On display at the 1901 Willunga show was 'The Buttercup', described as 'a modern and effective cream separator'. As this equipment designed for farm-scale operations increased in popularity, it became more profitable to separate on the farm and sell only the cream. The Aldinga butter factory was obliged to close in March 1901. Even in the 1930s, however, about 15 per cent of South Australian butter was still made on farms, and the Willunga and McLaren Flat shows included a section for homemade butter, as well as sections for bacon and ham. Nevertheless, the advent of milking machines in the 1920s and 1930s spelled the end of the small family dairy.

After 1926, when the Adelaide milk vendor came as far south as Willunga to collect milk to supply city consumers, fewer farmers did their own separating and butter production declined. Many local dairy farmers subsequently joined the Myponga Co-operative Dairying Society established in 1936 (in later years, it was known for its cheeses – Myponga tasty cheddar, edam and gouda). Though this factory closed in 1975, dairying and pig raising were, until relatively recently, important activities in the McLaren Vale region.

Poultry, like cows, were an integral part of the mixed farming tradition. When May Vivienne travelled through 'Sunny South Australia' in 1908 she was clearly impressed by the egg-laying abilities of hens and ducks on farms near McLaren Vale; hens, she reported, laid an average of 169 eggs a year and ducks 185. Competition was keen among amateur poultry fanciers in the district (including vigneron Frank Osborn, founder of the d'Arenberg vineyard), and the diversity of poultry at the annual shows of the McLaren Vale Poultry and Kennel Club in the early twentieth century was astounding. There were prizes for best cock and best hen in over ten different breeds, including the Plymouth Rock, Silver-spangled Hamburg, Andalusian, Indian Game and Black-red Malay. Bronzewing turkeys, Toulouse geese and Aylesbury, Rouen and Indian Runner ducks were also exhibited. For many years the poultry section, with over 160 different classes for fowl, ducks, geese and turkeys, remained a strong feature of the McLaren Flat Show.

Today the biggest poultry enterprise in the area, with farms at Blewitt Springs, Aldinga, Milang and Tooperang, is Aldinga Table Turkeys. For Terry Crabb and his father Brian it began in 1973 as a part-time family business but grew to become the largest producer of fresh turkey in South Australia. It processes around 200,000 turkeys annually and employs 50 people in addition to family members. Almost all the turkey is sold fresh, mostly as portions, though an increasing proportion now leaves the factory smoked or roast.

'The fairy in the dairy', inspired by the Amery dairy, c. 1920

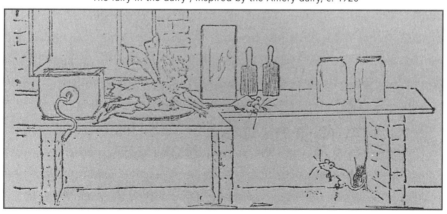

# ORCHARDS

The need to be self-reliant did not deter the first pioneers, who brought with them a strong tradition of farm orchards and kitchen gardens. In the early 1840s, soon after taking over the licence of the Bush Inn at Willunga, Edward Rowland wrote:

*We have peach, nectarine, apricot, cherry, and fig trees besides vines, and by the way, this is a splendid place for the vine – we have some magnificent vineyards. Next year, if I live, I intend planting mulberry trees, and if I could get some silk worms' eggs I should then have the honor of being the first to cultivate that valuable article.*

The Aldam family's garden, around the turn of the century:

*had every sort of fruit tree one could wish for. A long row of fig Trees & the Figs that grew on them one never forgot. Delicious great ones. Apricot Trees, Peach, Damson, Plums, Nectarine, Green Gage. Large dark and light plum trees. Apple.*

'All that remains in our Garden now,' wrote Maud Aldam around 1950, 'are 2 large Pear Trees. They are still always loaded with fruit, also one large Mulberry Tree, & Almond.'

While wheat was still profitable, the poor state of the roads hardly inclined farmers to establish commercial orchards. In July 1869 the *Register* reported that Mr Toll had more than 200 orange trees, yielding oranges as large as five inches (12 cm) in diameter, together with lemons and citrons, but added that the market for local fruit was limited, partly because of the difficulties and cost of transport. 'It seems a pity that oranges are so largely imported, when they can be grown to such perfection in the colony.'

Later, however, in the quest for ways of using the land to best advantage, fruit was reconsidered. In 1885 William McMurtrie fenced off two acres and planted an orchard of apricots, apples and peaches, said to be 'the best that could be possibly seen or wished for. They prove incontestably what the so-called worn-out land of the South can produce'. The fruit display at the 1883 Willunga Show, held at the beginning of March, included apples (both table and kitchen), pears, quinces, peaches, damsons, grapes and mulberries, together with dried apricots, peaches, currants and raisins, preserved figs, softshell almonds and 'colonial jams and jellies'. Some years later E.H. Hallack reported many new orchard plantings in the southern districts. Vineyard expansion began around the same time – between 1880 and 1890 over 300,000 vines were planted in the three District Councils of Aldinga, Willunga and Noarlunga. While most of the grapes were intended for wine-making, some were table grapes and others were grown for drying, as currants and raisins.

The region south of Adelaide was not the only area to have diversified into fruit production, and by 1893 there was a glut. No cold storage facilities were available, and for want of a reasonable return fruit was left to rot under the trees. People were advised to dry their fruit rather than let it go to waste, and a public meeting in Adelaide was called to discuss ways of providing a profitable market for fruitgrowers.

Drying currants, McLaren Vale, 1920

Attention had earlier been drawn to the potential for currants – in 1891, nearly 700,000 kilos of currants were imported into South Australia, enough for two kilos per person per year. Thomas Hardy planted currants in McLaren Vale around 1878, but these initial cuttings of unknown origin bore virtually no fruit. Known locally as 'Cape currants', they were probably the female variety of the seedless Muscat Hamburg, widely grown in tropical regions. Later Hardy acquired cuttings of the Zante currant and, after trialling them at his Bankside vineyard, introduced them to McLaren Vale, grafting them on to grenache vines. At the 1883 Willunga Show he was able to display an immense bunch of currant grapes from a two-year-old vine – despite the fact that Zante currants do not usually bear until much later than this.

Between 1900 and 1910 currant production in Willunga and Noarlunga District Councils increased almost seven-fold to more than 250,000 kilos. Raisins also were dried, though quantities were negligible. Often integrated with wine grapes, currants remained a major source of income for many farmers in the McLaren Vale–McLaren Flat area throughout the next decade, but the newer irrigation areas along the Murray River, which came into full production in the 1920s, soon dominated the dried vine-fruits market. The new vineyards specialised in sultanas, which gradually superseded currants – though these remained an important product of the McLaren Vale–McLaren Flat–Blewitt Springs district until the 1940s, along with dried apricots and prunes. Connor Sparrow, one of the region's hardest-working and most successful farmers, described the way fruit was dried in the 1920s:

*When the currants had dried you waited for a fairly warm day and in the cool of the evening you would rub them and shake them through the screen into a large box and that would sieve out the stalks and the oversized fruit called buck currants which have seeds in them ... the bucks went to a distillery to be made into wine spirits. There were 2000 trays and they would be filled twice most years.*

*Drying apricots ... the stones were cut out, and the halves were placed cut side up on the trays, and then the trays were put into a closed bin, where you burnt sulphur. This would help the drying and make them a good golden colour.*

*Prunes always seemed to be an endless job. From the time they started ripening you would have to go around every morning and pick up all that had fallen on the ground. When you had enough for a run of dipping you would prepare a caustic soda bath with boiling water, and then put the prunes in a wire basket and immerse them in it for a short time. This would crinkle the skin, and then they were spread on trays to dry.*

After currants, the next industry to be promoted was dried prunes and apricots, marketed through the McLaren Vale Fruit Packers which, until the formation of Almond Growers' Cooperative at Willunga, also handled almonds. Much of the dried fruit harvest was exported to England, but the district also developed a reputation for superb rich fruit cakes and plum puddings.

Many farms still have their fruit trees and, despite the conquering vine-yards, there are still commercial stone-fruit orchards in the area, many offering pick-your-own fruit in summer – cherries on the southern side of the Willunga hills; apricots, peaches, plums and nectarines around McLaren Vale, Blewitt Springs and Kangarilla.

## ELVA DYER'S GIN PRUNES

From Elva Dyer, born McLaren Flat in 1916:

*Fill a jar with prunes – they should be d'Agen prunes – and cover with gin. Leave for about six weeks. Take one in the morning and one at night, with a little of the thick syrup. Good for everything.*

# MEDITERRANEAN MODE

The Willunga Almond Blossom Festival at the end of each July affirms the region's reputation for fine quality almonds. Its assured rainfall and the absence of severe spring frosts offer natural advantages.

Recognising the region's Mediterranean climate, many early officials advised growing almonds, together with other Mediterranean fruits: figs, grapes and olives. A few almond trees were standard in farm orchards, but Thomas Atkinson was one of the first to plant them in large numbers, around his Ashley Farm. In the 1890s almond trees formed the borders of Malpas' vineyard, and in 1901 a ten-acre orchard of Brown Brandis, Nonpareil and Californian Paper Shell varieties was established off the Aldinga road. Between 1880 and 1900 the number of almond trees in the Willunga District Council more than doubled.

At the end of the nineteenth century, however, the Willunga region produced only a small proportion of the state's harvest, the Mitcham and Marion areas being far more significant. The second big increase in plantings occurred in the 1920s. Another 50 acres (Strout, Johnston and California Paper Shells) were added to the original ten of Strout's orchard in 1925, and in 1934 an additional 25 acres were planted. This 85-acre almond orchard was, at the time, the largest privately owned almond orchard in Australia. The nuts were harvested by hand; long thin wattle sticks would be used to knock the almonds on to hessian sheets stretched under each tree.

The increasing focus on almond growing in the Willunga district came about partly as a result of the subdivision of some of the original 80-acre blocks into smaller areas that were economically viable units for almond production. Ashley Farm, for example, was purchased in 1934 by the Almond Groves Company, planted to almonds and subdivided into smaller blocks. Around the same time, almonds began to disappear from the traditional growing areas around Adelaide as orchards were replaced by suburban housing allotments after the second world war and in the early 1950s.

# ALMOND VARIETIES

Around the turn of the century Mr A.C. Johnston, founder of the Pirramimma vineyard (still owned by the Johnston family), planted a patch of almonds near his cellars, using young trees received from an Adelaide nurseryman. One of these stood out from all the others, yielding large, good-flavoured almonds which were also easy to shell. It was named the Johnston's Prolific. Buddings from this single tree propagated the variety throughout the district. One of the most popular varieties in the 1940s, it is still grown and Johnston almonds are still in demand.

Then there is Strout's Papershell, a variety selected and planted by Tom Strout. One of the latest flowering almonds, its kernels are plump rather than flat. The Baxendale almond, also developed locally, is rarely grown today but its flowering time made it a good pollinator for the CPS (California Paper Shells).

In the 1950s the Willunga Show had separate sections for each of the principal varieties, both as shell almonds and kernels: Johnston, Strout, Chellaston, Californian Paper Shell, hard shells and unnamed softshells. These have continued in the McLaren Flat Show.

CPS almonds are usually sold as kernels, Johnston as shell almonds and Chellaston are often salted, smoked or devilled. The Almond Train at McLaren Vale offers the district's best selection of both natural and prepared almonds.

Almonds were important components of emergency ration packs in the second world war. In his memoirs Tom Strout noted that he was called up at the age of 18 but because of the demand for almonds (along with other nuts and dried fruit), he was sent back to his Willunga orchard for his war service.

Plantings around Willunga continued to increase until about the mid-1970s, when almond orchards covered approximately 5000 acres (just over 2000 hectares). In 1973 it was claimed that more than half of Australia's almonds came from the Willunga area. Yields doubled when bore water irrigation was introduced around the same time. In the 1990s, however, the profit potential of wine grapes enticed many growers to replace old trees with vines, and only six or so commercial orchardists remain.

More recently, the pistachio, another Mediterranean nut, has been introduced and, while not yet grown on a large scale, it has demonstrated its adaptability to the region.

## OLIVES

Olive cuttings arrived in South Australia with the *Buffalo*. In 1839 George Stevenson, editor of the *South Australian Gazette*, had four varieties of olive grown from these cuttings. In a public lecture he encouraged the growing of olives in the colony, as well as other Mediterranean crops. The South Australian Company also imported olives in the 1850s.

Possibly there was some resistance from English-born yeoman farmers to an unfamiliar tree, for olives were rare in the McLaren Vale region until the turn of the century. Some were planted for decorative purposes; an avenue of olive trees led to 'Sylvan Park', the gracious home built by Thomas Colton, second son of William Colton, in McLaren Vale in 1858. These trees are now part of the Gemmel Tassie Reserve, just off Main Road.

In 1880 there were just over 11,000 olive trees in the County of Adelaide (which extended as far west as the Barossa and as far south as Willunga), but less than one per cent of these were growing in the area of the McLaren Vale

region. Even in 1900, plantings here were relatively insignificant and it is doubtful that they contributed much to the colony's production of olive oil (most of which was crushed at Sir Samuel Davenport's Burnside mill).

In the 1890s A.C. Johnston planted the line of olive trees that lead to the Pirramimma cellars, though these were intended as a windbreak rather than a source of revenue. At Clarendon, too, olives were planted as a windbreak around Gillard's vineyard. Since the post-war arrival of Italians and Greeks in the district, however, the small elongated purplish-black berries from these trees have been picked and crushed for oil. Vince Scarfo's stone-press on Malpas Road began operation about ten years ago, crushing olives for the family's own use and for other Italians and Greeks who gathered fruit from hundreds of old trees and their descendants scattered through paddocks and along roads. In recent years State government funding has been provided to eradicate wild olives and many of the roadside trees have been cut down.

Thomas Hardy, who was one of the early enthusiasts, had a substantial olive grove at his Bankside vineyard (near the present suburb of Underdale) and later planted bands of olive trees through his McLaren Vale vineyards. Somehow, some of these developed into the Hardy's Mammoth variety, still propagated in Australia today and described as a dual-purpose variety. It's likely, too, that a good proportion of the wild olives in the district can trace their parentage to these trees.

One of Hardy's vineyards, complete with windbreaks and boundaries of olive trees – Hardy's Mammoth – was bought in the 1920s Joe Norman, who had an olive mill at suburban Brighton. Joe Norman continued to produce olive oil throughout the war years (it was considered an essential product) but in the late 1920s leased the property to Greek immigrant Emmanuel Giakoumis, today recognised as one of the founders of the modern olive oil industry in South Australia. Emmanuel eventually purchased the olive grove in 1972 and planted more olive trees, in particular the Kalamata variety.

In addition, he imported a traditional press from Italy, still used today on the McLaren Vale Olive Grove, as the property is not known. Today, if you nibble some olives or eat a salad tossed with olive oil in any of the local restaurants, there's a good chance you'll be eating the produce of the McLaren Vale Olive Grove. Kalamata olives (for pickling) make up about half the 22 hectares of bearing trees on the property, while other varieties such as Mission and Verdale are principally used for oil. Many of these original Hardy's Mammoth trees, now tall and spreading, with gnarled and twisted trunks, are still harvested, despite the difficulties; the large, fleshy fruit is excellent for pickling but also yields good oil. It's likely, too, that a good proportion of the wild olives in the district can trace their parentage to these trees.

Crushing of the Olive Grove's harvest takes place from about May through to August or September, and if you happen to arrive on a crushing day you can see the whole operation. The plant can produce up to 300 litres per day of crude oil, which is then filtered through cotton wool to yield the golden amber, extra virgin liquid available for sale, along with the various pickled olives, olive pastes and other local products and crafts.

Olive trees, both wild and named varieties, in ordered rows or scattered clumps, are now as much a part of the McLaren Vale region's landscape as vines and giant rolls of hay. Like almonds, olives go with wine and many wineries offer at cellar door their own pickled olives and smoked salted almonds. Coriole winery also produces some 5000 litres of olive oil per year, using local fruit of different varieties, all picked to order and crushed separately. The various oils – some soft and fruity, others stronger and peppery – are tasted at the end of winter and judiciously blended to yield extra virgin olive oil in both premium and standard qualities. Mark Lloyd's Coriole Diva oil was one of two McLaren Vale oils to win a High Commendation at the inaugural Australian Olive Oil Exhibition of 1997, an honour accorded only eight of the 30 entries. The other McLaren Vale oil, from Melia Olive Estate, is not yet available in commercial quantities.

# WATTLE BARK

All the agricultural activities imposed on the landscape by the early settlers involved imported plants, animals and techniques. Even bee-keeping, which brought in a little extra money on some small farms, relied on imported bees. One industry, however, took advantage of natural resources: wattle trees. In the nineteenth century the leather-forming properties of wattle bark were superior to any other known Australian tanning material.

Tannins have astringent and dehydrating properties which enable skins to be cured and become leather. Many trees have tannins in their bark, and the tanning properties of bark from wattle trees had been discovered by earlier arrivals to the other colonies. The main varieties were the broadleaf or golden wattle (*Acacia pycnantha*) and black wattle (*A. decurrens*). Well-grown broadleaf wattles yield, at seven or eight years of age, about 32 kilos of bark containing about 35 per cent tannic acid. Wattle wood was useful for cask staves, axle spokes, axe and pick handles, and for fencing; it was also the best wood for fuel stoves, giving a clearer and greater heat than other firewood. At the end of the nineteenth century wattles served as stakes for currant vines.

The season for collecting the bark was September to December, when the bark had the highest tannin content and was easily removed from the tree. In the 1860s bark could be delivered to the tannery at McLaren Vale, but once this shut down the Echunga tannery was probably the closest. Connor Sparrow described the operations:

*Wattle barking was done from the end of winter until around summer when the sap stopped flowing. You needed an axe and a tomahawk and a reasonably light trestle that a man could carry. Tapping the limbs with a tomahawk or hammer releases the bark . . . the method of getting the bark from the tree is to cut it about shoulder high and then run the bark down to the ground. You would lay the butt bark on two leather straps, and the toppings in the centre, and then tighten the straps, and then tie thick strings in place of the straps.*

*These bundles would weigh about 30 kilos and there was a factory at Echunga to which you had to deliver with horses in those days, and also factories in Adelaide which, when the railway started [in 1915] was much more convenient.*

By the 1870s and 1880s there was concern that the wild wattles were almost exhausted, and in several colonies official enquiries investigated the possibilities of wattle cultivation. Conclusions must have been favourable and wattle seed became a source of income for entrepreneurial locals. In his diary for 1889, Fred Low noted: 'Me and Lydia took 183 pounds of wattle seed to Harry Powells, what Lydia got, she got 6 pence a pound for it'. Travelling through the southern districts in the early 1890s, E.H. Hallack described a 'healthy-looking wattle plantation' east of Tatachilla and along the Aldinga road three wattle plantations belonging to a Mr Pengilly, while the Kay brothers

Gathering wattle bark, c. 1924

had 18 acres of wattles at Amery. These individual enterprises, however, were insignificant compared with the project of the Echunga Wattle Plantation Company, which had leased 2000 acres between Meadows and Echunga. As Hallack remarked, wattle plantations and vineyards seemed set to 'turn a tide in the affairs of the South'.

Production of wattle bark in South Australia increased until around the 1920s then gradually declined as new plantations in South and East Africa, established from Australian wattle seed, supplied the world market far more cheaply. Individuals continued to harvest bark for their own purposes; in the 1930s Adolphus Waye, a fisherman who lived near Silver Sands beach, cut wattle bark and tanned his own nets. By 1960, however, South Australian production of wattle bark was insignificant.

# FUTURE PLANNING

The handwritten diary of Fred Low of McLaren Flat, covering the years from 1888 to 1952, illustrates beautifully the changing face of farm production at the end of the nineteenth and beginning of the twentieth centuries. In 1888, at the age of 25, Fred married Lydia Mills and the couple moved to Rose Cottage, Tintara Vineyards (now Upper Tintara), where Fred worked. Three years later he bought a small farm at McLaren Flat, mostly planted to vines, and developed this property at the same time as working for Tintara. His first venture was beekeeping, and in later years Fred earned money from both the honey and the beeswax. In 1892 he grubbed out many of the old vines and trees (including almond and olive trees) and planted currant vines; the following year he planted a mixed orchard of apples, pears, apricots, peaches and plums, possibly for the family's own use but also for sale. In addition to these enterprises Fred grew field peas and potatoes in the early 1900s, and cut wattle bark. In 1911 he established an almond orchard of 26 trees, adding more the following year. The next wave of interest focused on dried fruits and in 1915 Fred planted 150 prune plum trees, together with a few apricots, followed by 299 apricot trees in 1922. By 1925, when the irrigation areas along the Murray were swamping the market with sultanas, currants and raisins, his currant vines were grafted to shiraz.

Today wine is the industry most immediately associated with the McLaren Vale region, and while vineyards occupy a sizeable area, land use is still characterised by a mix of complementary horticultural, agricultural and pastoral activities. Over the years different emphases have dominated at different times, but the end result is a rich and varied agricultural tradition that represents a cultural heritage to be valued and preserved.

The aesthetic value of such a landscape is also important to the region. State and local governments have recognised this, and in recent years have developed policies for the maintenance of the region's rural character. The Supplementary Development Plan prepared by the South Australian State Planning Authority in 1978 recommended prohibiting subdivision below a minimum area (16 hectares), and withholding permission for activities that were believed not to be in keeping with the character of the area, such as riding schools, dog kennels and tracks, intensive piggeries, feed lots, poultry batteries and hatcheries, and motor cycle and car circuits. Individual dwelling proposals would be required to conform to the 'spirit of place' in such matters as location, siting, form, colour and materials.

Subsequent reports continue to emphasise the importance of agriculture to the region while seeking to promote sustainable forms of agriculture. In 1994 the Willunga 2000 study identified certain rural activities to be encouraged in the Willunga Basin, based on their agronomic character and suitability to the region, their financial viability, and their impact on landscape, tourism and employment. The most favoured tended to be the value-adding ones, such as wineries, vineyards without wineries but selling wine made from their own grapes, olive processing establishments, the manufacture of jams and sauces from surplus berry fruit, pick-your-own stone fruit orchards, protea and banksia farms, plant nurseries and sheep dairies. Other activities recommended, but given a lower priority, were growing vines, almonds, fresh flowers, olives, stone fruit and speciality cereals, together with horse training and exercising, raising alpaca and goats and rearing poultry for meat.

At the same time future planning recognises the relationship between local agriculture and towns, and the compromise necessary between town expansion in order to sustain local business, and the value of rural land, not simply in terms of its suitability for agriculture but also in terms of the tourism attraction of agricultural landscapes. In the days of William Colton and Charles Hewett, the town, or what there was of it, was secondary to the farm – they might sell their crops for cash, but where could they spend it? Today the relationship is more one of interdependence; towns need rural industries as much as farming depends on the services the towns can offer.

# CHAPTER ROADS,

In the beginning were roads, lines of communication between settlements. They were built for a purpose – to link one end point to another. The Main South Road connected Adelaide with the whaling station at Encounter Bay, the road from Willunga to Aldinga connected farmers with the flour mills. Roads infiltrated and opened up the district, encouraging settlement and, in turn, the construction of new links. Inns were the stops along the way where horses and travellers, bullock teams and drivers could rest and refresh themselves.

Towns followed the roads. Some meandered and multiplied along the rough tracks, with no fixed plan in mind. A few clustered at strategic locations, such as Noarlunga at the crossing of the Onkaparinga River. Willunga – six hours' ride from Adelaide, six hours from the whaling station at Encounter Bay – was not only a convenient halfway stop but promised an easier route over the formidable hills. Relatively easier, at least, for, as James Hawker added, 'in hilly country all the roads went straight up', and bullock drays carried blocks and tackles to help them over the steepest sections.

# THREE
# TOWNS, INNS

The return trip from McLaren Vale to Adelaide took nearly a week. As E.H. Hallack commented in 1892, the old roads 'run down dales and up stone-capped hills utterly impassable for traffic'.

The common theme to roads, towns and inns is transport, the means of bringing news and goods to distant communities but more importantly, of taking wheat and wool, slate and hay to markets in Adelaide, other colonies and overseas where their value could be realised. The inadequacies of transport arrangements throughout most of the nineteenth century, and the disadvantages these meant to primary industry in the McLaren Vale region, appear as an underlying grievance in the chronicles of the period.

Today, paradoxically, the shrinking of distance and ease of travel between this region and the city of Adelaide have provoked concern because of their tendency to favour urban development. At the same time, however, they bring benefits in the form of tourism and visitors who support the local economy and look after the transport themselves.

Streamlined highways may have overtaken them, but the original roads have not completely disappeared. Some have become walking trails whose surfaces and gradients are insistent reminders of the arduousness of early travel.

At Willunga a narrow bush track to Willunga Hill summit traverses a section of the old Encounter Bay road, starting at the John Yeates Memorial Lookout just off the Victor Harbour road. The lookout and various vantage points on the trail present splendid views across the vineyards of McLaren Vale and, to the west, the Aldinga plains and wide waters of Gulf St Vincent.

The Coach Road Track over the Noarlunga hills in the Onkaparinga River Recreation Park follows the route taken by lumbering drays and well-laden coaches in the early days of settlement. Cross the river by the suspension bridge – or pick your way across the scattered stones in the shallow waters of the ford – and stroll along the river flats before turning to commence the climb along the ridge. Pause at the first rise to glance back on a scene reminiscent of rural England as the church of St Philip and St James stands solitary on a lonely hill. Continue around the sharp bend of the gully crossing, then take breath before the final steep stretch to the windswept crest. From here, enjoy magnificent panoramas across the farming lands and coastal suburbs to the sea, and bird's eye views of the township of (Old) Noarlunga.

From the Victory Hotel the old Sellicks Hill Road, narrow and rough, curls around the inner flanks of the precipitous hills, their smooth slopes interrupted at intervals by parallel bands of pale grey stones. Jagged shards of slate protrude like tombstones on some of the lower hills. Roadside cuttings illustrate graphically the shallowness of the soil layer, inspiring respect for the few spindly trees and shrubs that have managed to gain a foothold on this barren range.

# ROADS

In 1839, according to James Hawker, the route to Encounter Bay was not so much a road as a mere bullock-dray track. His first duty in the survey team was to 'commence a road to Yankalilla ... I was instructed to survey and clear a line of road from the Horseshoe to a police station and depot about to be formed where Willunga township is now located.' The original Encounter Bay road was, in his words, 'execrable where it crossed the range' near Mount Terrible – which, prior to the arrival of the pious Governor Gawler, had been called Mount Damnable.

Encounter Bay was not the only destination. As wheat became established, so roads were needed to take it to the ports or to the mills. Farmers from as far away as Yankalilla and Meadows used flour mills in the Aldinga/Willunga area, including Butterworth's mill whose ruins still stand on the south side of Aldinga Road, just west of Bayliss Road. A number of primitive tracks over Sellicks Range joined with other roads leading to the southern settlements of Myponga, Yankalilla, Normanville and Second Valley. The Loud's Hill Road was described in 1851 as 'execrable, nearly impassable', a 'break-neck spot of a road' and the worst, bar one, that the writer had ever travelled.

The initial track south from the Onkaparinga ford followed closely the 'native track' marked on John McLaren's map, straight up and over the hill. It may have been rough and ready, but by February 1840 a twice-weekly service was carrying both passengers and goods from Adelaide to Willunga, making stops at 'the Horseshoe Ford, Onkaparinga; Tarranga, McLaren's Vale; Mr Hewett's farm; the Bay of Biscay'; and finally the police station at Willunga. A month later it had become a daily service.

Some of the transport difficulties were alleviated when the first bridge across the Onkaparinga was completed in early 1841. From here, the south west curve of the river near the end of Baron Street, the road mounted the hill to a point near today's South Road–Quarry Road intersection and, still following the line drawn by McLaren, made a meandering descent into

McLaren Vale. Clearing the route was fairly easy until this last section, heavily timbered and with fallen gum trees across the line of the road. James Hawker requested gunpowder and fuses to remove these massive obstacles but after an accident in which 'nearly 20 lb of sporting gunpowder' exploded before he had a chance to get clear – the consequence of faulty fuses – Hawker was instructed to clear by hand as much as possible and to cut down

large trees about one metre above ground level. The presence of these stumps led to its being christened Stump Hill Road.

With the opening in the late 1840s of a new bridge over the Onkaparinga, this time on the northern edge of the Horseshoe, the road south took a slightly different route as it climbed the hill to the west of Noarlunga then split in two, as it does today. In 1853 this network was officially listed as one of the three Main Roads of South Australia – the Great Southern Road 'to

Noarlunga and Willunga, with branches westward to Yankalilla and Cape Jervis, and eastward to the Meadows and Encounter Bay'.

All roads designated 'main' roads were the responsibility of the Central Board of Main Roads, while 'district' roads were to be maintained by District Boards. The District Roads Board for the Hundred of Willunga was established in 1849 and met at many of the local inns – the Bush Inn in Willunga,

the Devonshire or Mrs Gumpr's Hotel in McLaren Vale. Once the government had approved the formation of district councils the Board was replaced by the Willunga District Council, proclaimed in August 1853. Council still had responsibility for district roads – and three years later, disputes over roads led to Noarlunga and Aldinga seceding and forming independent district councils. The principal cause of disagreement was the route of a new road south to Myponga, eventually settled in favour of the Sellicks Hill route.

# VICTORY HOTEL

First licensed in 1858 as Sellicks Hill Hotel, the name was quickly changed to Norman's Victory Hotel to commemorate John Norman's victory in the matter of the new southern road.

John Norman was Chairman of Aldinga District Council and founder of Normanville; he was also the genial host of the first Willunga ploughing match, held on his property in July 1848, and reputedly renowned for his superior breed of pigs.

The controversy over the best route began in 1854. The virtual impassibility of so many roads in winter made a proper all-weather north-south link vitally important. Norman favoured the route by way of Sellicks Hill, shorter by four miles; his opponents, pointing out that farmers on the western side were already amply serviced by road and sea transport, preferred a more easterly route that passed closer to the flour mills.

Eventually, the matter was resolved at a public meeting in March 1858, when both sides had the opportunity to argue their case. 'Mr Norman also addressed the meeting,' reported the *Register*, 'and concluded by stating he should fight it out to the last to obtain a good road over the ranges about that point, as leading most directly to the districts south of Aldinga, and at the same time benefiting the greatest number of settlers in Aldinga, besides being the most direct line to the port, which by this route the distance would be shortened in every case.' Put to the vote, Norman's amendment for carrying the line past Sellicks Hill was adopted by large majority. On 20 March 1858, the *Register* commented: 'In its perfect incomprehensibility to the uninitiated, it rivals the ancient controversy between the Nominalists and the Realists; while, in the pertinacity with which it is maintained, and the bad blood it occasions, it almost parallels the Wars of the Roses.'

Opened in March 1859 by Jane Norman, one of John Norman's family of seven daughters, the original road ran straight up the slope past the Victory Hotel, but soon after completion was diverted around the top of the hill to make travelling easier. In the era of motorised transport even this road, with its steep and winding gradients, was hard going, especially for low-powered cars, though motorcyclists apparently relished the challenge of the hill climb. A new, sealed road was completed in 1929. The present road, which sweeps around the western face of the range, was opened in 1969.

The hotel remained Norman's Victory until 1946, but since then has been simply known as the Victory. The original cellar now stocks one of the best commercial wine collections of the district and the dining room, which over-looks the alluring coast, serves satisfying, unfussy meals.

# BY SEA AND RAIL

In the nineteenth century road transport was laborious, slow and expensive – and uneconomical. For bounteous wheat harvests and massive slate exports envisaged by the early settlers, sea and rail were the preferred alternatives, both requiring investment by either private individuals or government.

Interest in a jetty at Port Willunga began in 1850 when the Port Willunga Wharf Company was formed, but the lure of the goldfields left the region depleted of manpower and it was not until 1854 that the first jetty was completed. Perhaps it was built too hastily, for small boats were needed to take cargo from the end of the jetty to waiting ships, and it was replaced by a new jetty in 1868. In *Hope Farm Chronicle*, Geoffrey Manning has described the opening as his great-great-grandfather, George Pitches Manning, might have experienced it.

*Thursday 6 February 1868 dawned bright and sunny, with a light south-westerly breeze. My wife, Jane, had, by nine am, packed a picnic hamper and shortly thereafter our family set off on what was to be a gala day ... Upon our arrival the jetty was crowded with spectators, while several picnic parties had established themselves on the beach, where vendors were dispensing eats and drinks. Promptly at one pm the official party proceeded down the cutting to the jetty and after several speeches were made, Miss Stewart, the daughter of Duncan Stewart, summarily opened the jetty by breaking a bottle of wine upon the structure. After lunch, which was washed down by a bottle of my 1866 claret, my mind drifted back ...*

By the end of 1855 Port Noarlunga also had a jetty and tramway but it, too, did not extend far enough for vessels to dock alongside, so wheat and flour still had to be ferried by small boats. It was extended a few years later, and again in 1878, but about five years later the Noarlunga mill had ceased operation, and in any case sea links were beginning to appear less urgent and less attractive than rail. Storms and high seas gradually weakened and washed away these man-made structures and although deputations requested a new

Port Willunga jetty in 1915 – ironically, the year the railway arrived – the era of sea transport was effectively over.

The idea of a railway was first mooted in the 1860s, when the northern line was being extended to Burra. In 1880, when the line to Blackwood was under way, local politicians again lobbied for construction of a line from Marino to Willunga. At least this time the Commissioner of Public Works went so far as to count freight and passengers to and from Willunga as a kind of feasibility study, but the project was dropped in 1883. The idea was revived in 1899, but it was not until 1915, just over a year after the opening of the line to Brighton, that a train service south to Willunga became a reality.

Steam train to Willunga, 1919

January 20, 1915 was a day of celebration for the whole community. Early in the morning the first train from Willunga departed with a group of local schoolchildren on board, picking up more at the various stations on the way to Brighton then returning to Willunga. From the city came a train carrying members of the public plus a special train to transport the Governor, Sir Henry Galway, and the parliamentary party, who were welcomed by the schoolchildren singing 'Song of Australia'. The Governor officially opened the line, waving the green flag that was a cue to the engine driver to steam

Pro-railway group, c. 1913

ahead and burst through the blue and yellow ribbons stretched across it. While the Governor and officials retired for lunch and interminable toasts, the children enjoyed a day of sports and games on the oval.

Ships might have been suitable for transporting bulk goods but railways also served people. Although from 1883 people could take advantage of a coach service connecting with the railway at Blackwood, the communities were still quite isolated. Roads were not yet sealed, and in winter were often difficult to negotiate. Around the turn of the century, when Fred Low wanted to take his honey, beeswax or currants to Adelaide, the trip by horse and dray would take about seven hours. Having completed his business that afternoon, he would stay with family overnight and perhaps make some purchases in town before returning home the next day.

The arrival of the train service shortened the travel time, but made little difference to the number of trips Fred made to Adelaide each year. For his wife and family, however, the convenience of rail travel meant far more frequent visits to town to shop or see the sights, and made it possible for his youngest daughter to study in Adelaide. It broadened the family's horizons, enlarged the circles of contact, extended the links by marriage. The railway opened the local community to a wider world.

It also brought changes to some of the towns. In the 1880s towns were the business and service centres for farmers, with their banks and post offices, general stores and butchers, blacksmiths and bootmakers. With the railway, and particularly in Willunga, came a range of new occupations to be fitted into the social hierarchy – engine driver, station master, rail guard, porters and gangers – and a multiplication of agricultural services through stock agents and contractors. Willunga became a transport hub. Passengers for Yankalilla arrived by train, lunched in the tea rooms of Mrs Richards, then changed to a coach for the remainder of the journey.

The railway benefited agriculture by offering an efficient service to transport livestock, grain and cans of cream to Adelaide, and at the same time generated employment in the towns and increased their population. Indirectly, however, it may also have precipitated their decline. Children took the train to Adelaide to attend high school, though it meant leaving home around seven and not returning until 12 hours later. People shopped in Adelaide more easily and more often, to the detriment of local businesses. But perhaps more importantly, the train accustomed people to feel close to the city, so that when the roads were bitumenised and a bus service introduced – a service significantly faster than the train, which was obliged to stop at many level crossings – they switched their patronage to this more time-efficient form of transport and, in a way, turned their backs on the local towns.

The last passenger service to Willunga was on 18 May 1957. The freight service continued, on a weekly frequency, until November 1963 but thereafter the only trains to use the line before it closed in 1969 were special excursion services organised by the Railway Historical Society. In 1986 the strip of land once occupied by the final section of the line starting at Field Street, McLaren Vale and ending at the Rose Garden at Willunga, was proclaimed a linear park for walking, cycling and horse riding.

# THE BUSH INN

Built in December 1839, Willunga's first inn – and the first in the McLaren Vale region – was actually named Lincolnshire House, after the English county where Thomas Atkinson and his brothers were born. Their initial building, on the corner of St James Street and Atkinson Drive, was a straw-thatched mud hut. The locals referred to it as the Bush Inn and this name was officially adopted when it was replaced by a solid brick building in 1844.

It was at the Bush Inn that the dinner and prizegiving for the district's first ploughing match was held in 1848. About a hundred 'gentlemen and farmers' attended, numerous toasts were proposed – including one to Noarlunga brewer 'Mr Edmonds and our Internal Interests' – and a small group of stayers 'kept up the conviviality till a more advanced period of the night, during which some good songs and glees afforded much gratification to the company, thus concluding a day of evidently high interest in all present'.

The Bush Inn was a lively focus of community activity – or as Mary Maud Aldam remembered it, 'a home from home'. Ploughing Match banquets were still held there in the late nineteenth century, with roast beef and plum pudding gracing the menu. It was from the Bush Inn, she wrote, that 'the Huntsmen met with the Hounds, before starting for the Day's Hunting the Dingo & Kangaroo or rounding up the mobs of cattle to be brought back to the Settlement'.

In turn this building was demolished, though its stables are still standing behind the present Bush Inn, built in 1901.

# WILLUNGA

Halfway between Adelaide and Encounter Bay, at the foot of the challenging hills and offering a way over them, Willunga was the government's natural choice for a depot and other services. The area was surveyed by John McLaren in 1839 and the first police station and Bush Inn were in place even before completion of the town plan in 1840. The unusual feature of this plan was its choice of a religious theme for street names, with eight saints honoured in the town.

Progress was slow. Four years later the town had only ten or so buildings including the second Bush Inn – 'handsome and commodious … built of brick, with stables, stockyard, &c', according to a contemporary description. There was a police station, the local sergeant also acting as postmaster and

High Street, Willunga, c. 1880

caretaker of the house erected by the government for the accommodation of its officers. About eight private dwellings had been built, some of stone and others of brick and pisé, all with slate roofs; most were occupied by workmen from the slate quarry. It was, however, an important stopping place on the north–south route. 'Not a dray passes to Myponga, Bangala, Yankalillah, Rapid Bay, or Encounter Bay, but calls at Willunga,' noted the *Adelaide Observer* in 1844.

By the 1850s Willunga was prospering. In 1851 the *South Australian Register* supported its claims to be the most picturesque township in South Australia, saying that 'it possesses an inestimable advantage in the view of the ocean, whose broad expanse here bounds the view to the westward'. Willunga had four churches, four butchers and two doctors – but no bakery; bread either came from Noarlunga or was baked at home. (William Morton's cottage, built at the end of the 1850s, had its own bread oven, as did many other dwellings.) In 1854 a total of 91 girls and boys attended James Bassett's school, Buckland House Academy, in St Lukes Street. A store-cum-post office was built in 1850 and a Telegraph Station in 1858. The courthouse and new police station opened in the 1850s, together with one more hotel (the Alma) in the town and one more (the Cornwall) just outside, on the road to Aldinga.

*Quiz's Tourists' Guide* described Willunga in 1893 as 'a town of some importance. Perhaps to a Londoner it may appear somewhat rustic, but we are not Londoners.' *Quiz* enjoyed the hospitality of the Bush Inn – 'Mine Host ... must find us rather unprofitable lodgers, and the way in which we demolish the contents of the cream jug must come in the light of a revelation to the bucolic mind' – but found the town had few amusements. 'At one time there existed a skating rink ... It was an admirable spot for flirtations, and ought to have been encouraged by impecunious clergymen.'

Until the turn of the century Willunga was the principal town in the region. Its population of 450 in 1900 was nearly three times that of McLaren Vale or Noarlunga. With the arrival of the railway the town doubled in size but in its later expansion could not keep pace with the other two.

# WILLIAM MORTON'S CANE CHAIRS

Around 1871 William Morton arrived in Willunga and planted willows along the creek, with the intention of continuing the trade for which he was trained in England: making cane baskets and chairs. Willows grow well wherever there is a running stream, and Morton's land ran down to the creek. He built his cottage, Upalong, at the top of St James Street.

Cutting back the willows once or twice a year causes them to send out a proliferation of pliable shoots which can be woven into baskets; larger canes are split before being used for chairs. Morton exhibited his 'thoroughly well-made cane chairs, cradles, &c.' at the Willunga Show, and in 1892 E.H. Hallack commended the 'really creditable specimens of handicraft' turned out by the 'basket and chairmaker of Willunga'. Mary Maud Aldam remembered the 'comfortable great arm chairs & baskets from willows planted along the creek'. A fairly large basket cost about 1/6 at a time when it cost 2d to send a standard letter or buy a loaf of bread.

Morton made his chairs and baskets for about 40 years. They were popular in the district and obviously found a ready market, and can often be identified in old photos where the gentle curves of cane contrast with the stiff pose and dress. A Morton chair is displayed in Willunga Courthouse.

Taking tea, Aldinga, late 1890s. The lady on the left sits in one of William Morton's chairs.

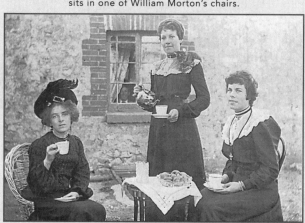

# NOARLUNGA

The land set aside for the township of Noarlunga was owned by the South Australian Company, which offered allotments for sale in April 1840. With plentiful fresh water upstream from the fords, it was an ideal staging post for coaches and bullock teams. One of the first buildings, also serving as the town's first post office, was the Horseshoe Inn, which opened in July 1840 directly opposite the vehicle ford. A month later the *Adelaide Chronicle* could describe the plan for the 'beautiful township of the South Australian Company, called Noarlunga' as being:

'most tastefully laid out in a romantic valley, formed by a singular bend of the river, the great south road, to Encounter Bay, running through the centre of it. Within the limits of the town a market-place has been reserved by the company, which is about to be fenced in; and, in the course of a few months, a market is to be held.'

The South Australian Company's elegant plan for a township was never fully realised. The town's first school, built in 1860, occupied the block set aside for a government reserve and in the 1920s took over Stephens Square as its recreation area. The bridge shown in the plan was not constructed until

South Australian Company town plan for Noarlunga

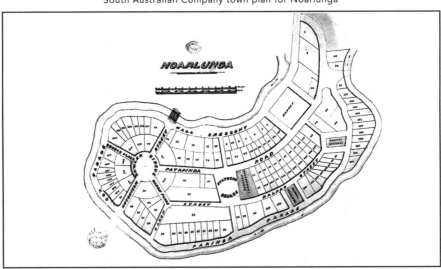

the late 1840s, the first bridge crossing the river near Baron Street. On the western sweep of the river, below the Horseshoe Inn, designated blocks of waterfrontage land remain open space, and the space around Gawler Circus in the crook of river has been used as a recreation area since early this century. Parkland borders Paringa Parade, while from Hutchinson Reserve, which extends along the banks as far as Baron Street, cable gliders on red wings can be seen swooping down the gullies. On the other side of the town, a boardwalk and path skirt the water's edge from the bridge as far as the site of market reserve, now a park. Beyond this, on a wide bay, is the old mill and next to it a limestone cottage built around 1844 for the harbour master. Being tidal near the ford, the river was designated a harbour and the volume of river traffic in the early days, together with its anticipated increase, warranted the appointment of a harbour master, who also acted as customs officer.

Unlike Willunga, which developed as a kind of provincial capital, Noarlunga was more of a market town. The town planners had reserved land for a market square, and the colony's first livestock show was held in here in March 1841. Pioneer farmers of the district were well represented: Mr Hewett exhibited 'a very fine red bull' and won a prize for the best-bred cow and for the best boar and sow while Mr McLeod, of Tarranga, entered a bull and a team of bullocks. The success of this show prompted McLeod to propose a regular market, to be held on the first Wednesday of each month, plus a fair every three months. In the 1850s Noarlunga had one of the busiest stockyards in the state.

On the river and just behind the market square was Noarlunga's mill, the first steam-driven mill in South Australia, which started taking wheat in 1844. A few years later Edmonds' brewery commenced operations almost opposite the Horseshoe Inn. A second hotel, the Jolly Miller (now the Noarlunga Hotel), opened in 1850, when the town had about 150 inhabitants and forty houses, many of which are still in use and classified in the Noarlunga Local Heritage Inventory. By 1882 the town had an office of the Bank of Adelaide, a Post and Telegraph office, public school and Institute, bootmaker,

Horseshoe Hotel, c. 1899

blacksmith, wheelwright and coachbuilder, butcher and three storekeepers. In the 1920s and 1930s Noarlunga was the most populous town in the district. Old residents of the town remember the busy Saturdays earlier this century when shops would be open until eight and local families would come to town to do their shopping at the three butchers and the three or four general stores, catching up on news and gossip at one of the two inns.

The town was also a popular sporting destination. The image of a penny farthing cyclist above the verandah of the Noarlunga Hotel recalls the weekend cycle races that finished at the Horseshoe. They were organised by the Norwood Cycling Club, which had a clubhouse at Port Noarlunga in the 1920s and 1930s. Before the completion of the Mount Bold reservoir in 1938, the Onkaparinga used to flow strongly every winter and offer excellent fishing. In 1929 a 'Back to Noarlunga' pamphlet described the fishing as equal to any in the state, adding that 'local residents can point out many paddocks where quail provide excellent sport for those fond of shooting, and rabbits, hares and foxes are also to be found in the neighbouring fields. There are few towns, even in rural districts, that offer better facilities for picnic parties.'

The opening up of Moana and the southern beaches in the 1920s meant vastly increased weekend traffic along the Main South Road through the town. The new road which now bypasses the town opened in 1972 – at almost the same time as a large new shopping centre opened at the 'new' Noarlunga in the centre of the urban spread along the coast and directly linked to the city by rail. With the transfer of business, the town settled into retirement and from 1978 was officially known as Old Noarlunga.

⟶    M c L A R E N   V A L E    ⟵

The parade of banners at the northern entrance to McLaren Vale proclaims its identity as a wine town, with two major wineries in its Main Street and many more signposted nearby. Since Thomas Hardy bought the old flour mill and turned it into a wine cellar, the town's fortunes have followed those of the wine industry, which has provided employment and, more recently, brought tourism to the region.

The name McLaren Vale originally referred to the whole valley that opens out beneath the Onkaparinga ridge. As the *Adelaide Observer* of 1844 reported, McLaren Vale 'ramifies into different small vales and flats with various local names, as, Douglas Flat, Boon's Valley, Wattle Valley, McLaren Vale proper, and so on [to] the … beautiful open plain … the so-called "Bay of Biscay"'. It was not until 1923, when part of section 156 was developed as a new subdivision under the name of McLaren Vale, that this became the official name of the township.

But almost as soon as there was some semblance of community it was commonly known as McLaren Vale or simply 'the Vale'. The advertisement for the twice-weekly goods and passenger service from Adelaide to Willunga in 1840 listed 'McLaren's Vale' as one of the scheduled stops.

According to the *Adelaide Observer* of 1844, the town was named after John McLaren, surveyor, though a competing claim later nominated David McLaren, at that time manager of the South Australian Company. The first time the name officially appeared was on John McLaren's map of 1840, applied to a stretch of what is now known as Pedler Creek; but the sections of land through which the creek runs were owned at the time by the South Australian Company. In his journal of 1839 (published in 1899) James Hawker, assistant surveyor under John McLaren, referred to the MacLaren Plains as being south of the sections bought and occupied by James McLeod. In his journal Hawker consistently used 'Maclaren' when referring to David McLaren, and 'McLaren' when speaking of John McLaren; his spelling of the location as 'MacLaren Plains' seems to favour naming rights going to David McLaren.

Both claims have some legitimacy, but the sentimental favourite must surely be John McLaren. He arrived in Adelaide in 1838 with his wife, who accompanied him during his pioneering survey of the region ('a most kind, motherly Scotch body', wrote James Hawker). John McLaren remained in South Australia and was appointed Deputy Surveyor General in 1847.

For the past 50 or so years McLaren Vale has been implicitly recognised as the commercial and service centre of the area. It was the logical choice in 1945 for the site of the district hospital. But this reputation was slow to develop. In 1867 the *Southern Argus* referred to McLaren Vale as 'what country Townships ought to be. Houses well scattered along the road and well separated from each other by flourishing gardens – a Township showing a straggling, self-contented, leisurely aspect'.

Perhaps there was a hint of irony in this description; unlike Willunga and Noarlunga, McLaren Vale was never planned. It began as two tiny settlements along what is now Main Road, the first a subdivision in 1851 of section 157 just south of the cluster of houses and outbuildings on the farms of William Colton and Charles Hewett, extending to near the Salopian Inn. This village was named Gloucester – though Colton's hotel, opened in 1849 on the northern edge of the village, was called Devonshire House.

The second village was named Bellevue, after Richard Bell who in the early 1850s bought part of section 135 from Charles Hewett and constructed a huddle of little pug houses, followed in 1857 by a hotel which he called the

Clifton. Subsequently purchased and enlarged by Thomas Hardy – who also bought the flour mill adjacent and much of the property nearby to house his employees – the hotel was renamed the Bellevue wine saloon, then Hotel Bellevue, and is now the Hotel McLaren.

The two settlements were further separated by an invisible line passing through the spot where the Almond Train now stands, representing the border between the District Councils of Willunga and Noarlunga, an anomaly corrected in 1987. Perhaps the nebulous character of this divide, combined with the ridiculously short distance between the two villages, contributed to their lack of individual identity. The *South Australian Gazeteer* of 1862 referred to 'McLaren's Vale, or Bellevue', meaning the combined settlement. In the 1866 *Town and Country Directory*, addresses are simply given as McLaren Vale, whether in the listing for the District Council of Willunga or that for the District Council of Noarlunga. However, the name of Bellevue was later attached to the railway siding to the north-west of the main McLaren Vale station.

Main Street, McLaren Vale, during Bushing Festival

# THE BARN

This low slung, whitewashed, 1860s cottage at the Bellevue end of McLaren Vale, today an art gallery and restaurant, once served as a stopping place for coaches and bullock teams plying the north-south road. Like many other Bellevue properties it was acquired in the 1880s by Thomas Hardy, who used the stables at the back to house his work horses.

At the start of the McLaren Vale wine renaissance, artist David Dridan and David Hardy, one of Thomas's great-grandsons, bought the premises with the idea of combining art, wine and food in a 'relaxed and comfortable' setting. The original building, now the gallery, bar area and ghost-inhabited cellar of the restaurant, was extended around a vine-shaded courtyard with the help of sturdy beams rescued from Gillard's old winery at Clarendon.

Named 'The Barn', it opened to the public in February 1970 as McLaren Vale's first restaurant. 'It'll never work,' was the usual reaction from locals –

The Barn c. 1900

but with the support of the wine fraternity it achieved its aims of encouraging conviviality and bringing art to the community. Frequent art exhibitions attracted people to stay for dinner and it became the regular stopping place for motorists between Adelaide and the southern coast, echoing its earlier vocation.

Anticipating the present trend towards regionalism by nearly 30 years, David Hardy promoted local foods such as almonds and olives in the restaurant. It was at David Dridan's instigation that in 1969 South Australian licensing regulations were amended to permit any bona fide art gallery or museum in a wine-producing area to be granted a licence to sell wine both by the bottle and the glass. At the same time the wine licence was modified to make it possible for food to be sold. The first of these new licences went to the Barn.

# INNS

Inns were meeting places and rest and refreshment stops for travellers. For scattered populations, the inn was the focus of community life. Ploughing match dinners were held there, topics of community interest – such as the building of a jetty at Port Willunga in 1850 – discussed within its rooms. The Bush Inn was the venue for meetings of the Willunga Farmers' and Stockholders' Club. For the club's annual meeting in 1844 'a good and substantial dinner was provided by Mine Host … which the members assembled seemed duly to appreciate'.

The district boasted fourteen inns in the 1860s: two at Noarlunga, three at McLaren Vale, one at Sellicks Hill, two each at Aldinga and Port Willunga and four in the Willunga district – some of which were actually outside the township, catering to thirsty teamsters carting wheat to the Aldinga and Willunga mills from as far away as Meadows, Bull Creek and Finiss River.

In 1839 inns were open until ten in the evening for six days a week, but on Sunday – when the community meeting place became the church – opening hours were restricted to between 1.30 and 3.00 pm, and even then only regular customers not drinking on the premises and bona fide travellers could buy alcohol. There was some local opposition to William Colton opening his inn on a Sunday in 1849; in possibly divine retribution, Colton died of a heart attack that same night.

In 1855 the weekday closing time was extended to 11.00 pm, and two periods of trading (one to three and eight to ten) were permitted on Sundays. Nevertheless, for dinner parties or balls or any other social occasions – such as the dinner following the annual show or ploughing match – the licensee could use his discretion and entertain guests beyond the official closing hour. Sunday opening was discontinued from 1891, and in 1915 additional restrictions were introduced, with closing time brought forward to six pm. The six o'clock closing remained in force until 1967.

The gradual introduction of such disciplinary measures went hand-in-hand with the growing strength of the temperance movement. Wesleyan

Outside Noarlunga Hotel, c. 1914

Methodists were strongly in favour of temperance, and in 1870 Reverend John Greer delivered a lecture on temperance in the Willunga Chapel, reported to have been well-attended. His message was sustained through gatherings of the Band of Hope, two groups meeting regularly in the district. The International Order of Good Templars built a Temperance Hall in Kangarilla in 1875 to be used for public and social events, and the following year temperance advocate Matthew Barnett visited the area. Having won over the locals to his cause, he succeeded in having the Kangarilla hotel converted to a boarding house and temperance hotel.

The best-known of the temperance hotels in this region was the Aldinga Temperance Hotel which operated as a boarding and eating house from the 1860s until 1920 and probably influenced the remaining hotel at Port Willunga to renounce its licence in 1895 and also become a temperance hotel.

# THE SALOPIAN INN

Since it opened as a restaurant in 1985, the Salopian Inn – on the Willunga Road, just out of McLaren Vale – has quietly built a solid reputation for the quality of its cuisine which, so far as possible, utilises the best of local produce of the McLaren Vale and Fleurieu regions – from the olive oil produced almost on its doorstep to goat cheeses from further south.

The building started off in 1851 as an inn, Gumprs', under licensee James Gumprs. In 1854 it had a brief life as the Salopian, a name meaning 'native to Shropshire' (the alternative name for this county was Salop). After losing its licence in 1879 it became the family home of the McMurtries for over 60 years.

Kerry and Zannie Flanagan bought the property, at the time scheduled for demolition, in 1984, having sold their previous restaurant, Prewett's at Kangarilla. The once spacious cellars had accumulated dirt and debris, the crumbling walls were covered by wisteria, and the toilet sat over a deep well. When the old galvanised iron was taken off the roof, they discovered a primitive roof of stringybark shingles. Their restoration aimed to preserve as much as possible of the original structure and character. The cellars were patiently cleared out by hand, cedar fire surrounds and cupboards retained, walls rebuilt using the same stones, and slate floors relaid.

The Salopian's first chef was Russell Jeavons. Initially influenced by Japanese cuisine and its distinctive, clean flavours, he also admired its ascetic philosophy. A meeting with Emmanuel Giakoumis, his olive oil and the force of his tradition transformed Russell's culinary career, encouraging him to turn to his immediate environment for inspiration. Japanese ingredients had no part in a sustainable local economy, he realised. Russell remained chef for another five years after Pip Forrester bought the restaurant in 1988, sharing her belief in good food sourced from the region and prepared simply so that the flavours speak for themselves.

The pleasures of the table are paramount in Pip's vision for the Salopian. It is a place where wine and food are equal and complementary and where formality plays second fiddle. With fond memories of the cafés of Paris (where she grew up) and the pubs of England (where she went to school), she has re-invented the Salopian in its original vocation, as a convivial meeting place where people share food, wine and ideas.

# SALOPIAN INN, AUTUMN 1998

*Chilli & lime blue swimmer crab with rice cakes*

*Goats cheese and fig tart with rocket salad*

*Tilbaroo veal with pancetta, sage, pappardelle pasta and preserved lemon cream sauce*

*Corned hogget with tomato & mustard seed pie and bayleaf-scented jus*

*Tagine of Kangaroo Island chicken with spiced couscous and baked quince*

*Terrine of poached peaches, apricots & peacherines and botrytis jelly with crème fraîche and a crisp waffle*

*Passionfruit and Paris Creek quark brulée with shortbread*

# CHAPTER
# BUILDINGS

Old Noarlunga and Willunga could probably both qualify as heritage towns merely by virtue of their density of historically interesting and significant buildings – not only the grand, formal public buildings such as churches and institutes but also humble cottages.

Arriving in McLaren Vale in January 1840, the Hewett family is supposed to have made its home in the hollow of a huge gum tree, domestic comfort having a lower priority than occupying the land. Other pioneers made makeshift shelters of bark or simple slabs and later, more permanent structures of mud (pug) or pisé. They built in a vernacular style, using easily accessible materials – and since these came from the land, their buildings harmonised with the natural environment.

Some made use of the wattle-and-daub style of construction. The name 'wattle' was probably first applied to trees of the *Acacia* species around the end of the eighteenth century and derives from an old English term for the rods or stakes that were interlaced with twigs and branches to form fences

# FOUR
# AND
# ARCHITECTURE

and walls. When these were plastered with clay or mud the construction was known as 'wattle-and-daub'. In Australia acacias supplied the long pliant branches, and hence the trees were known as wattles. The house on Wirra Wirra vineyard in which Connor Sparrow was born in 1906 was built of wattle-and-daub. It had five rooms, an enclosed back verandah, floors of slate and a roof of galvanised iron. The separate cool room was of similar construction but had a thatched roof.

More substantial buildings were made of stone – limestone, ironstone, sandstone, bluestone, or whatever was locally available. Their durability sometimes depended on the quality of the mortar, which in early years was variable. Many early buildings have simply crumbled away, but the warm, golden tones of these stone ruins make them favourite subjects for painters.

The natural choice for roofing material was slate from Willunga, and this combination of weathered red and subtle grey, stone-and-slate, has come to characterise the region.

# ~ SLATE ~

The slate industry in Willunga is as old as the town. Anyone who ventures into the Willunga hills, to the south-west of the town, can hardly fail to notice the seams of slate breaking the surface of the slopes. Certainly Edward Loud, newly arrived in the colony, recognised what he saw while out quail hunting early in 1840. By June 1840 Loud's quarry was in operation, employing about twelve families, and a few months later a second quarry opened in Beltunga gully, behind the town.

Loud's quarry produced an inferior kind of slate, described as purple slate, and eventually closed when better slate was found at Delabole quarry. In the next ten years numerous quarrying operations were begun, some under licence and others defiantly illegal. In 1846 investigations by the Willunga police constable uncovered several people quarrying slate on Crown Lands, including Thomas Williams and Sampson Bastian, both from Cornwall, who had been quarrying slate under a timber licence.

Many of the pioneers of the slate industry were of Cornish extraction. Thomas Martin decided to emigrate after learning about the copper mines at Burra. He heard about the slate on arrival in 1847, and immediately changed his destination. John Allen was another Cornishman who landed in 1847 – he later bought the Delabole quarry.

The slate was easily quarried, being so close to the surface and so readily accessible. The difficulty, as always, was negotiating the distance between producer and market. In the very early days it was shipped from Aldinga Bay, but this still involved a journey of ten kilometres over a road that was always rough and almost impassable after heavy rains. At the southern end of Aldinga Bay, where the beach is steeper, ships' longboats could approach to within a metre or so of the shore, facilitating loading, but this was only practicable during calm weather. In 1841, while waiting in the bay to take on slate, the *John Pirie* was driven ashore by a south-westerly gale. One alternative discussed was to float the slate to the sea by barge along the Onkaparinga.

Bill Heverley and Jack Kernick splitting slate for roofing, 1921

The heaviness of the cargo, the shallow and variable depth of the river, the occasional protruding rocks and the difficulties imposed by the sandbar at the mouth of the river made that idea impractical. In the 1840s, however, demand in Sydney for roofing slate – and the Willunga quarries specialised in roofing tiles, paving slate being more often sourced from Mintaro – was such that it was profitable to export from Aldinga Bay. In 1843 a record 241,000 roofing tiles were exported.

One of the motives for building a jetty at Port Willunga was the advantage this would offer the slate industry, but neither the first nor second jetty was totally suitable. Further, transport was almost prohibitively expensive. In the late nineteenth century slate imported from England and America – often as ballast – sold in Melbourne for £12 per 1000 tiles, while Willunga slate delivered to Melbourne cost £17. The price in Adelaide was £10/10/- per 1000 tiles. Even to get the slate from the quarries to Aldinga cost £3.

Until about the end of the nineteenth century, four quarries were in operation: Bangor, Bastian's, Delabole and Martin's. Bangor and Delabole were named after famous slate quarries in Wales and Cornwall. While wheat growing declined in the 1870s, the slate quarries worked steadily on, reaching peak production in the late 1880s and early 1890s; in 1891 two vessels left Port Willunga every week, carrying between them 20,000 slates.

Then came galvanised iron, considerably cheaper than slates for roofing, and asphalt, considerably cheaper for paths and paving. Demand for slate suddenly evaporated. From employing about 60 men in 1873, the quarries had work for only 18 in 1893. A minor resurgence occurred during the First World War, when the price of galvanised iron rose steeply, but it was short-lived. A galvanised iron roof in 1925 cost only half the price of a slate roof. Terracotta tiles offered another cheaper alternative from 1928. Only the Bangor quarry has continued operating throughout this century, though intermittently and with several changes of ownership. Production of the Willunga quarries from 1840 until 1975 has been estimated at 22 million roofing slates plus 60,000 tonnes of flagging, paving and walling slate.

# SLATE QUARRIES

In a high enclosed valley above Willunga, a substantial half of a hilltop has been removed, revealing the interior of the hill: slightly tilted, tightly packed plates of bleached grey and weathered brown. Vertical marks on one section of the cliff face indicate where workers once used hand chisels to extract slabs of slate. On exposed ledges a few hardy olive trees have found a precarious foothold.

This is the Bangor quarry, opened in 1842 by Thomas Williams. At its entrance, on the steep hillside, is the old foreman's office, built of slate in the 1850s. Even from a close distance the hut is dwarfed by the massive planes of slate, though the quarry face is nowhere near the height of 60 metres it once reached. At its peak it employed as many as 100 men but today, among the echoes, there are only two.

After the turn-of-century decline of the slate industry, Bangor quarry was bought by a Sydney consortium that included the architect John Dunstan. In 1920 it was transferred to Australian Slate Quarries Limited, a company of which John Dunstan was managing director and chairman, while two of his sons were employed as works manager and engineer. This company invested a great deal of money in buildings, plant and machinery and in 1921 opened on the site a new mill capable of an annual production of two million slates, for roofing and damp courses as well as doorsteps, fireplaces, shelves, cricket pitches, verandah floors, with waste pieces being used for crazy paving. By this time blasting powder was being used to dislodge large slabs of slate, then reduced to smaller blocks which were split by hand using wide chisels and mallets.

At the same time the company unveiled plans for a unique house, almost solely of slate, to be erected in Willunga as the residence of the managing director. This type of construction is relatively common in Wales and USA, but 'Glantawe' at 20 St Andrews Terrace, built in 1924 and 1925, is the only example in Australia and is now on the State Heritage Register. It has vertical slate panels as both external and internal walls; the roof is of slate, as are floors and ceilings, lintels and shelves and even wash troughs. John Dunstan's son Basil, who succeeded him as manager in 1937, was also District Clerk from 1929 to 1963, and used a small front room of the house as the office where local rates were paid.

There is little machinery in evidence now, and the slate is still split with chisels. Roofing slates are trimmed in a silent old treadle machine whose blade revolves like that of a lawnmower. Manufactured in 1881 and imported from Bangor USA, it has been lovingly restored to full operation by Murray Roberts, the present owner of Bangor quarry.

The site of the old mill today bears stacks of cut slates of varying sizes and thicknesses – some for floors, some for outdoor paving, the thinnest ones for roofs. On odd tiles, broken edges sparkle with glints of quartz. So often is slate described as grey that the range of colours, on close inspection, is quite amazing: a whole series of greys, from blue-grey to olive-grey to flannel suit-grey to almost black. Then there is the soft aubergine of the so-called 'purple' slate, marbled sections where tones of ochre and honey-brown swirl into depths of grey, and mottled blends of all these shades.

The next deep valley to the west secludes the Delabole quarry, which seems to have begun operations in the late 1840s, probably under the ownership of Sampson Dawe, previously manager of Edward Loud's quarry. Here, in a succession of cutaways, the massive planes of slate are almost vertical, the sheer faces softened by green mantels of grass.

Lower down the valley crumbling pillars stand like a miniature Stonehenge as a reminder of human occupation. The same warm terracotta colour as the eroded bank of the hillside, these pillars are all that remain of a settlement once dependent on the quarry. Hillsides now criss-crossed with sheep tracks would once have been home to perhaps a dozen Cornish families, some from the old Delabole quarry in Cornwall and others from American quarries. A visitor to the quarry in 1869 described the rows of cottages on either side of the valley, 'with here and there a little garden'.

In this isolated setting, about six kilometres from the village of Willunga, they built their homes of materials most readily accessible. Mixed with chips of rock and slate, the packed earth made walls while slate served as foundations, lintels, shelves and sometimes floors. Had the roofs been of slate, too, the buildings might have lasted longer – pisé erodes quickly if not protected from rain. The almond trees they planted still blossom around the ruins in late winter, next to the blackberries and dogroses; in the tiny creek white arum lilies run wild.

Above the quarry and houses, where a gap in the hills offers glimpses of the nearby coast, is a small, simple Wesleyan chapel, built of slate in 1867. Many Cornish were devoutly religious, and the erection of their own tiny chapel saved them walking the five kilometres or so into Willunga and back every Sunday. The pews from this chapel are now in the Sunday School of the Willunga Uniting Church.

Archeological studies show that most of the dwellings were double houses, with a common middle wall and shared central chimney. This traditional form of housing was common in south-west England; it can also be seen in the Cornish cottages of Paxton's Row in Burra. The houses were small, two rooms only with an area of less than forty square metres, though some had an additional slate-lined area outside the back door that probably served as a coolstore. One of the rooms would have been a bedroom, the other a living room/kitchen. The hearths where the women cooked and baked their bread stand as the most enduring and symbolic reminder of human presence.

## THE USES OF SLATE

Willunga could be nicknamed 'slate village'. Slate is everywhere, in the most unlikely settings as well as on roofs and footpaths, sills and steps. In Kookaburra Court in Willunga's garden village, a miniature slate house, complete with sagging verandah, serves as a letter box.

Thick slabs of slate line and cover a channel underneath St Jude's Street near the Methodist church, allowing water to trickle through to the other side. Next door is an old cottage, reached by a slate bridge across another watercourse. Its oldest section, probably dating to the 1850s, has slate walls – the better-quality, more durable grey slate in the lower part, above that the softer yellow slate that occurs closer to the surface – and a slate roof, from which rainwater drains into an open slate tank. Such tanks are relatively common; the old courthouse has several. Made of five large squares, bolted and banded together, they could hold up to 800 gallons (3600 litres); some were roofed with slate as well. Slate was also used to build wine fermenting vats but its tendency to flake meant that tiny pockets of bacteria could infect and spoil successive batches of wine, and the practice was discontinued. Kays' Amery winery has an shallow slate trough once used for washing winery equipment.

Verandahs are paved with slate – as at the courthouse and the handsome two-storey residence at 19 St Andrews Terrace, built in the late 1850s by the district's leading builder, George Sara, for Sampson Dawe. Mantelpieces were carved of slate. It was considered the ideal flooring and shelving for kitchens and dairies. Even fenceposts were made of slate.

Walls of dry slate construction stabilise slopes (such as outside the foreman's hut at Bangor quarry) and support bridges – such as 'Morton's

A wall of tightly packed slate, Willunga

bridge', crossing the willow-bordered creek near the cottage where basket-maker William Morton once lived. Near the top of Delabole hill the sides of a sunken waterhole for stock are partly lined with slate. The old dairy at Waverley Park, built in 1846, has immaculate walls of 'bookleaf' slate, sawn slabs of even thickness laid one on top of the other.

In the Willunga cemeteries are slate sarcophagi and headstones, many beautifully incised in the meticulously sober script of George Sara. A slate column in the Gemmel Tassie Reserve in McLaren Vale honours the fifty years' anniversary of the end of the second world war, while in a corner of the grounds of the Willunga Courthouse a solid slab of slate – from Bangor quarry, donated by Murray Roberts – commemorates 150 years of settle-ment in the Willunga district, from 1839 to 1989.

The principal use of slate, however, was for roofs. It is durable and fire-proof and, as a natural material, is also aesthetically pleasing. In the nine-teenth century almost every house in Willunga had a slate roof. Describing the town in 1867, the *Southern Argus* reported: 'In the matter of houses, every man has been his own architect, and the only visible point of agreement is the roofs, which are all of slate.' Slate tiles graced important public build-ings in the city of Adelaide, as well as the governor's summer residence in the Adelaide hills. Today Willunga slate can be seen on the roofs of the Adelaide GPO, Adelaide Town Hall, the old Legislative Council building, Bonython Hall at the University of Adelaide, the Royal Adelaide Hospital and St Francis Xavier Cathedral. The Melbourne GPO, built in 1867, was both roofed and paved with Willunga slate.

The original blackboard was a leaf of slate; boys who attended James Bassett's Willunga school in the 1860s wrote their schoolwork on slates, some of which can be seen through the windows of the building, now restored by the National Trust and listed on the State Heritage Register. And at Russell Jeavons' restaurant, a slab of slate records the list of pizzas.

# RUSSELL'S

Blacksmith Henry Harker's house (and later, the Primitive Methodist manse), with its walls, floor and roof all of slate, was one of the first in Willunga. It seems that Henry Harker also planted the first garden in High Street. The *South Australian Register* of 26 March 1851 reported that 'the best kept fruit and flower garden we saw, belonged to Harker, the blacksmith and wheel-wright, at the corner of the road. The trees of all kinds promised abundance of fruit, and the garden had scarcely a weed in it.' Though long past their prime of life, some of these fruit trees – the mulberry and pear – remain to this day.

Like the dwellings at Delabole, Harker's original house had just two small rooms. These have been converted into a single space which is now the main dining room of Russell Jeavons' restaurant. The larger of the two orig-inal rooms, probably the kitchen/living room, boasted a wide, deep fire-place. A narrow slate-paved verandah ran along the longer wall that faced north-west. A separate underground cellar was dug later, and then the house was extended with an addition at the back – now Russell's kitchen, where he has built a dome-shaped brick oven, its galvanised-iron exterior covering layers of insulating material.

The oven is heated by a wood fire – Russell prefers mallee roots and heavy red gum to generate a good heat, but makes use of other available fuels, including olive pressings. It takes about four hours, from completely cold, to heat the oven for baking bread. The oven can take about 30 loaves of bread, but with pizzas Russell usually cooks only four at a time – directly on the floor of the oven, previously raked and mopped clean. Five minutes is all it takes to bake a pizza – served directly to Russell's red gum tables on a wooden board.

Russell is a passionate enthusiast for slate. Above the oven squares of slate in different colours form a subtly muted checkerboard, and the toilets boast floors of tessellated slate. The 'blackboard' menu is written on a large slate

propped on the mantelpiece in the kitchen, and a smaller slate alongside lists the wines.

He is also a passionate advocate of simple, honest food – food which is true to its origins. As far as possible he sources his ingredients from the region – olives and olive oil, fresh stone fruit and almonds come from growers in the immediate vicinity, greens and herbs from Mount Compass.

One of the specialities of the restaurant is dukkah, a Middle Eastern nut-and-spice mix that Russell has popularised in South Australia, particularly in the McLaren Vale region. Traditionally eaten with bread dipped in olive oil, its usual ingredients are sesame seed, coriander seed, cumin and coarsely ground hazelnuts. Russell's version expresses the character of the region by substituting local almonds for the hazelnuts, and replacing cumin with seeds from the wild fennel that grows prolifically in the backblocks. He takes advantage of the gentle heat of the cooling oven to dry and slightly roast the seeds and nuts to enhance their flavour, before grinding each component sep-arately and blending them according to the proportions of his unique recipe.

Russell Jeavons at his oven

# HISTORIC WILLUNGA

In 1851 the *South Australian Register* reported of Willunga:

*The houses are of various materials, chiefly brick and stone, with roofs of slate from the quarries near, and a few of wood. The fencing is almost entirely post-and-rail, and the occupied lands are substantially enclosed.*

Brickmaking, using local clay, began in 1840, Mr William Atkinson (brother of Thomas) advertising in the *Register* 'good bricks' at £3/5- per 1000, cash. Willunga bricks could be distinguished by thumb-and-finger imprints, the result of their being turned by hand during firing.

The earliest buildings in the town were the police station, survey and post offices, and the rough-and-ready original Bush Inn. A regular mail and passenger service to Willunga was soon in operation, Willunga having one of only six post offices in the colony in 1841. From the late 1840s postal operations were run by Henry Malpas from his general store at 1 St Peters Terrace. Henry was happy enough to act as postmaster in a voluntary capacity, possibly because his general store profited from the arrangement, but the Colonial Secretary recommended that he be paid since Willunga had more business than any other of the southern post offices. The gracious building in St Peters Terrace now known as Willunga House was built in several stages, a small, slate-floored single storey cottage added to the store-cum-post office in the 1850s, the upper storey with its wide balconies added in 1864. Possibly at the same time the ground floor facade was altered to incorporate bay windows. The kitchen, which also seems to have been built in several stages, was separate from the main house, though the spacious cellars were excavated beneath the post office part of the building. Generations of the Malpas family lived in the house for over a century; today Willunga House offers bed-and-breakfast accommodation to visitors.

In 1858 the post office moved to new premises which it shared with the telegraph station, opposite the courthouse at the top of High Street. The original single storey building of local stone with a shingled roof was soon enhanced by a verandah, and a two-storey addition completed in 1865. In its essentials the building is still as it was then, an excellent example of early rural colonial architecture and, in its use of local materials, an illustration of the self-sufficiency of local builders. Henry Pounsett, postmaster from 1861 to 1891, would signal the arrival of mail from England by hoisting a blue flag from the flagpole. He would also leave a barrel of apples on the verandah, for the enjoyment of customers and travellers.

Willunga had a police station in the early years but no courthouse; the local court was held in a room at the Bush Inn. It was hardly a satisfactory arrangement, and more than a few complaints were received. In 1854 a magistrate reported that:

*the greatest degree of difficulty has been experienced in maintaining in the present room, that degree of order and decorum, which is required in a court of justice, and on Wednesday all propriety was grossly outraged and public business disrupted by repeated disturbances and quarrelling in the public house by persons intended to be witnesses in cases before the court, but who had become drunk . . .*

A request was made for the court to be moved 'to the old buildings called Government House', the magistrates being willing 'to submit to very inferior accommodation rather than again hold the Court in a public house'. Despite their plea, however, no alternative was available. The two-roomed government hut built in 1839 – known locally as 'Government House' after Lady Franklin and her companions stayed there on their way to Encounter Bay in 1840 – needed major repairs. According to the Commissioner of Police in 1854, 'Nothing useful can be made out of the rubbish now standing.' In December, tenders were called for the erection of a courthouse and police station, and work started two months later.

Built of sandstone from the quarry on the opposite side of the creek, the courthouse began basically as the courtroom and a single cell, directly opposite the entrance door, with an adjacent constable's room and rear kitchen.

The magistrate's chambers, with its slate mantelpiece, was added in 1864 together with the cells at the back of the courthouse, the slate-paved verandah, and the stables with their wooden-louvred windows. The exercise yard and stables, paved with smooth, bleached, rounded stones from the nearby coast, were probably completed at the same time.

One of the early magistrates was Buxton Forbes Laurie, SM. Although a chemist by training, he was appointed a country magistrate soon after his arrival in South Australia, and by 1874 he had become the chief stipendiary magistrate for the entire southern district, attending Yankalilla on the first Tuesday of the month, Willunga the following Wednesday and other local courts in succession. He participated in local affairs, giving a reading at the quarterly soiree of the Willunga Mechanics Institute in 1871. Perhaps his chief claim is as superintendent of the construction of the Port Elliot–Goolwa tramway, the first public line with iron rails laid in Australia. (Since it used horse power, strictly speaking it was not a railway.) Buxton Forbes Laurie established his home at 'Southcote', Port Elliot, and was one of the earliest vignerons in that district, planting his first vines in 1853. Coincidentally, two of his descendants – great-great-grandson d'Arry Osborn and great-grandson Keith Genders – continued this association with wine.

Willunga was originally a post for mounted policemen. Of the team of three in 1840, two were supposed to be stationed, one on the move. One of the policemen stationed at Willunga towards the end of the century was Constable Tuohy, who received a gold medal for his role in rescuing victims of the *Star of Greece* shipwreck in 1888. In 1892 his two daughters planted a lemon and an orange tree near the eastern wall of the building, celebrating the event by recording on the soft sandstone walls: 'This orange (lemon) tree was planted by Eileen M. Tuohy (Kathleen Tuohy) August 19th 1892.' To commemorate their deeds, two new citrus were planted at the time of the opening of the museum in 1970. Constable Tuohy himself left his name on one of the walls of the exercise yard.

The building remained a courthouse and police station until 1929. Saved from demolition in the late 1960s, it was restored by the Junior Group of the National Trust of South Australia, and in February 1970 opened as a National Trust museum, its interior rebuilt according to the original plans which are displayed in the courthouse. On the magistrate's left, near the door to the cells, is the prisoner's box with its well-worn floor, and on his right the six-man jury box and witness box. Five years later, the restored stables were opened amid great festivity, including a street procession of locals in period costume, horses and traps, brass and pipe bands, and the symbolic offering of a 'peppercorn rent' to Willunga District Council.

Before it was used as a courthouse, however, the building housed single female immigrants, mainly Irish, who had been brought to Australia to work as domestic servants. This brief period of occupancy was not without its drama. Until they obtained employment, the girls were under the supervision of a matron for the time they were at the 'depot', as it was known, and this supervision implied a strict curfew. On one occasion in 1856, several girls went to visit a friend who had found a position some way out of the town, and as a result were late in arriving back. A rule was then imposed by local notable and chairman of Willunga District Council, Thomas Smith Kell, forbidding the women to 'go to a distance in the country' because, he seemed to assume, this inevitably meant their returning at all hours of the night. Understandably, the rule aroused opposition, and on his next visit Mr Kell claimed to have been assaulted by one of the girls, Catherine Leary, who threatened to murder him next time he came to the depot. Local police had to be called to settle the dispute.

T.S. Kell was one of the earliest settlers in Willunga and a pioneer of the short-lived flax industry. He once owned the whole of St Peters Terrace, and lent his name to Kell Street, which bordered his property, Waverley Park. The homestead, built in 1846, has been greatly modified by subsequent owners but still boasts elegant marble fireplaces in the original bedrooms and drawing room. A photograph, probably taken in the 1920s, shows a simple colonial dwelling surrounded by a verandah on three sides and with a kitchen

At Waverley Park, Willunga, 1898

wing at the rear, near the old dairy. In its rural setting the house appears insignificant, dwarfed by the massive red gums growing along the creek behind the house, many with bases over one metre in diameter.

In 1879 Waverley Park was acquired by John Allen, owner of Delabole slate quarry from 1861 until 1903, and until 1971 remained in the Allen family. It is remembered today in the range of wines produced by Willunga High School and in the Herbert Allen Memorial Park, established on 10 hectares (25 acres) of land bequeathed in trust to the Willunga Council by Miss Maude Allen, who lived in the house until her death in 1971. This portion of the property, adjacent to land earlier donated to the Willunga Bowling Club, became the first nine holes of the Willunga golf course.

# EARLY WINERIES

When Thomas Hardy began to make wine at McLaren Vale, he took advantage of the disused flour mill, converting it to process grapes instead of wheat. The vignerons who followed him had to develop their own winemaking facilities. Between 1894 and 1897 Ryecroft, Amery, Katunga and Pirramimma wineries each opened cellars in annual succession, while in the Happy Valley district large wineries were built at Vale Royal, Horndale and Mount Hurtle. Wirra Wirra, The Wattles and the original Tatachilla followed in the early 1900s.

The essential stages in winemaking are crushing (to release the juice), fermentation (to produce the alcohol), settling, fining or filtering, then bottling. Most red wines undergo an additional stage of maturation in wooden casks before bottling. At the end of each stage the must or wine has to be transferred for the next phase of the operation. Electric pumps do the job quickly and efficiently today, but nineteenth-century winery design took advantage of gravity.

The principles of gravity flow are clearly in evidence in the massive stone winery at Horndale and in the old Amery cellars, constructed for the Kay brothers according to plans developed by John Kelly, at that time co-owner of Tatachilla. Situated on a relatively steep slope and partly dug into the hillside, the Amery winery was built in several stages. The earliest section, completed in 1896, housed the 24 open fermenting vats that received the must, the grapes having been crushed at a slightly higher level. With the assistance of hand pumps, the wine was transferred to settling tanks at the next level, thence to casks. This structure still has its original galvanised iron roof – or rather, roofs, both of galvanised iron, with an insulating layer of dried seaweed in between. The 1901 addition, plans for which can be viewed at the winery, was essentially for storage in large vats and casks, eventually carted away from the lowest level of the winery complex. The same gravitational principles were applied at Pirramimma and the original Wirra Wirra winery which, after years of disuse, was barely a ruin when Greg and Roger Trott bought the property in 1969. They have since rebuilt the cellars according to the basic design.

In the main street of McLaren Vale the new Tatachilla winery occupies the cellars built in 1901 by Horace and Cyril Pridmore to replace an earlier cellar of wattle slabs – hence the original name, The Wattles. A plaque over the arched doorway of this dark ironstone building reads 'Laid by C. E. P. Feb$^y$ 15, 1901'. Again, this structure took advantage of a slightly sloping site, the grapes being received at the higher level. When Penfolds bought the winery in 1910 the cellars were greatly enlarged; but by this time the age of galvanised iron had arrived, and the broad, spacious building that now serves as barrel storage area for the new Tatachilla was constructed simply of corrugated iron. Wooden louvres at the peaks of the three hipped roofs ensure ample ventilation in summer.

What amazes most is the scale of operations in those early days. Under Penfolds' ownership there would probably have been as many as 80 cement tanks, though not all would have been full at the same time. Similarly at the original Tatachilla on Tatachilla Road, then the largest single vineyard in the southern hemisphere, the rows and rows of open concrete fermenting vats would, if joined together, have stretched for 100 metres or more. According to a report in the *Wine and Spirit News and Australian Vigneron* in 1913 – the year the winery opened – the floor space covered just over 23,000 square metres, and the 42 fermenting vats had a capacity of 230,000 litres.

In its heyday the old Tatachilla was a thoroughly modern winery with competent pumping machinery to obviate dependence on simple gravity. The imposing limestone edifice – pale pinky beige with defining lines of red brick, massive internal supports of oregon and a galvanised iron roof – was built by the English exporting company, Stephen Smith & Company Limited. An earlier winery of galvanised iron had been built in 1903 by John Kelly, anticipating a vintage in excess of the district's winemaking capacity, and a distillery added in 1909. Kelly, however, soon sold out to Stephen Smith, a company whose shareholders were practically all English and which shipped its entire production to England, where the wine – often promoted for its medicinal virtues – sold under the name of Keystone Burgundy.

Winemaking at Tatachilla ceased soon after it was purchased in 1962 by Emu Wines, which sold the property almost immediately, the buildings and surrounding land being bought by the Lutheran church in 1964 for a camp site. Today, while the external structure is virtually unchanged and the huge rainwater tanks incorporated into the building still collect and store water, the upper-level cask hall serves now as an auditorium for students, and the idle banks of fermenting tanks store spare mattresses and other paraphernalia.

Tatachilla cellars, 1930s

Given the potential of present technology to overcome almost any natural situation, the harnessing of gravity by McLaren Vale's newest winery, Maxwell's, appears almost obtusely primitive. This three-level hillside winery of warm Western Australian sandstone with plenty of glass is, however, simply a sensible response to increasingly sophisticated technology: if gravity will do the trick, let it.

# DOMESTIC BUILDINGS

The earliest building in McLaren Vale – even before it was known as McLaren Vale – was William Colton's farmhouse, Daringa, its name echoing the word the Kaurna people used to describe that swampy area. Built of bricks, possibly those made by William Atkinson in Willunga, set on thick foundation slabs of slate and roofed with slate, the original cottage probably had just four rooms and an outside kitchen. Red gum forms the lintels over low doorways. Though progressively enlarged, it was not until the 1870s that the kitchen was actually part of the house, tacked on at one corner. Ken Maxwell remembers this slate-floored room as it was when his family came to the house in 1927, its big wood stove and baker's oven along one wall, and a sunken half cellar adjoining.

Another very early dwelling, and only a few kilometres to the north, is the Oliver family homestead at White Hill, built in the 1850s. It is unusual in having a complete below-ground level of four main rooms, floored with slate that was initially laid directly on the clay substrate. The original house, since modified and enlarged, had no plumbing connected. The kitchen, scullery and, presumably, the washhouse were in a separate building behind the main one, a covered breezeway separating the two.

Such a design was not unusual. In many early Australian houses the kitchen was separate and outside or a lean-to on the back; Willunga House, built by Henry Malpas in the 1850s, offers a good example. Often the original and primitive shelter was later used as a kitchen after the construction of a more substantial homestead, as might have happened at Daringa.

In the early days cooking was done over an open wood fire, the hearth generally slightly raised above floor level. Each morning the fire would be rekindled from the warm coals remaining, and each evening the coals would be raked to the centre and covered in ash. This procedure for making the fire safe without extinguishing it completely was called 'damping', and lent its name to 'damper', bread cooked in the ashes.

Many nineteenth-century kitchens included a small bread oven, just big enough to bake the three or four loaves the household required. The vast bread oven built into the back wall of the narrow kitchen wing at the rear of the former Seaview Hotel at Port Willunga – which began licensed life in 1856 as the Lewis Arms, then became the Jervis Arms, the Louis Arms and the Jervis Arms again – is big enough to have baked enough bread for the whole district. Well built and very well insulated, this efficient commercial oven, very modern for its era, was heated by a separate fire to one side of the low, arched, brick-lined chamber in which the bread – and probably many other dishes – baked.

The old Clark farmhouse at Coriole winery, with its inside kitchen and slate-floored hallway, must have been a superior style of dwelling. Beautifully situated on the crest of a gentle rise against the backdrop of a higher ridge, with views across McLaren Vale to the profile of the Willunga scarp, the little white cottage crouches low as if to cause the least possible disruption to the landscape. Dating to the 1860s, both the cottage (now winery office) and neighbouring barn (now the tasting room) seem to have been built to last, with walls of local bluestone and dark, almost black, ironstone and with large, airy cellars excavated underneath.

By contrast, the 1880s building known as the Harbourmaster's Cottage at Port Willunga had the primitive design of a four-roomed dwelling with a front verandah and half-cellar at the back, dug into the side of the hill. A fifth room was later added on the western side. Now within the Port Willunga Linear Park, the ruins of this cottage, constructed of coastal limestone and quartzite beach cobbles, are part of what was originally the Martin family farm, the first European settlement at Port Willunga. Together with the ruins of the larger building, once the Pier Hotel owned by Thomas Martin and known locally as Uncle Tom's Cabin, the cottage has been investigated by an archeological team from Flinders University and the University of Adelaide. Among the relics are sauce and pickle bottles, and a few patent medicine bottles – Chamberlain's Elixir and Scott's Emulsion.

It could almost have been the Harbourmaster's Cottage that the Kaines family rented in the summer of 1899. English visitor Maisie Smith accompanied them and described their holiday accommodation in her almost daily letters home to her mother. This correspondence has since been edited and published by her grand-daughter Joan Kyffin Willington in the book *Maisie*:

Plan of Harbourmaster's Cottage

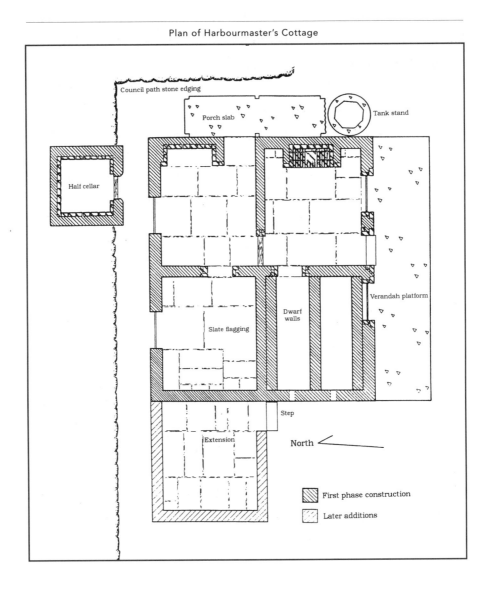

Harbourmaster's Cottage, Port Willunga

*Such a comic cottage – a parlour, a kitchen and two bedrooms and an outside bedroom [as well as a front verandah] … We all feed in the kitchen, a great luxury because we can keep things hot. Such a lovely huge open fireplace – takes up one side of the little kitchen entirely … and all the floors are stone, even in the bedrooms. There is a nice little cellar outside, made expressly for the comfort and convenience of the blowflies and ants, into which we put all our meat, with obvious results. A pigsty has been built just outside, and cocks and hens come to feed outside and also inside our back door and upset our pots and pans deliberately if we attempt to shoo them away … The front door opens straight on to the parlour, and the parlour opens on to Laura's bedroom and the kitchen, and my bedroom opens from the kitchen.*

# LIMEBURNER'S COTTAGE

Now incorporated into the Marienberg Limeburner's Centre at McLaren Vale, a restaurant and cellar door tasting room for Marienberg wines, this modest 1880s cottage was for a time the home of bricklayer Simeon Dunstone. Dunstone's house was probably built over an earlier structure, constructed in the 1850s when the Bellevue settlement was beginning. The front rooms and cellar have retained the original timber floors, the adjoining room its original slate. This room was probably the kitchen with a 'colonial oven', heated from both below and above, in place of the present fireplace.

Traces of lime, coal and charcoal discovered at the back of the restaurant kitchen, behind the tasting room, indicate the spot where 'the limeburner' burnt limestone to make the mortar needed in bricklaying. The logical source of this limestone would have been but a short walk away at the end of Chalk Hill Road, where Maxwell's winery now stands. A cutting into the hillside behind the building shows how close to the surface the limestone is. The tunnel dug into the hillside below the winery gives an even better indication of the ease of excavation of the limestone. In the early twentieth century, this tunnel was used for mushroom cultivation.

# MODERN BUILDINGS

The old buildings of the nineteenth century shared a common feature: their reliance on local materials. Earth and clay, timber and stone, slate and bark were all valuable resources to professional builders and bush carpenters.

The development of new materials such as galvanised iron, together with a reduction in the region's isolation through improved means of transport, diminished this distinctive character. Recognition of the value of heritage, however, means that local government now encourages sympathetic development in 'historic township zones' by insisting on compatibility in design, materials and colour schemes. Guidelines have been established for Old Reynella, (Old) Noarlunga, Clarendon, Willunga, Port Willunga and Aldinga.

One of the newest types of building construction demonstrates a return to materials that are both local and natural. The rammed earth technology (now known as stabilised earth) was developed in Western Australia in the 1970s. For Ian Collett, the first to experiment with stabilised earth in South Australia and founder of Stabilised Earth Adelaide, the process accorded with his interest in permaculture, the principles of which emphasise the harmonious integration of humans and nature.

With a background in horticulture, Ian Collett never intended to end up a builder. 'What I really want to do,' he said, 'is cook for my friends, but to do that properly you've got to grow the ingredients, and that means setting up a system' – in his case, permaculture. The permaculture garden will come later, together with the animal sanctuary he is developing on land adjacent to the Willunga garden village, establishing native trees, shrubs and grasses in a mix as close as possible to the original ecosystem.

The garden village, twenty blocks of land surrounding a central common area with garden, fruit trees and swimming pool, is a unique concept in South Australia. On the eastern edge of Willunga, it was originally farming land where Ian grew oats. Township boundaries were moved to accommodate his development, and over two years subdivision plans were drawn, roads constructed and underground services installed. The first block of land was purchased in 1987 and now all but one have been sold.

A diverse population has been attracted to the village – from retired couples to families with young children – and all residents have chosen to use stabilised earth, partly for its insulating advantages, partly for its warm appeal and touch-inviting texture. Within this unifying theme there is great variety of size, shape and form. Traditional peaked roofs of red galvanised iron are juxtaposed with gentle curves of soft bluish grey; teal blue window frames contrast with the warm honey tones of natural timber and sprawling flower gardens bloom alongside sombre walls. The depth and shade of colour vary, some houses tending towards pink, others more akin to ochre. For all their mass, these buildings give the appearance of 'sitting lightly on the earth'.

In the McLaren Vale region, stabilised earth has been used to construct domestic dwellings, wineries and wine stores (Wirilda Creek, Pirramimma), restaurants (Woodstock Coterie), schools (Waldorf school) and public buildings (McLaren Vale & Fleurieu Visitor Centre). Compared to bricks, which need to be fired, the material itself is energy efficient, and additional efficiencies can be incorporated into the buildings through appropriate design and orientation. Construction is quick, with less than two weeks needed to erect the walls of an average house. Kerry Flanagan chose stabilised earth for the Wirilda Creek winery because it is both eco-sensitive and aesthetically pleasing, 'like a cellar above ground'.

## WILLUNGA WALDORF SCHOOL

Stabilised earth was chosen for the Willunga Waldorf school partly for its appearance and temperature-moderating properties, but also because of its low toxicity. The cluster of separate buildings, all displaying a different colour scheme, illustrate the school's philosophy of complementarity between the classroom, the curriculum and the stages of child development. The kindergarten unit is rounded and reassuring, its external walls a dusky mushroom pink with lolly-pink door and window trims beneath a deep pinkish-red roof.

Much of the design detail is the inspiration of Jeremy (Jerry) Keyte, who also constructed the whimsically rustic Snugglepot-and-Cuddlepie benches in Willunga's High Street. In one corner rounded timber shingles overlap like the petals of a flower and, surrounding a door, they become the protective wings of Athena's owl of wisdom. With their gently domed roofs and curved timber trims disguising the angles, these classrooms give the impression of being designed on a child's scale, for a child's imagination to transform into spaceships or fairy mushrooms.

Stabilised earth construction of Pirramimma wine store

# CHAPTER
# WINE

English colonists were quick to realise that the Australian climate should allow them to grow grapes and make wine. In New South Wales vineyards were established early in the nineteenth century, and pioneers such as James Busby and William Macarthur, seriously intent on making quality wine in Australia, toured the vineyards of Europe selecting suitable grape varieties. They imported cuttings, principally from France and Spain, and these acclimatised vines provided stock for the fledgling South Australian wine industry some twenty years later.

South Australian vineyards account for almost half Australia's annual wine production of nearly 600 million litres and the 50-odd wineries of McLaren Vale contribute slightly under ten per cent of the state total, their 1997 vintage yielding the equivalent of about 37 million bottles of wine. Almost 60 per cent of the grapes crushed in 1997 (around 40,000 tonnes) were red wine varieties, principally shiraz, cabernet sauvignon and grenache, varieties that were among the earliest plantings in the area and have sustained the region for almost a century and a half.

# FIVE

The official McLaren Vale Wine Region, bounded by the Sellicks Hill Range to the south, extends eastwards as far as Mount Bold Reserve, taking in the eastern side of Clarendon, and beyond the Reynella district to the north. All but a few patches of vineyard, however, are concentrated south of the Onkaparinga. Even in in this small area, however, the diversity of environments, from the coastal plains to the ridges of Blewitt Springs 200 metres above sea level, yields a pronounced diversity of styles.

The standard-bearers for the region, shiraz and chardonnay, produce unique regional wines that are highly acclaimed in Australia and increasingly recognised overseas. Partly this is due to the beneficent climate – reliable winter rains, hot summers tempered by sea breezes, and an extended autumn, typically warm and dry. These favours of nature ensure fruit of consistently high quality, year after year, and give McLaren Vale wines their distinctive richness of flavour.

# WINE PIONEERS

The honour of the colony's first vines probably goes to John Barton Hack, who brought vines from Launceston in Tasmania and planted them on his North Adelaide property in 1837. The following year, apparently independently of one another, it seems that John Reynell and Richard Hamilton planted vines. These two pioneers of the South Australian wine industry both have an association with the McLaren Vale region.

Reynell seems to have had a consumer's interest in wine as well as an eye on possible profits, while Hamilton, who regarded wine as a tonic, was at least partly motivated by concerns for the health of his family. Reynell's vineyard, at the northern edge of the McLaren Vale viticultural region, was purchased by Thomas Hardy & Sons in 1982 and is now the headquarters of the BRL Hardy Wine Company. Descendants of some of Reynell's original cabernet vines are still bearing and his hand-dug, grass-roofed cellar, completed in 1845, is still in use. Richard Hamilton's land was in the Marion district, just south of Adelaide, but since 1947 his descendants have been established in McLaren Vale.

Though most of his land was devoted to farming and sheep grazing, Reynell gradually expanded his vineyard from half an acre in 1844 to 15 acres in 1862. His interest in wine was decidedly more serious than most other early settlers who also planted vines and established small vineyards. Edward Rowland had vines at the Bush Inn in the early 1840s and Thomas Atkinson planted a vineyard at Willunga district. In her memoirs of the late nineteenth century Mary Maud Aldam wrote of the 'good wine' made by the local farmers, which they gave to their workmen 'every day with lunch, as tea in those days was very scarce'.

One such farmer was George Pitches Manning, who in 1850 bought two sections of land north-east of McLaren Vale, naming his property Hope Farm. The following year, at the instigation of his daughter's father-in-law, Congregationalist minister Reverend Thomas Stow, Manning planted cuttings from Stow's vineyard: cabernet sauvignon, mataro, grenache and shiraz.

Thomas Stow was himself the owner of a small vineyard north-east of Adelaide, and had been impressed by the local wines he had sampled on his rounds. Following his first vintage in 1855, Manning was one of five exhibitors in the wine section at the second Willunga Show of 1857: 'Best sample of colonial wine, not less than six bottles, the manufacture of the exhibitor'. He also made some of the first brandies and ports in South Australia, setting up a still on the edge of his duckpond. Hope Farm is better known today as Seaview winery; at the end of one of the winery's cask-lined corridors a com-memorative plaque stands before a face of the chalky white subsoil from which George Pitches Manning's original cellar was hewn.

The Clarendon Vineyard, mid-1870s

Another district pioneer was Edward Peake of the Clarendon vineyard, high on the hills west of the township. According to E.H. Hallack, these vines were originally planted by John Morphett in 1848 or 1849 (though William Leigh is also credited with establishing grapes in the area). The land was later sold to Edward Peake who built the winery in 1858. Joseph Gillard bought the property in 1882, and still owned it in 1908 when May Vivienne visited and described the township of Clarendon as 'nestling among the lovely vineclad hills like a little bird in a nest of lovely green'.

By 1862 small vineyards must have been almost commonplace in the McLaren Vale region, the *Register* reporting on 23 April of that year that most of the vineyard proprietors had finished wine-making. The writer added:

*The climate and soil here seems exceedingly well adapted for the growth of red wines, and now every description of agricultural produce sell so low, I have no doubt that many of the residents will turn their attention to the culture of the vine, which, at a moderate price for wine, promises to be more remunerative than farming ... The frost has never been known to materially injure any vines in this neighbourhood, which is a great advantage.*

Few of these early farmers, many from the south of England, would have had any experience or knowledge of grapegrowing or winemaking. Undaunted, and encouraged by others' apparent success, they launched themselves into this new venture with rash enthusiasm, learning as they went, swapping advice and tips along with a bundle of vine cuttings.

There is no way of knowing from written comments and judgments of the day what these wines tasted like; nor can we necessarily trust the palates of those who judged them. 'I cannot say anything in praise of his wine,' wrote the *Register* reporter in his account of a visit to Mr Loud's farm at Willunga in 1863, 'but he [Loud] accounts for its inferiority by saying that the good wine is drunk during the first part of the season, and the worst left till afterwards.' In the same year the *Register* described a visit to Atkinson's orchard and vineyard, where the vines – mainly mataro, grenache and black Portugal – were sufficiently old to produce several hogsheads of wine. 'I tasted some thoroughly good sound wine. It was much too strong for general use; but when fully matured it must be a very saleable comodity.' Heartened by such remarks, more farmers planted vineyards as a sideline, and more wine was produced. Between 1854 and 1862 South Australia's vineyard area increased tenfold, though the McLaren Vale area accounted for only about 10 per cent of the state total.

Manning's wine, portrayed as full bodied, dry, deep in colour and heavy with tannin, found a ready market in the district and in Adelaide. It also inspired Dr A.C. Kelly to persuade a number of influential and wealthy Adelaide businessmen to invest in this promising new industry. Kelly bought land adjacent to Manning's Hope Farm and in 1862 planted the first 90 acres of the Tintara vineyard with cuttings of shiraz, cabernet, mataro, grenache and sauvignon blanc from Manning's vines.

Previously, in 1842, Kelly had planted vines at Morphett Vale, using cuttings from Macarthur's vineyard at Camden, New South Wales. His Trinity vineyard was not too far south of John Reynell but far enough from main roads for transport to be a problem. In any case, his ideas were grander than his twelve or so acres. In his first book, *The Vine in Australia* (1861), he wrote:

*The prospects of wine growing in the Australian colonies are much more hopeful than wheat growing ever was or perhaps is now; and when we compare our soil and climate with those of the wine countries of Europe, we are warranted in coming to the conclusion that the future of the wine growing interests in Australia is as promising as any of her permanent resources.*

Stirring sentiments – but he had not calculated for the economic depression of the mid-1860s. While production had increased, demand for local wine sales plummeted, and exporting to other states was uneconomic because of tariffs imposed to protect their own wine industries. George Manning, stuck with a cellar full of wine, was saved by Thomas Hardy, who bought half of it. Hoping to increase overseas sales, Kelly headed for England in 1871, and small quantities of Tintara wine were optimistically shipped to London. Sadly, freight, distance and lack of recognition of Australian wines conspired against Kelly and his company, and when the 700 acres of vineyards, the Tintara cellars and other improvements were eventually offered for sale, it was again Thomas Hardy who saved the day, buying the lot. Kelly's efforts, however, were instrumental in establishing the base on which an export industry could be built.

# THOMAS HARDY

Thomas Hardy is acclaimed as the father of the South Australian wine industry, and in particular of wine in McLaren Vale, where a memorial to him stands in the Apex Park, incongruously at the Gloucester end of the town. Extraordinarily vigorous, industrious, astute, enterprising and far-sighted, he founded a family company, Thomas Hardy & Sons, that became South Australia's largest wine producer.

Thomas Hardy's introduction to grape-growing and winemaking in Australia was a year's work on John Reynell's farm soon after arriving in 1850 at the age of 20. Seven years later, after investing the profits from a brief foray to the Victorian goldfields in land at Bankside, west of Adelaide, Thomas was crushing his first grapes. In 1862 his vintage of 1500 gallons represented five per cent of the state's production. He acquired the Tintara vineyard and the old flour mill at McLaren Vale, and by 1880 he held 200,000 gallons of wine, the largest stock in Australia. He had also won nearly 100 prizes, including medals from Paris, Philadelphia, Sydney and Melbourne. A gold medal at the Bordeaux Exhibition of 1892 added more lustre to his reputation, and in 1895 the Hardy vintage contributed 22 per cent of South Australian wine production for that year.

While the Bankside cellars were the centre of his winemaking operations in the 1860s and 1870s, many of the grapes came from southern districts, including Brighton and Mitcham. Hardy seemed to have an uncanny ability to find markets for his product; even though rail freight for wine was twice that for beer, he sent his wines to the northern towns – where he was also assiduously earmarking land for future wine saloons. In 1872 the cheapest wines – 'good sound wines not less than three years old' – both red and white, cost threepence per pint bottle if bought by the dozen, approximately the same price as half a pound of colonial cheese or a pound of mutton. His pint bottles of Morooroo shiraz – advertised as 'One of the best full, dry wines, and an excellent one to mix with water as a summer drink' – sold for 10 shillings per dozen.

Thomas Hardy in his vineyard

In so many ways, Thomas Hardy was ahead of his time. While he offered no explanation for the 'Morooroo' name, his 1875 'Oomoo' label (both red and white wines) picked up a word used by the Dieyerie Aboriginal people of Central Australia, said to mean 'good', 'nice', 'pleasant to the eye'. The Oomoo wines, he claimed, represented a 'fair sample of the FULLBODIED, GENEROUS, UNFORTIFIED wines of South Australia', the red version being 'a full dry wine of the Burgundy character ... made principally from the Shiraz or Hermitage Grape, with a certain proportion of Carbenet and Malbec'.

After the purchase of the Tintara operation and its stock of wine – which he was able to sell, and thus finance the deal – Hardy's operations were increasingly centred on McLaren Vale. At Tintara he cleared more land, enlarging the vineyard and planting better varieties, and experimented with contour cultivation – following Kelly's example – as a way of preventing soil erosion. Having acquired the former flour mill, he bought up just about everything else at the Bellevue end of McLaren Vale, including the Bellevue hotel, which became his headquarters during his weekly visits. Until the 1940s, the terms of the hotel's lease required that a room always be kept vacant should a member of the Hardy family visit.

A.C. Kelly's sketch of Tintara Vineyard, 1874

In 1884 Hardy purchased additional land next to Tintara, his McLaren Vale holdings then covering nearly 1500 acres, of which about one-third was vineyards. The company Thomas Hardy & Sons Limited was formed in 1887, and by the mid-1890s it was the largest winemaker in South Australia, producing over 80 per cent of McLaren Vale wine and employing over 100 hands at vintage time.

In recognition of this transfer of interest Hardy's Vintage Festival, which had been celebrated at Bankside since the early 1860s, shifted to McLaren Vale in 1890. With its afternoon sports – always including a tug-of-war, vintage hands versus the rest – high tea and evening social, it was truly a community festivity. Fred Low wrote in his diary for 4 May 1891:

*Lydia Mabel and I went to the Vintage Picnic at McLaren Vale wine cellars and it was a nice day. Harry and Lew Townsend got first prize for the three legged race 15/- and Harrold and I got second prize 5/-, Frank Whiting won a Boys race 10/-, the Vintage hands won the tug of war, Lydia and Mabel came home with Grandfather after they had their tea, I stayed to the ball till 2 o'clock in the morning. Fanny Liverton and Fanny Whiting were there.*

Thomas Hardy was a prolific contributor to local newspapers and magazines, where he displayed his wide reading and knowledge. In the first year of *Garden & Field* in 1875, his 'Notes for the Month' covered such topics as pruning, trellising, fermentation, fining wines and vine diseases. On crushing he wrote:

*I find that the practice of treading out the grapes by the naked feet is still thought by some to be the best ... [but] very much stronger arguments will have to be used in favor of treading before I shall give up the rollers and go back to that very old system.*

When travelling through the wine districts of Portugal, Spain, France and Germany in 1884 Hardy penned a series of articles for the *Observer*, reporting on the foods and wines he encountered. At Pinhao, near Oporto in Portugal:

*we were right royally entertained. The dishes we liked best were curried fowl and rice and delicious pork sausages; for dessert the small green fig and magnificent grapes; and for drink, a good dry red wine – but not port; indeed, we never saw port drank anywhere, except by English visitors, in this country.*

Incidentally, Hardy also reported on the ravages of the phylloxera root louse in Europe. Back home, he campaigned strongly to keep South Australia phylloxera-free, often addressing meetings of the Vignerons' and Wine-growers' Associations. He was also a fervent supporter of federation – though perhaps as businessman more than patriot, for federation of the separate Australian states included the promise of free trade between states. Indeed, soon after federation South Australian wine sales to other Australian states exceeded exports to England.

Thomas Hardy was an innovator and educator. He practised soil conservation measures, and initiated pruning competitions that were the first in the state and possibly the first in Australia. His reading kept him informed of the latest technology, and independently he developed a system whereby water was pumped through a series of pipes in the fermenting vats as a means of controlling temperature – a system 'not yet even used in France', reported the *Advertiser* in 1895. He is also acknowledged as the pioneer of the currant industry in South Australia. Not until Hardy had proven success, at his Bankside property, were widespread plantings made in other regions.

Thomas Hardy died in January 1912. Thomas Hardy & Sons continued as a family business, acquiring Emu Wines in 1976, Reynella and Rhinecastle Wines in 1982 and Stanley Leasingham in 1987. In 1992, it merged with Berri Renmano to form the BRL Hardy Wine Company, the second largest wine producer in Australia and proprietor of vineyards in France.

# CREATING MARKETS

With the drop in demand caused by depression, the area of vineyards in the colony decreased by about one-third between 1865 and 1880. South Australian winemakers were able to make a palatable product; the difficulty, as always, was how and where to sell it. Addressing this dilemma, 'IN VINO VERITAS' wrote to the *Chronicle* on 26 May 1860:

*The excellent quality of South Australian wines is now acknowledged, not only in England, but also in the neighbouring colonies; and judges of wine in both places have stated that the first class wines of South Australia possess a flavour peculiarly their own ... I am of opinion that in order to introduce colonial wine to an extensive consumption in the colony itself, it should be offered to the public cheaper than imported drinks; but as only publicans, paying the customary high licence, are now permitted to retail it, they have the power of fixing an arbitrary price; so that no person desirous of drinking a glass of colonial wine can obtain the luxury for a smaller sum than sixpence a glass, which is the price of imported sherries and ports.*

*Would it not be possible to issue licences expressly for the sale of colonial wines ... Respectable, and perhaps elegant establishments would be opened for the sale of this very important colonial production. In the places which I would have established there ought to be refreshments of an edible character as well, and perhaps a supply of newspapers and magazines, chessboards, &c. There is no doubt that such establishments would be more conducive to temperance and comfort than are many public bars, taprooms or bar parlours.*

As John Bleasdale noted in his essay 'On Colonial Wines' (1873), Australians were not yet wine drinkers, 'else we should consume the produce of the colony in less than a month'. The market for Australian wine was elsewhere – but where? In his 1871 report to the Chief Secretary, the Government Statist, J. Boothby, remarked:

*It is lamentable fact that the colonial wine is now, and has for years, suffered great depression from inability to secure a foreign market. The want of success in this respect has not been from the absence of persistent effort, or from want of excellence in the product itself ... but rather to the existence of hostile tariffs, which impose the same rate of duty upon the light and cheap wines of this colony as upon the costlier products of France, Spain and Germany. The large amount of capital invested in vineyards, the numerous branches of labor fostered, and the capability of unlimited extension, alike call for the early removal of the restriction which now paralyzes this most important industry.*

With markets in neighbouring Australian colonies virtually closed, the only other possibility was England but very little headway had been achieved; between 1866 and 1871 South Australian exports amounted to less than one per cent of production.

When Dr Kelly went to London in 1871 he took with him a letter of introduction to William Colton, brother of Thomas Colton of McLaren Vale (son of the pioneer William Colton), and through him met the wine merchant P.B. Burgoyne. Burgoyne's appointment as the English agent for Tintara wine marked the beginning of a long – and sometimes acrimonious – association between his company and McLaren Vale winemakers. Initial results were not promising. Tintara wines were shipped to London and sold there – but at such prices that after paying expenses the exporters were left with a substantial debt. In a letter to Dr Kelly in 1877, Burgoyne wrote:

*I am afraid I cannot give a satisfactory account of our sales indeed less Enquiry appears to be made for Australian wines than ever, and the great drink is our Claret, and aerated drinks are greatly in demand ...*

Persistence eventually paid off, as the publication *South Australia: Its history, resources, and productions* noted in 1876:

*The manufacture of wine may now be regarded as an established industry, although it has not been so pecuniarily successful as it was once expected to be. But this has arisen from want of skill in making it, and in managing the cellar ... After years of labour and much bitter disappointment, we are now getting a good market for our native wines in England. There is one thing in*

Unloading grapes, Tatachilla, c. 1900

*their favour. They are the juice of the grape, without adulteration, and in most cases without being brandied. The taste for pure wine needs to be formed and cultivated in England, and when that is done there will undoubtedly be a great demand for it.*

South Australians were, too, drinking more wine. 'The greater part of the wine grown here is consumed in the colony, where a taste for the good and pure article is gradually and steadily growing,' reported the *Register* in 1879. The government publication *South Australia: its history, productions and natural resources* claimed that by 1883 'the colonial wine has largely supplanted the colonial beer in the harvest field, in cafes, and in private houses', though in fact the annual vintage always fell far short of brewery production.

South Australian exports of wine to England averaged 14,000 gallons (64,400 litres) annually in the decade from 1872 to 1881, double the average of the previous decade, and continued to increase during the 1880s and 1890s, reaching a peak of nearly four million litres in 1902. Simultaneously, vineyards expanded; in the three district council areas of Aldinga, Noarlunga and Willunga, vineyard acreage trebled between 1880 and 1890, and more than doubled again between 1890 and 1910.

# THE IMAGE OF AUSTRALIAN WINES IN THE NINETEENTH CENTURY

Australian exports in the nineteenth century were dry, full-bodied red table wines – albeit high in alcohol. Not only were fortified wines like ports and sherries more expensive to make, they attracted higher duties in England, where the Australian product had to compete with cheaper wines from Spain and Portugal.

Such 'Burgundy style' wine, as it was then called, was exactly the style of wine being produced in the McLaren Vale – full-bodied, dry, high in alcohol, deep in colour and heavy with tannin. Dr Kelly, placing his faith in a kind of 'sympathetic' medicine, favoured the dark, heavy, 'ferruginous' wines produced by Manning and others as useful for invalids and convalescents. Like some of today's wines, many contained over 15 per cent alcohol, a level unheard of in true Burgundies, which were more likely to have around 12 per cent alcohol. Indeed, critics such as the well-respected English chemist Dr Thudicum declared it impossible for natural fermentation to yield this percentage of alcohol, and that the wines must have been fortified. P.B. Burgoyne was one who refuted these claims, asserting in a letter to the London *Times* in 1873 that Dr Kelly's wines did indeed generate high proportions of alcohol, and that no brandy was ever added. This dispute could hardly have enhanced the image of Australian wines in the eyes of the British public – and, it must be admitted, it was not unknown for a little brandy to be administered occasionally, to sedate the wine during the long sea voyage.

Given the long, hot summers in the McLaren Vale region, the crude technologies employed in winemaking, and the absolute lack of experience on the part of most winemakers, it would be ridiculous to expect its wines to have had any resemblance to French wines – yet, given that these were what the English knew, perhaps this was the only way to market them. What was tactfully called the 'lack of recognition' of Australian wines probably acted against them, but their mixed success in the English marketplace in the

1870s may also have been associated with variable, and possibly poor, quality. After his visit to Australia in the early 1870s, novelist Anthony Trollope confessed:

*I cannot say that I liked the South Australian wines. They seemed to me heady, and were certainly unpalatable … I was told that I was prejudiced, and that my taste had been formed on brandied wines, suited to the English market. It may be so; – but if so, the brandied wines suited to the English market not only suit my palate, but do not seem to threaten that a second or third glass will make me tipsy. The South Australian wines had a heaviness about them, – which made me afraid of them even when I would have willingly sacrificed my palate to please a host.*

Throughout the century, the quality of Australian wines gradually improved. After the Vienna Exhibition of 1873, Australian wines were reported to have 'much improved', and to 'have generally a full, rich, vigorous character and quality'. Nevertheless, that South Australian wines did not compare with French wines was made clear by comments on samples sent to the Bordeaux Exhibition of 1892:

*1. The jurors found that you collect the black grapes when they are too ripe.*
*2. They believe that you put brandy in the wine, which dries it and takes away the freshness [la fraîcheur] and the softness[leur moëlleux].*
*7. They judge that your wines should have no more than 13° Gay-Lussac. The less the grapes are ripe, the less the wine is strong, the less sweet it is …*
*10. Avoid leaving your grapes in the sun as much as you can when they are cut, otherwise the stock gives a harsh taste to the wine.*

On the British market, South Australian wines were competing against European wines and being judged in those terms; on their home ground, however, cellar palates invariably deemed the wines excellent. P.B. Burgoyne's provocative comments in the *Register*, at the end of his visit in 1893, came as a shock to colonial winemakers, especially since he was seen as a supporter and promoter of Australian wine, and South Australian wine in particular. He began:

*In many of your vineyards, the 'heavy-bearing' vines have been planted, and no regard whatever has been paid to quality. Quality is not a matter of concern to the farmer – the grapegrower – and the winemaker, turning aside from his higher instincts, his natural ambition to make a name for himself and his colony, has, in the vain hope that the public is the proverbial ass so erroneously imagined, continued year after year, with perhaps a little feeble protest, to purchase those inferior grapes, and to make such poor, vapid, characterless liquids as I find in almost every cellar.*

This was only the start. Burgoyne continued:

*Many winegrowers, to render their flabby, poor things at all marketable, level down their choicest productions to cover their deficiencies. ... We [the public] require with our meals that which is pure, refreshing, invigorating, and health-giving: a wine of the claret, Burgundy, or hock class, without taint of acidity, carrying firmness of texture, and an aroma, flavour, and consistency in close accord, a solid combined whole.*

Then came his accusation:

*I contend that you have not been purveying for public taste, you have been ignoring the middle class wine-drinker, and have been cultivating a taste for so-called ports and sherries. They are as unlike their generic types as can well be. It is the nastiest use to which your grapes can be put.*

'For goodness sake don't make it too easy to sell your bad wines in England,' he concluded. 'You will discredit the whole trade.'

The uproar from South Australian winemakers can well be imagined. It is 'not a fair and honest criticism [but] the vulgar tirade of an irascible trader', replied Mr J.H. Symon, proprietor of the Auldana vineyards, who believed that Australian winemakers were at the mercy of such merchants. Also, he added, Burgoyne had practically a monopoly on South Australian wine exports, and therefore sought to discourage the establishment of a South Australian wine depot in London.

A more measured response came from Thomas Hardy:

*The truth is often unpalatable, but still does good. Mr Burgoyne is right in saying that inferior varieties of grapes have been largely planted ... [but] the charge that we have been pandering to vitiated tastes and not endeavouring to supply pure unfortified wines, is not the whole truth ... We have had to deal largely with people who had rarely drank wine before, but who almost invariably refuse to take any but sweet wines ... I believe that notwith-standing some things, which had better have been left unsaid, Mr Burgoyne's letter will do good in showing the vinegrowers and winemakers that their only hope of holding the English market lies in improving the quality of the wines of the colony, and that can only be done by growing the best varieties of grapes on the most suitable soils.*

Hardy initiated the quest for quality by announcing a reduction in prices paid for common grape varieties and a premium for 'the better sort of grapes, such as Carbinet, Malbec and Shiraz'.

Certainly, Burgoyne was in a position of power in England, and even after the opening of the South Australian Wine and Produce Depot in London in 1894 his company still controlled about two-thirds of the market. The Depot ceased trading in 1903, but during its brief existence it managed to increase the South Australian share of wine sales in England. While the Burgoyne vs. South Australia conflict can be seen as the clash of two 'cellar palates', it is unlikely that Burgoyne's criticisms were motivated by avarice. As others conceded, Australian wines probably were, on average, unequal to those from Europe.

A measure of the distance between Burgoyne and Australia can be gleaned from an old photograph, now displayed in the Wirra Wirra winery's tasting room, that shows Cuthbert Burgoyne (son of P.B.B.) seated with a group of McLaren Vale winemakers in 1903. With their country hats and bushy, droopy moustaches, the Australians seem very much the colonial cousins, while clean-shaven, square-jawed Cuthbert, in his well-tailored suit and high, button-up boots, exudes absolute assurance and superiority.

Cuthbert Burgoyne at McLaren Vale, 1903. At rear, l to r: A.C. Johnston, Herbert Kay, Frederick Kay, Frederick Wilkinson, Fred Shipster. Seated, l to r: Walter Bagenal, Robert Wigley, Bob Russell, Cuthbert Burgoyne, Cyril Pridmore.

In view of later developments, it is significant that Australian wines could make headway in England at a time when average English wine consumption was less than half a gallon (about two litres) per head, and when it was said that the average Englishman only drank wine when he could get cheap, sweet, fortified wine. Burgoyne accused Australian wines of corrupting English taste, but perhaps Burgoyne's representation of public taste was inaccurate, and English tastes were already corrupted. In 1861 Dr Kelly commented that 'the habit of drinking strong brandied wines and their counterfeits have so vitiated the tastes of the people that a pure wine would not be relished by the majority of the British', and attributed this state of affairs to the fact that, until 1860, Spanish and Portuguese wines had been charged a lower duty than French wines.

# EXPANSION 1880-1900

Despite past difficulties, the future seemed sufficiently promising to entice many newcomers into the wine industry in the McLaren Vale area. Until the turn of the century, the predominant occupation in the region, as recorded in the annual directories, was 'farmer'. In 1880 only two vignerons – E.H. and G.P. Manning, sons of George Pitches Manning – were listed, but by 1900 there were 21 proud vignerons (including Fred Low) and, ten years later, 30 vignerons plus 'W. Neilson, wine expert'. As vineyard plantings increased – for both currants and wine – so did the number of self-proclaimed vignerons, reaching 45 in 1921, when there were also two vineyard managers, two cellar managers and one excise officer.

Grapepickers at Amery vineyards, c. 1900

McLaren Vale was beginning to realise its vocation as a regional wine centre. Thomas Hardy had bought and planted additional land adjacent to the original Tintara – known as Lower and Upper Tintara respectively – and transformed the old Mill into a winery. By 1885 maturing stocks amounted to 40,000 gallons, mostly Tintara claret, a blended wine sold in bulk to P.B. Burgoyne. Hardy had the only winery able to absorb additional quantities of grapes and he bought the harvests of small local growers. Fred Low recorded in his diary on 18 May 1896:

*I went to the Mill and got paid for our grapes we had 13 cwt 2 qrs Frontignac grapes 10 cwt 2 qrs white grapes and 6 cwt Shiraz grapes and 3 ton 6 cwt 2 qrs mixed red grapes they were £1/10/- a ton most of them we had £8/4/- worth all together.*

Following Hardy's example, investment in vineyards proceeded apace at the end of the nineteenth century. Ryecroft was established in 1884, Tatachilla in 1887, Amery in 1891, Pirramimma, Katunga and The Wattles in 1892, Wirra Wirra in 1893. Vines multiplied miraculously, existing vineyards providing stock for the new expansions. In 1892 the Kay brothers at Amery supplied John Kelly at Tatachilla with riesling cuttings, at the same time buying white hermitage vines from Thomas Hardy and 'carbonet' and malbec cuttings from W.H. Craven, who that year had bought out Manning's vineyard.

Even greater expansion was occurring around Reynella, not far from where John Reynell had introduced the first vines. Vineyards were planted at Horndale and Glenloth around 1896, Vale Royal in about 1888, and Mount Hurtle in 1890. Their owners' faith in the future of the wine industry is evident from the extent of their plantings – 80 hectares (200 acres) at Horndale, 60 hectares (150 acres) at Mount Hurtle – and the grandiose scale of the wineries and cellars. The vast Horndale winery (now used by Beresford Wines) had 23 fermenting tanks, each with a capacity of 1,500 gallons (6900 litres); the cellars could store 350,000 gallons (1.6 million litres), and by 1903 the vintage yielded 75,000 gallons (345,000 litres) of wine.

Capital, dedication and a propensity for hard work were the all-important attributes of most of these fledgling vignerons. Only Robert Wigley at Wirra Wirra, and John Kelly, son of Dr A.C. Kelly, had any previous experience, both having worked under Thomas Hardy. Perhaps it was another example of Hardy's foresight and generosity that he instituted, in 1892, the first of the annual 'pruning matches', which were designed not only to test expertise but also to train pruners in the appropriate techniques. Fred Low wrote in his 1894 diary:

*Sat.Jun 23rd. Mr Townsend brought us 7 Apple trees from Town, they came from Pitts, in the afternoon I went to a Pruning match held on Mr Hardy's hill at McLaren Vale. I got second prize it was £1/5/-.*

At the close of the century South Australian vineyards produced about one-third of Australian wines, McLaren Vale contributing about 11 per cent of the state total. Victorian vineyards, which had shown so much early promise, were decimated by the root louse *Phylloxera vastatrix*, first noticed about 1877. A similar occurrence in South Australia would have been disastrous, and in 1885 a regulation was brought into effect to prohibit the importing of the insect into the state – hardly the most effective measure, since vines could still be brought in. Eventually, with the passing of the Phylloxera Act in 1899, strict quarantine was imposed and South Australia increased its domination of the Australian wine industry, producing over three-quarters of the national vintage in the 1930s.

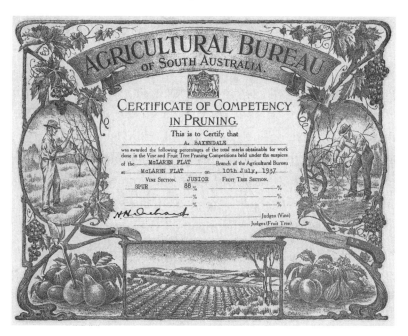

# JOHN BULL'S VINEYARD

Hubert de Castella gave this prophetic title to his 1886 book, drawing 'John Bull's' attention to Australia's 'most valuable vineyards, which may bring him money and health, two things he is very fond of'. He also urged Australians to develop a wine-drinking tradition and to take pride in Australian wine, valuing age and quality as they would with French wines. Thomas Hardy undoubtedly supported these ideas, often using customers' testimonials such as this one to promote his product:

*Port Adelaide Nov. 6, 1875*
*Dear Mr Hardy – I have tasted with much satisfaction your Red Oomoo Wine. It is a very pure and unfortified wine, and I can recommend it to any who prefer the pure unadulterated wines of the south of Europe to the fortified wines usually sold in England. – H. Duncan, M.D.*

Speaking at Hardy's vintage fête of 1899, Mr W. J. Blacker MP said he was 'pleased to know that the young people in the district were not at all given to drinking wine to excess. That bore out what been often said, that the people in winegrowing countries were the most sober of any'. Seconding his remarks, Mr A. McDonald MP, expressed his pleasure at seeing South Australian fine light claret and white wines so generally on the tables of the best hotels and restaurants.

In the McLaren Vale region the cluster of cellars established at the end of the previous century, together with those on the northern side of the Onkaparinga at vineyards such as Reynella, Horndale and Glenloth, diligently continued to produce heavy, dry table wines in the style that seemed to be required by the bulk wine merchants and exporters such as Burgoyne's and Stephen Smith and Company. Stephen Smith exported Tatachilla's entire output; its Keystone Burgundy was reputedly the largest-selling single brand of Australian wine in England. With virtually no wine-drinking tradition behind them, winemakers were hardly likely to switch to making lighter wines – despite Dr Cleland's plea in 1880 that winemakers reduce the alcoholic strength of South Australian wines – and the limited local market offered little encouragement.

Since about the 1870s, however, the forces of temperance had been gathering strength. From 1891 hotels were no longer open on Sundays and in 1916 six o'clock closing was introduced. With contraction of the domestic market a greater proportion of wine was exported, and there was probably a gradual shift to making fortified wines. They were less trouble to transport and plenty of fortifying spirit was available, spirit production almost trebling between 1900 and 1910. Some was matured into brandy; Horndale brandy won an enviable reputation, and was served at the exclusive Adelaide Club in the 1930s.

The English market had its ups and downs during the first few decades of the twentieth century, and in any case was less important than interstate sales. But overseas exports soared after the introduction of the Wine Export Bounty by the Australian government in 1924 and of Imperial Preference in the UK

Cask storage, Tatachilla winery, c. 1920

in 1925. The Bounty applied to all wines exported from Australia that contained at least 34 per cent proof spirit (about 20 per cent alcohol), while Imperial Preference meant lower tariffs on Australian wines. These measures encouraged the production of fortified wines, and exports were predominantly of port-style wines that could now compete more favourably with Portuguese and Spanish wines. In a strongly competitive market prices were cut drastically; the minimum price recommended by the Wine Overseas Marketing Board quickly became the maximum. Australian wine exports to England almost trebled between 1920 and 1930 and continued to increase throughout the 1930s. In 1939/40 exports represented about 25 per cent of production.

The largest South Australian exporter in the 1930s was the Emu Wine Company, based at Morphett Vale, which made its own wine and purchased huge quantities, made to the company's specifications, from local wineries such as Ryecroft, d'Arenberg and Seaview. Shiraz was favoured for port-style wines; Fred Low's diary records that in 1925 he grafted shiraz on to his

Emu Winery, Morphett Vale, c. 1930s

currant vines. For decades Australian wine in England was synonymous with cheap port and inevitably associated with the incongruous 'emu' image.

Nevertheless, dry table wines continued to be made, and while few were drinking them in the Depression years local sales began to increase after the first world war. At the Adelaide Wine Shows of the 1930s, twelve of the 30 classes were for table wines, in both 'export' and 'merchant' categories. Of the clarets in 1935, the judges reported: 'A large entry of generally fine wines with some good wines of Burgundy type included'. In the 1930s the Kay brothers' output was predominantly dry red wines for the English market, and even in the 1950s 'Australian Burgundy' was still being shipped to England. The South Australian Coronation Dinner, held at Grosvenor House, London, on 27 May 1953, featured a 1947 Tatachilla Burgundy.

McLaren Vale winemaker d'Arry Osborn's first vintages of the 1940s were sold in bulk to Hardy's, Penfolds, Emu and Angove's, but barrels of wine were also shipped to Agostino, a wine merchant in Melbourne, who would bottle it for sale. The barrels were often old whisky barrels, while others were of stringybark, waxed on the inside. L.S. Booth, a local firm that undertook most of the transport, has since become one of the biggest wine transporters in the country. At the same time there were direct sales to customers who would bring flagons and stone jars to be filled. 'Cud' Kay has similar memories of the cellar door trade, mostly flagons of sweet sherry and port, but dry red and dry white wines were also sold in flagons.

Since most was sold in bulk, McLaren Vale wines tended to lose their identity in blends bottled elsewhere in Australia. It was not until 1951 that Ben Chaffey began small bottlings of table wines under the Seaview label. At d'Arenberg winery the first bottling took place in 1958, wines being siphoned out and the bottles filled from a hose. Tatachilla also began bottling small parcels of selected wines in 1958, but for many other McLaren Vale vineyards bulk sales were the rule until the late 1960s. With the change in the licensing regulations about the same time, wineries began to establish tasting facilities and promote cellar door sales.

Wine Week 1946 opened with the annual meeting of the Federal Viticultural Council, at which it was announced that the 1945/46 vintage of 24.7 million gallons (114 million litres) was the largest on record. About 80 per cent of this came from South Australia.

According to Mr K.T. Hardy, president of the Council, 'the home market at present was favourable and the greatly increased demand which developed during the war was being maintained.' In Great Britain 'there appeared to be an unprecedented demand for Australian wines ... [which] could not be satisfied at present owing to the control of wine imports by the British Ministry of Food'.

The purpose of Wine Week was to give vignerons and winemakers from different regions opportunities to meet, talk and socialise, both at the celebratory dinner (in 1946 held at the South Australian Hotel) and at an informal picnic for delegates and spouses. In 1946 the picnic was held at Tintara vineyard, where trestle tables were set with bottles of wine, both fortified and table varieties, red and white, and guests ate finger food of sandwiches and pasties, cold chicken drumsticks and barbecued lamb chops, followed by cheese and biscuits.

# THE WINE REVIVAL

In 1950, fortified wine represented 84 per cent of South Australian production, and more than half the wine made was distilled for grape spirits. Average wine consumption was less than five litres per person – which at least was considerably more than the 2.7 litres per person at the end of the 1930s. It was not until the late 1960s that people were drinking almost as much table wine as fortified; of today's consumption of about 18 litres per head (or about 25 litres for everyone over the age of 18 years), over 90 per cent is table and sparkling wine.

Wine was not part of the Australian way of life in the mid-twentieth century. In most households, the only wine was the bottle of sweet sherry to add to the Christmas cake and pudding. In Adelaide in 1950 there were only six restaurants permitted to serve dry wine and cider to customers ordering a 'bona fide' meal, and then only between midday and two, and between six and eight, Monday to Saturday. Hotels could also serve wine in the dining room between six and eight, if they were in the habit of serving meals, and if the person was 'bona fide' taking a meal of not less than two courses.

A different attitude began to emerge during the 1950s. Licensed restaurants started to blossom and by 1955 Adelaide had about 35 such establishments, many owned by European immigrants and bearing such nostalgic names as Blue Danube, Paprika Grill, Hungarian Cafe and Beograd Cafe. People came together to form food and wine clubs; in Adelaide, the Bacchus Club, the Beefsteak and Burgundy Club and the Wine Lovers' Club of Adelaide all sprang up in the 1950s. The McLaren Vale branch of the Bacchus Club, established in June 1956, was the seventh wine and food club to be launched in the country districts of South Australia, and the fifteenth in the state. One of the most active and progressive of the Bacchus clubs, its foodmaster for many years was Clive Whitrow, licensee of the Port Noarlunga Hotel. Many memorable dinners took place in its dining room, some boldly featuring kangaroo, emu, mutton birds and marlin steaks long before such Australiana became fashionable.

For this new class of enthusiastic drinkers, Hardy's introduced in 1957 its Barbecue Burgundy – at a chop-and-sausage barbecue picnic at its McLaren Vale winery. It was in the next decade, however, that the real revolution in drinking customs occurred, with significant numbers of Australians taking a serious interest in wines. Wine-and-cheese parties were fashionable in the sixties, as were home wine bottlings. By 1967 the number of restaurant permits in South Australia had increased to 124. Licensing reforms introduced that year extended the closing hour for hotels to 10.00 pm, and the restaurant permit was replaced by a far more liberal restaurant licence. In the five years between 1959/60 and 1964/65 average wine consumption in Australia increased by the equivalent of a bottle per person, and in the next five years by the equivalent of over four bottles per person. Further, the increase was in table wines at the expense of fortified wines. The invention of the bag-in-the-box wine cask in the mid-1970s was a further encouragement to the drinking of table wines, especially white wines. In the 1980s over five times as much white wine as red wine was sold, and of this more than half was cask white.

Wine tasting party, c. 1968

| WINE | AREA | GRAPE TYPE | PRICE |
|------|------|-----------|-------|
| 1 McWilliams Mt Pleasant | Hunter River | Pinot | Medium |
| 2 All Saints Claret | NE. Victoria | Shiraz | Medium |
| 3 Mildara | Blended at Mildura | Shiraz from McLaren Vale Cabernet from Coonawarra | Medium |
| 4 Gt Western Dry Red | West Victoria | Shiraz | Medium |
| 5 Barossa Hermitage | Barossa Valley SA | Shiraz | Medium |
| 6 Wynn— Coonawarra Cabernet | Coonawarra | Cabernet-Sauvignon | Medium |
| 7 Houghton's Hermitage | Swan Valley WA | Black Shiraz | Medium |
| 8 Bulk Red | McLaren Vale SA | Shiraz | Low |

In 1952 there were only nine wineries in the McLaren Vale/McLaren Flat area; north of the Onkaparinga, Reynella, Horndale, Glenloth and Emu were still in operation. Tatachilla (Stephen Smith & Company) was taken over by Emu Wine Company in 1962. In the mid-1960s, however, McLaren Vale began to stir. Perhaps it was the visit of wine connoisseur André Simon that drew attention to the region and its wines, or perhaps it was simply a belated recognition of its high quality dry red wines – a far cry from the early Australian Burgundy – that were increasingly sold under the name of the individual vineyard.

André Simon, founder of the London-based Wine and Food Society, visited Australia for the first time in the summer of 1964, recording his impressions in the autumn 1964 issue of the society's *Wine & Food* journal.

*Monday, 27th January, Australia Day and a Bank Holiday. Mr Ken Hardy, Managing Director of Thomas Hardy & Co., and his son John called for us and drove us to Tintara ...*

*After visiting the Winery we motored through many acres of vineyards down to Lower Tintara and up to the crest of a hill where Mr David Hardy, a cousin, his wife and young children have their home. There we had a barbecue lunch in the garden with some of the neighbours, friendly rival winegrowers and their wives: quite a party. We had grilled smoked garfish, which was excellent, and delicious yabees (écrevisses) which were on ice, not barbecued, and kebabs with the choice of mutton or kangaroo for meat between mushrooms and peppers – I thought the mutton better than the kangaroo. The heat was great but not humid and quite bearable, and there was no risk, of course, of anybody being dehydrated, both white and red wines from the Tintara and nearby Seaview vineyards flowing freely.*

*Before returning to Adelaide we called at the Edwards and Chaffey winery, also in the McLaren Vale, in a sea of vines, and with the great sea miles away in the haze, which is why the firm's wines are marketed under the brand of Seaview. There Mr Ben Chaffey had a number of his wines to taste, as well as olives from his own olive groves.*

André Simon with 'Cud' Kay (left) and David Hardy (centre)

In 1966, when Dan Murphy wrote the *Australian Wine Guide*, the first comprehensive guide to Australian wines for the ordinary consumer, he singled out only two McLaren Vale wines – Seaview Rhine Riesling and Moselle – among the sixty-odd 'above average' dry white wines, and recommended ten red wines from McLaren Vale in his selection of dry reds. All were from long-established vineyards – Reynella, Tintara (including Tintara St Thomas Burgundy – the founding father having been elevated to sainthood!), Ingoldby, Ryecroft and d'Arenberg. Of these, d'Arenberg was the youngest, having been purchased by Frank Osborn in 1912.

McLaren Vale wines were simply not much known at this time, and without proper identification it was difficult to get to know them. Max Lake's *Classic Wines of Australia*, published in the same year, honoured a mere three wines from McLaren Vale: Seaview Rhine Riesling, Seaview Cabernet Sauvignon and Hardy's McLaren Vale Cabernet. Made from a central strip of vines in lower Tintara, the Hardy's wines were described as having a superb berry bouquet, rather robust fruity flavour with excellent balance, and the deep, soft, red depth of colour typical of the region.

One of the first initiatives encouraging recognition of the region was the formation of McLaren Vale Wine Pty Limited by Jim Ingoldby in 1965. The aim of this company was to market selected wines as high quality regional wines by bottling them under a McLaren Vale label while at the same time giving details of the individual vineyard or winemaker. For smaller producers, this was an alternative to disposing of their vintage in bulk.

The 1960s and 1970s was a period of huge expansion in the McLaren Vale region, even as suburban spread began to engulf the northern section. Urban expansion motivated the Patritti family, with a winery at Dover Gardens near Adelaide, to buy land and develop vineyards at Blewitt Springs and Aldinga North. Between 1966 and 1979, 26 new wineries were established; Wirra Wirra, which was not exactly new but had not made wine for many years, became the sixteenth winery in the region when it re-opened in 1969. Some were associated with new vineyards; others, such as Coriole, were established vineyards acquired by new owners.

In addition, wineries were becoming increasingly specialised. While many of the larger concerns continued to supply a complete range of red and white, sweet and dry table wines, together with sherries, muscat, vintage and tawny ports and marsala, the newer, smaller wineries concentrated on producing a small number of distinctive table wines, in particular shiraz, cabernet and blends of these two.

| | |
|---|---|
| Marienberg | 1966 |
| Coriole | 1967 |
| Genders | 1968 |
| Settlement | 1968 |
| Noon | 1969 |
| Norman's | 1969 |
| Wirra Wirra | 1969 |
| Berenyi | 1970 |
| Oliverhill | 1970 |
| St Francis | 1970 |
| Woodstock | 1970 |
| Merrivale | 1971 |
| Trennert | 1971 |
| Richard Hamilton | 1972 |
| Maglieri | 1972 |
| Taranga | 1973 |
| Daringa (now Dennis of McLaren Vale) | 1974 |
| Palladio | 1974 |
| Cambrai (now Kangarilla Road) | 1975 |
| Dridan's Skottowe | 1975 |
| Elysium | 1975 |
| Thomas Fernhill Estate | 1975 |
| Donolga (now Aldinga Bay Vineyards) | 1976 |
| Dyson | 1977 |
| Maxwell | 1979 |
| Scarpantoni | 1979 |

# GRAPE VARIETIES

Given the region's reputation, first as a producer of heavy 'Burgundy-style' wines and then of port-style wines, it is no surprise that red wines should dominate – indeed, shiraz, grenache and cabernet accounted for about three-quarters of the vineyard area in the 1970s. Red grape varieties are still paramount, the proportion of red to white now about 3:2. Though high trellises are rapidly taking over the region, century-old grenache bush vines still yield superb wines.

Shiraz and grenache, together with mataro and carignan, were amongst the original plantings of the McLaren Vale district. These varieties, popular in the south of France, probably came from James Busby's collection in the Sydney Botanic Gardens, gathered during Busby's tour of France and Spain in 1831. Other vines were supplied by William Macarthur's vineyard in New South Wales, and a miscellany of varieties imported from Spain. Even in those early days, it seems that vignerons were looking to climatically similar regions in the northern hemisphere for their stock.

At the turn of the century Hardy's crush comprised doradillo, mataro, grenache, carignan, shiraz and 'carbenet' (cabernet). Cabernet seems to have been a relatively new variety in the region; Hardy was successfully grafting it on to mataro stock. The region's new vignerons followed Hardy's example – omitting doradillo, mostly used for brandy. At Pirramimma A.C. Johnston planted cabernet, shiraz, malbec and currants; Tatachilla was mainly mataro, with shiraz, carignan and cabernet; while Ryecroft had cabernet and shiraz.

The Amery vineyard, when the Kay brothers bought it in 1891, contained mataro and grenache plus a host of other varieties – grec, doradillo, lady fingers, currant, frontignac, cinsaut, sweetwater, palomino, semillon, muscatel, shiraz – but in their own plantings they concentrated on shiraz, mataro, cabernet, and frontignac, reputed to yield an outstanding long-living wine not unlike Portuguese tawny port. The shiraz vines planted in 1892, grown from cuttings taken from Kelly's old vineyard on the other side of the valley, are still bearing and have themselves provided the basis of many other vineyards in

No. 4.

From *The Vine in Australia*, by A.C. Kelly

the district. Their wine, bottled as Block 6 Shiraz, is an old-fashioned McLaren Vale classic, richly coloured, robust and high in alcohol. Colin Kay intends to replicate Block 6 on one of his new plantings. If only Dr Kelly could have known that his work was not in vain!

Among white wine varieties, chardonnay has come to dominate over the last ten years. Chardonnay vines were first planted in the district by Richard Hamilton in 1975. Semillon, Rhine riesling and sauvignon blanc are grown in lesser quantities. 'Cud' Kay of Amery was the first with riesling, selling in bulk and supplying wines to be bottled under the Seaview label until his own bottlings commenced in the mid-1960s. Sauvignon blanc was one of the original Tintara varieties planted by Dr Kelly, who apparently started with cuttings from Manning's vineyard. Descendants of these returned to Seaview in the 1950s and contributed to the popular Seaview white burgundies. Later generations of the same vines continue to garner awards for Hardy's sauvignon blanc and Seaview sauvignon blanc.

## VINEYARD RATIONALISATION

The vineyard expansion of the 1970s was perhaps too rapid. Soon there was a glut of grapes. This was partly because Britain had joined the European Common Market, reducing the market for dried raisins, sultanas and currants. Grapes that would previously have been dried were diverted into winemaking. From the mid-1970s, expansion of vineyards in the immediate vicinity of the town of McLaren Vale failed to compensate for loss of vineyards in the older area north of the Onkaparinga, victims of suburban sprawl. The announcement of the 1985 government-sponsored vine-pull scheme, whereby growers were compensated for grubbed vines, resulted in a further decrease in vineyard area.

At the same time, however, vineyards became more productive. The first help to nature came in the early 1970s in the form of thin black plastic tubes alongside the trunks of the vines, delivering water in opportune amounts at opportune times and doubling yields. While the extent of irrigation was minuscule in 1970, it increased by 50 per cent in the next five years. Today 90 per cent or more of the region's vines receive supplementary water. Water usage has become more efficient, with irrigation taking place at times when stress on the vines is likely to compromise fruit quality.

As people recognised that underground water supplies are not infinite, the Willunga Basin was proclaimed a 'prescribed wells area' in 1990 and controls on the use of ground water were introduced. A moratorium was declared over an area east of Blewitt Springs in 1993, also considered to be a major recharge zone, and no more water harvesting for irrigation purposes is allowed – controls apply to both surface and ground water. The area has since been shown to be less significant for the Willunga Basin groundwater than originally believed but the moratorium has continued, landowners in the region conscious of long-term effects. In future, however, treated waste-water may become a valuable resource. Wastewater from Aldinga was used on a small scale in 1997/98, and from 1999 treated wastewater piped from the Christies Beach Treatment Plant will make additional irrigation possible.

Mechanisation has defiantly made its presence seen, if not felt, in the past few years. In autumn tall, lumbering mechanical pickers straddle the rows, their strong fibreglass fingers separating the berries from the mother vine. Even old bush vines have been trellised so they can be mechanically harvested and pruned, though this is not everywhere possible. Aesthetically, such mechanisation diminishes the region's natural attraction. The strong, sharp, symmetric silhouettes of meticulously hand-pruned vines (rod-and-spur system) are increasingly rare amongst a winter landscape featuring fistfuls of thin brown sticks, like straw brooms gone to rack and ruin. But as 'Cud' Kay says:

*It's been gradually discovered, to the horror of a lot of us who are perfectionists, that [hand pruning] was a bit of a waste of time. You might as well prune them roughly, and you get just as good results, and it takes much less time to do it.*

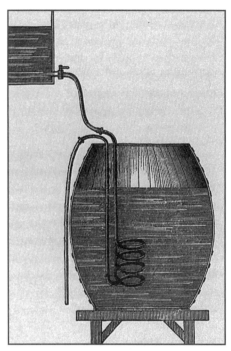

Dr Kelly's cooling system

Materially, the benefits of mechanisation increasingly outweigh other considerations. Both judicious irrigation – at times when vines are most stressed – and mechanical pruning give greater yield without affecting quality. With cabernet, for example, irrigation can ensure more bunches of smaller berries with more flavour. Mechanical harvesters make it possible to pick grapes at night when they are cooler, with consequent advantages in wine-making procedures.

In winemaking, too, technology has come to the fore. A.C. Kelly warned in 1861 of the dangers of high temperatures during fermen-tation and many of the early winemakers improvised ways of reducing must tempera-tures. Kays' still have the copper serpentine coils – introduced over a century ago and used until the 1970s – through which cooled water was pumped in order to reduce the temperature in the fermenting tanks by several critical degrees. At Hardy's winery similar coils are still in use. The introduction of temperature-controlling stainless steel tanks has revolutionised fermentation processes, especially for white wines.

The progress in winemaking technology and in the ability to control fer-mentation and subsequent processes has progressed to such a degree that scope for further developments is limited. As a result, more attention is being paid to the vineyard and to the quality of the fruit, the aim being to produce high-quality grapes at low cost. New grape varieties are being tested, including viognier, marsanne, rousanne, three (white) compatriots of shiraz in the Rhone Valley in France. Verdelho, one of the old varieties planted by Kelly following Macarthur's recommendation, is also being reintroduced. New ways of growing the grapes are being studied. The Hamilton Wine Group practises 'economically sensible organic agriculture' using the V-shaped or 'lyre' trellis. While more expensive to install, it reduces the need for chemical sprays, the vines being exposed to more sunlight and greater air flow. Biological methods of pest control, such as the use of microscopic wasps to control other insect pests, also offer distinct advantages for the future.

Another exciting innovation involves the recycling of grape marc (the leftover skins and pips) through worms, to be returned to the vines as fertiliser. Marc has previously been used as a mulch or fertiliser, but only after it has been allowed to stand 12 to 18 months to reduce its acidity. Worms seem to love the marc, and in two months convert it into castings constituting a very good, non-acid, slow-release fertiliser which becomes potassium-enriched if crushed grape seeds are fed to the worms as well.

In 1995 Greg Trott of Wirra Wirra winery and Sandy Sylow formed a partnership to experiment with worms and worm castings. Some of Wirra Wirra's vineyards have since had applications of worm castings, either in combination with a straw mulch or as a mulch-cum-fertiliser, in which castings are mixed with pelletised newspaper. Additional trials on other vineyards are being undertaken by the CSIRO. The liquid that seeps out from the worm 'cots' also contains nutrients; as a natural organic liquid fertiliser it could either be sprayed on to vines or fed through the irrigation drippers. This product, too, is still in the experimental stage but initial results are very promising; some garden shops in Adelaide are already stocking bottles of 'Wormalizer'.

Greg Trott sees enormous potential in harnessing worms to treat otherwise unusable material – which could eventually include household waste presently dumped at the Pedler Creek tip – and convert it into a product offering advantages to grape growers and the environment. The fertiliser-mulch treatment means less weed growth, reducing the use of herbicides and the amount of tractor work, while increasing the efficiency of irrigation. Whether or not the goal of a totally organic vineyard is achieved, enterprising developments such as these move the region one step closer to the ideal of sustainability.

None of the early vignerons had any formal training in vine-growing or wine-making but rather learnt from one another and from experience. Versatile and resourceful, they could turn their hands to ploughing, milking, building or repairing pumps.

In contrast, today's generation of winemakers are tertiary-trained, have served their apprenticeship under a respected master winemaker, and often have experience of vineyards and winemaking in other countries.

Colin Kay, winemaker at Amery, completed an oenology degree, worked in a Barossa winery and travelled extensively overseas before taking over from his father 'Cud' Kay. His grandfather and great-uncle, on the other hand, had virtually no experience on the land when, in 1891, they bought the farm with its seven acres of vineyard, making their first vintage in 1895. 'Cud' Kay's expertise was acquired first hand, next to his father and uncle, though his studies in bacteriology at the Waite Institute equipped him to detect and treat problems in wines.

A.C. Johnston was also inexperienced when he purchased Pirramimma in 1892, but he immediately planted 100 acres of vines and, five years later, built a winery. After his death, control passed to his sons Lex and Digby, who both had some scientific and technical training in winemaking. Lex's son Alex, who became winemaker in the late 1970s, studied oenology at Roseworthy College; the current winemaker is Geoffrey Johnston, Alex's cousin, who has a bachelor of science degree in winemaking from Charles Sturt University, Wagga Wagga.

When Frank Osborn bought the property that became d'Arenberg in 1912, he simply sold his grapes to other wineries, later building his own winery and acquiring winemaking skills on the spot. His son, d'Arry, also learnt on the job but d'Arry's son, Chester, graduated from Roseworthy Agricultural College with a degree in oenology before becoming winemaker at d'Arenberg.

Between 1988/89 and 1992/93, the area of vineyards in the McLaren Vale increased by more than 600 hectares, and investment in new vineyards over this period, in establishment costs alone, has been estimated at a minimum of $20 million. Since then expansion has continued apace, vineyards replacing farmlands and orchards. On Delabole hill, behind Willunga, where the lower slopes have been planted to vines, shearing sheds may soon be transformed into wineries.

New wineries have been established, old ones modernised, and in previously untried locales superb wines are being made. On the southern side of the Willunga hills, just outside the proclaimed McLaren Vale wine region, Geoff Hardy's Kuitpo vineyard yields grapes for the wines under his name and also under the Pertaringa label. The old Southern Vales Cooperative in the main street of McLaren Vale, which began life as The Wattles under H.V. Pridmore, now houses the reinvented Tatachilla Winery. No connection to the original Tatachilla, it continues to buy grapes from contracted growers and also has vineyards outside Clarendon. Meanwhile Simon Hackett, last chief winemaker at the Cooperative, has recently bought the old Taranga winery, having launched his own label in 1981.

The century-old Horndale Winery has become the home of Beresford wines, while the former distillery and spirit store houses Horndale Winery. Nearby, Geoff Merrill has breathed new life into Mount Hurtle winery, originally built in 1897. On the edge of Reynella township, the old Reynella distillery and spirit store, built in 1900 by John Reynell's grandson Carew Reynell, is today part of the St Francis Winery complex, while Chateau Reynella's former 'port paddock' yields table wines under the Wylpena Vineyard label.

Winemakers who once worked for others have established themselves independently: Nick Holmes moved from Ryecroft to found Shottesbrooke in 1984; Warren Randall and Warren Ward, both previously with Andrew Garrett, took over Manning Park Wines in 1994 after having bought

| | |
|---|---|
| Blewitt Springs | 1987 |
| Curtis Wines | 1988 |
| Hastwell & Lightfoot | 1988 |
| Mount Hurtle | 1988 |
| Beresford | 1989 |
| Clarendon Hills (previously Elysium) | 1989 |
| Hugh Hamilton | 1990 |
| Hillstowe | 1991 |
| Wirilda Creek | 1992 |
| Wylpena Vineyard | 1993 |
| Fern Hill Estate (previously Thomas Fernhill) | 1994 |
| Wayne Thomas Wines | 1994 |
| Fox Creek | 1995 |
| Hoffmann's | 1995 |
| Koltz | 1995 |
| Penny's Hill | 1995 |
| Dowie Doole | 1996 |
| Kangarilla Road (previously Cambrai) | 1997 |
| Twelve Staves | 1997 |

Tinlin's. The Hugo family once sold their grapes to wineries but now make wine themselves at Hugo Winery.

Substantial outside investment in the McLaren Vale region is a clear indication of faith in the quality of the region's wines and in its future. In 1992 the Rosemount company, based in the Hunter Valley of New South Wales, took over the old Ryecroft winery and in 1994 another Hunter company, Tyrrell's – which for years purchased bulk wines from McLaren Vale – bought an established vineyard and has since constructed its own winery. The Mildara Blass company, now part of the Foster's Brewing Group, acquired the Andrew Garrett and Ingoldby operations in 1995. In turn, the previous owner/winemaker of Ingoldby, Walter Clappis, bought the then-defunct Middlebrook winery and in 1998 relaunched the Middlebrook label.

Interest has been shown by the legendary Chapoutier family of Tain l'Hermitage in France, home of shiraz (or syrah, as it is known there). Chapoutier is looking to establish a vineyard in the McLaren Vale region or the near vicinity, to be planted, in part, with cuttings from the French vine-yards and maintained biodynamically, as is the parent vineyard in France. The company has an informal arrangement with the Hamilton Wine Group that has allowed winemakers from each to work a vintage with the other, and in 1997 it contracted Hamilton's to make a quantity of wine, using mostly McLaren Vale grapes, for the international market. The Hamilton Wine Group has also imported cuttings from Chapoutier's 500-year-old vines that will produce wine for the twenty-first century.

Such investment is a sign of the premium associated with the region as consumers increasingly recognise and value wines identified as being from McLaren Vale. Rosemount proudly proclaims the origin of its McLaren Vale range and Seaview, now part of the Southcorp group, has relaunched the Seaview and Edwards & Chaffey brands for its 100 per cent McLaren Vale varietals. In 1997 Hardy's resuscitated the old Tintara name which, etched into dark glass in the distinctive old-style script, now dignifies both a grenache and a shiraz wine made entirely from McLaren Vale grapes. Record prices have been paid for vineyards and vineyard land, and exports are once again big business, with a number of wineries exporting around 30 per cent of production – at Mount Hurtle, Geoff Merrill sells closer to 75 per cent of output overseas. Exports, in turn, have altered outside perceptions of McLaren Vale and given winemakers more confidence.

Mt Hurtle Winery

These developments are in part a result of the Australian Label Integrity Program, which specifies that a wine must contain at least 85 per cent of the variety named on the label, at least 85 per cent must come from the named region and 85 per cent from the named vintage year. Since 1990 the Australian Wine and Brandy Corporation has had the power to audit winery records to check that this program is being followed, also ensuring that McLaren Vale contributions to blended wines are acknowledged.

The maturity and confidence of the McLaren Vale region is seen in the increasing numbers of visitors and tourists, especially during festivals such as the Sea & Vines festival, the Continuous Picnic weekend in October and the Wine Bushing Festival. Recognising the potential of tourism, a number of wineries have added restaurants or catering facilities. The first was Haselgrove, which started its weekend cellar lunches in 1982. McLaren's on the Lake, a restaurant and motel complex adjacent to the Andrew Garrett winery, opened in 1983. In recent years Woodstock has added a popular restaurant and gallery; Wirilda Creek has incorporated a cafe in its winery design; and in 1996 d'Arenberg launched d'Arry's Verandah restaurant, a superbly sited, elegantly informal dining room where chef Andrew Davies and his team serve food of rare finesse, impeccably prepared in the best traditions of classical French cuisine. Marienberg's restaurant in the old limeburner's cottage in McLaren Vale opened in early 1997, the new Maxwell winery includes catering facilities and at White Hill, the old Oliver family farm, Oliver's offers 'country cuisine'.

A spirit of camaraderie, collaboration and generosity has always characterised the McLaren Vale wine industry, beginning in the earliest days when everyone learnt from each others' successes and failures. Wineries all join forces for the McLaren Vale Wine Bushing Festival and celebrate the start of vintage, signalled since 1991 by the ringing of Wirra Wirra's massive bell by whichever winemaker crushes the first grapes. This same spirit of cooperation is evident in the general willingness to manage water resources rationally, showing responsibility for the environment and for future generations of farmers and vignerons.

McLaren Vale Winemakers Incorporated was one of the driving forces behind the new McLaren Vale & Fleurieu Visitors' Centre, contributing about 25 per cent of its initial funding. Volunteers have planted their own vine cuttings around the building, and the wine these eventually yield will be sold in the Centre and generate income for it. In the meantime, a financial contribution will come from sales of The Fleurieu Shiraz produced by some of the region's finest shiraz producers. The 1994 wine was released in 1997.

Another community venture is the cellar-door get-togethers initiated by Ruth Wallace. These informal meetings have been held monthly for the past ten years and give cellar-door staff, together with restaurant staff and

Winemakers' Luncheon at McLaren Vale Wine Bushing Festival

bed-and-breakfast operators, the opportunity to visit and learn about a winery and taste its wines, as well as wines from two or three other vineyards, while a local restaurant or caterer provides a sample of its cuisine. Over a year all wineries get a chance to show their latest wines, and cellar door staff can keep up-to-date on advice for visitors: where to eat, where to stay, where to take the kids, where to buy almonds and olive oil, where to find zinfandel (the answer: Kangarilla Road) or taste Australia's only varietal wines made from the petit verdot grape, one of the lesser red wine varieties of Bordeaux (the answer: Pirramimma).

Shiraz and chardonnay wines from McLaren Vale are recognised among the elite wines of Australia and the world.

At the 1997 International Wine challenge, held in London, 22 out of the 30 gold medals awarded in the section for Rhone-style wines went to Australia, eight of these 22 being from McLaren Vale.

The 1997 Great Australian Shiraz Challenge was dominated by McLaren Vale. It was won by 1995 Steve Maglieri Shiraz, with 1995 Tatachilla Foundation Shiraz second and 1995 Rosemount Estate Balmoral Syrah third, closely followed by 1996 Scarpantoni Block 3 Shiraz. Nine of the top ten wines were from McLaren Vale (including a predominately McLaren Vale blend). Not only did a Steve Maglieri wine gain first prize but others from the same maker were placed eighth, twelfth and thirteenth. In the previous year the winner was 1994 Wirra Wirra RSW Shiraz, and five of the top dozen wines came from McLaren Vale. The inaugural competition in 1995 was won by 1993 Geoff Hardy Kuitpo Shiraz.

In 1996 *Wine & Spirits* magazine in America ranked Richard Hamilton's Burton's Vineyard 1996 Grenache-shiraz equal second in a tasting of Australian wines, after Penfold's 1991 Grange.

In a 1996 tasting of 100 premium shiraz wines from around the world, London's *Wine* magazine voted Rosemount's Balmoral Syrah top shiraz.

In *Wine Spectator*'s top 100 wines for 1996, Chateau Reynella Basket Pressed Shiraz, 1994 vintage, was ranked eighteenth among the world's best wines.

James Halliday's top 100 Australian wines for 1997 included three McLaren Vale wines among the 20 best white wines under $20: 1997 Seaview Chardonnay; 1997 Ingoldby Chardonnay; and 1997 Geoff Merrill Premium Sauvignon Blanc. Among the best 40 red wines were eight from McLaren Vale: 1996 Tatachilla Keystone Grenache Shiraz; 1995 d'Arenberg d'Arry's Original and Old Vine Shiraz; 1995 Maglieri Shiraz; 1995 Hardy's Tintara

Grenache and Tintara Shiraz; 1995 Tatachilla Foundation Shiraz; and 1995 Wirra Wirra RSW Shiraz.

The 1996 d'Arenberg Olive Grove Chardonnay topped its class at the 1997 'Chardonnay du Monde' competition in Burgundy, France, while the 1996 d'Arenberg The Other Side Chardonnay won one of four gold medals in its class of nearly 600 entries at the 1998 'Chardonnay du Monde'.

In 1997 the 1994 Rosemount Estate Show Reserve McLaren Vale Shiraz was awarded the 1997 George Mackey Memorial Trophy, an annual prize for export wines. All Australian wines for export must be tasted by a panel of wine inspectors, who make a preliminary selection of wines to be entered for the prize; in this instance they chose 109 wines from the 5,500 submitted for export, and the final choice was made by the Adelaide Wine show judges.

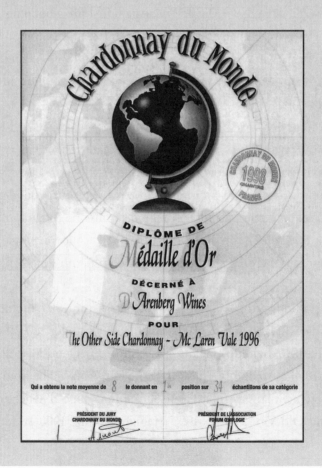

'Willunga High School – Home of Waverley Park Wines' proclaims a large sign in a corner of the school grounds. Behind it is the school vineyard, where senior students can study viticulture and progress to making their own wine at the school.

A small area of vines was planted when the school opened. Students learnt a little about vineyard management as part of a general agriculture course, but only so far as harvesting, the grapes being sold. In 1994, however, at the instigation of teacher Andrew Oliver and with the encouragement of the McLaren Vale Winemakers' Association, the students not only picked the grapes but observed all the subsequent operations through to bottling the wine. The following year the viticulture course was introduced, its curriculum developed by the South Australian Wine and Brandy Industry Association.

Planted to shiraz, cabernet and chardonnay, the school vineyard produces about 250 dozen bottles of red wine and 150 dozen chardonnay. Since 1994, the wines have been made by local winemaker Nick Haselgrove at Kay's cellars.

Andrew Oliver is a descendant of William Oliver who settled in the McLaren Vale area – at White Hill, near Oliver's Road – in 1841 and who was one of the early farmers in the area making wine for home consumption, with a little left over to sell.

WAVERLEY PARK

JOHN ALLEN
BLEND
CLASS OF 1995

Andrew's paternal grandmother was Kathleen Allen, grand-daughter of John Allen who, at the end of the nineteenth century, owned the Delabole slate quarry and lived in the Waverley Park homestead. The land Willunga High School occupies was once part of Waverley Park, and was sold to the Department of Education by Maude Allen in 1957. The school's three Waverley Park wines are named after John Allen, his son Herbert and Herbert's daughter Marguerite, sister of both Kathleen and Maude.

# CHAPTER
# FESTIVITIES

Since the earliest days of European settlement, festivities have played an important role in the life of the McLaren Vale region, beginning with the harvest thanksgiving festival of February 1844 when the handful of hard-working pioneers came together in McLaren Vale to rejoice in their good fortune and future prosperity.

The first farmers and townspeople in this relatively isolated and sparsely settled district organised their own entertainments – sporting events, ploughing matches, district shows. Even without the name, these became festivals in the old-fashioned sense: feast days, holidays, letting-your-hair-down days, days for revelling and relaxing and exchanging news and gossip. The customary festivals of Christmas and New Year were also celebrated, gradually taking on a particular local character.

Australia Day celebrations were popular around the turn of the century, with processions of decorated carts and vehicles followed by a picnic and sports day. In later years Australia Day seemed to lose its significance, but more recently, enthusiasm has been revived. Since 1988 a flag-raising

# SIX

ceremony has been held at the old Willunga Courthouse, and the McLaren Vale Rotary Club and local council have combined to offer a special Australia Day breakfast – orange juice, fruit, cereal, bacon and eggs, tea and coffee. Until 1998 it was also the occasion for the citizenship ceremony for local residents adopting Australian citizenship, and for the announcement of the Citizen and Junior Citizen of the Year. These formal events are now under the auspices of the amalgamated City of Onkaparinga.

In time festivities developed that were also for sharing with visitors and the outside world. Some, such as the Willunga Almond Blossom Festival and the McLaren Vale Wine Bushing Festival, have became features of the regional calendar and serve to affirm a sense of regional identity.

Virtually all the festivities have involved eating and drinking and music. Whether a church supper with hymn singing and pots of tea; roasts and toasts and bawdy songs after the annual cricket match; or the food, wine and music formula of contemporary events, festivity is synonymous with conviviality and sharing, and the pleasure which flows from these.

# EARLY FESTIVITIES

The focal points of community life in the early settlements were the church and the inn, and festivities naturally centred on these establishments. Church festivals such as the annual thanksgiving after the harvest in late summer and the Sunday School picnic attracted large crowds. In February 1852, the *Register* reported that about 70 people sat down to a harvest thanksgiving tea at the Wesleyan (Methodist) chapel, 'the ample and various provisions for which, gratuitously furnished by several ladies of Willunga, did infinite credit to their taste and hospitality'. For the fourth annual picnic at the Anglican church in Willunga in 1860, more than 100 'gathered for the long anticipated treat', according to the *Chronicle*; 'and the day being breezy and fine they enjoyed themselves to their heart's content, until the hill sides echoed with their gleeful shouts. An abundance of childhood's luxuries, cake, fruit, tea, &c., was supplied them'.

The inn was more like a local club, the publican truly deserving of the epithet 'Mine Host'. Public meetings were held there, and it was always to the inn that everyone repaired after a friendly cricket game or ploughing match.

Australia Day celebrations at Aldinga, 1915

Australia Day parade at Aldinga, 1915

Testimonial dinners, such as one for Thomas Kell in 1860 to honour his
service to the Willunga District Council, were held in the local hotel. The
whole district was invited to the New Year feasts at the Devonshire Arms in
McLaren Vale when Alexander Stewart Malcolm, licensee from 1863 to 1875,
welcomed the year in traditional Scottish style. Sucking-pigs and chickens
were roasted outdoors and carved on long trestle tables, and Malcolm produced the haggis he made for all special occasions. Then came sweets and
cakes which, in keeping with Scottish custom, would probably have included
a Black Bun, together with large dishes of raisins flamed in brandy.

The public holidays of New Year's Day, Christmas Day and Boxing Day
were often the stimulus for public festivities. In 1854 a Boxing Day sports
carnival was organised at McLaren Vale, with 'rural sports and old English
pastimes', together with 'the noble and now fashionable game of cricket'. The
*Register* reported that 'a large number of the neighbouring settlers, of both
sexes, visited the focus of attraction during the day, which, as in Adelaide, was
kept as a general holiday by young and old'. Before too long the tradition of
the beach picnic on these summer holidays was well established, and large
crowds would gather at Port Noarlunga and Port Willunga. Recollecting

the Christmases of his childhood early this century, Connor Sparrow wrote:

*My family had Christmas Dinner on the nearest Sunday. I suppose this came about because of going to the beach on Christmas Day when we were young, or it may have been more convenient for more of the family to get home [on a Sunday].*

Then there were events such as the annual Oddfellows' picnics, at Willunga often held by the creek at Waverley Park. In 1873 the Noarlunga Lodge of Oddfellows had a picnic at Dalkeith Farm near Pedler Creek, after assembling in the main street of Noarlunga and marching through the town to the accompaniment of the Aldinga brass band. After lunch, provided by Mr Dungey, licensee of the Horseshoe at Noarlunga, games were organised. The *Register* reported:

*In spite of intense heat cricket, croquet, quoits, skittles, dancing and other amusements secured attention, and from 300 to 400 visitors at least were present from Willunga, McLaren Vale, Aldinga, Reynella, Morphett Vale, and Noarlunga. At night a soirée was held in Mr P. Ryder's schoolroom, which was crowded.*

Within twenty years of the district's settlement racing carnivals were held. They continued until the early years of the twentieth century, Maud Aldam remembering enjoyable outings at the picnic races at Noarlunga and Moana. The Southern Racecourse, near Port Noarlunga, was said to be the only one in South Australia purchased expressly for sporting purposes. The 'race-horses' – including All-the-Go, Whalebone, Snoozer and Stick-in-the-Mud – were local nags and rules seem to have been fairly lax. Reporting on the race meeting of 23 March 1858, the *Register* summarised one race over two miles:

*Only Johnny and Coronet started. They ran together for rather more than a mile, when the latter bolted. Johnny came in at a trot, which he later dropped to a walk before passing the chair, Coronet following at a canter and making no effort to regain his place.*

In an era of do-it-yourself entertainment, people were not too shy to show their talents. Concerts and the more elegant-sounding 'soirées' were held in local halls and other premises, with programs of musical items, singing and recitations. At a concert organised by the Willunga Mechanics' Institute in June 1866, a Mr Hutton sang a song of his own composition, 'Slate, Slate, Slate; or the Delabole Hat', and according to the *Chronicle* 'convulsed the audience by having a slate hat brought on to the platform, the allusions to which seemed to be thoroughly understood and enjoyed by those present'.

From around the turn of the century dances have been very popular, often doubling as fundraisers, especially for church and community organisations but also for public events such as the McLaren Flat show and the Willunga Almond Blossom Festival. 'Cud' Kay remembers dances in the McLaren Vale Institute and in the Vintage House at the back of Amery homestead. 'There would be occasionally a dance there and we would have a chap playing the accordion.' Fred Low often played his violin at dances around the turn of the century, daughter Mabel 'vamping' an accompaniment. At all the dances a lavish homemade supper would be offered.

Strawberry Fete 1915

# STRAWBERRY FETES

Strawberry fetes were another fundraising festivity, particularly popular in the early twentieth century. Old residents remember the strawberry fetes at (Old) Noarlunga, held each year around November in the Institute Hall to raise money for the Methodist church. 'As children it'd make your mouth water. ... Threepence a saucer full, and well piled up with cream on it. Oh, it was really something,' recalled Kathleen Dungey, a former resident of (Old) Noarlunga.

The beginning of summer seems to have been marked by a succession of strawberry fetes in the region. There used to be one at the Kay family vineyard – 'a strawberries and cream sort of thing' – which attracted lots of locals and people from as far away as Kangarilla. 'So many people had strawberries ... no lack of strawberries', says 'Cud' Kay, though for the fetes the strawberries might have been purchased from commercial growers in the region.

Strawberries were the stars of the strawberry fetes, but there were also ice-cream and homemade lollies, needlework and produce. Chrystabel Duell, born in Noarlunga in 1915, remembers setting up stalls the night before the fete, decorating them with bamboo and crêpe paper, and attending an evening concert after the fete. Fred Low noted in his diary of 22 December 1909:

'At night we had a Strawberry Fete over to the Chappel [most probably McLaren Flat Bible Christian] in ade of the new organ, we all went there but Lydia, there was ice cream and fruit and lolies and drink there.'

Wonderful strawberries are still grown in the region, though the vineyard sprawl is reducing the number of growers. Some of the best come from Glaetzer's Blueberry Farm, just south of Willunga. Fresh strawberries have long been a feature of the Bushing Fair, and strawberry fairs and fetes continue to raise money for local churches and, since the early 1980s, for the Madge Sexton Kindergarten at McLaren Vale.

# THE ANNUAL SHOW

The first South Australian show took place in 1843 on Adelaide's northern parklands, with marquees and tents and a large pavilion for the main exhibits. By the 1850s a number of country centres had formed agricultural and horticultural societies that organised not only an annual show but also the local ploughing match. Willunga's annual ploughing match very quickly became a gala day for the local community, the *Register* of 9 September 1851 reporting that:

*The people availed themselves of the fine weather and came from all parts of the district in great numbers to witness the work and participate in the enjoyment of what seemed to be, by general consent, a district holiday ... Here was knot of rustic youngsters, whose boisterous merriment extorted the ringing laughter of a gay group of village girls. There lads and lasses more 'sober, steadfast and demure' strolled leisurely in couples over the ground, apparently discussing matters in which they felt peculiarly interested ... The more mature of the male sex paid frequent visits to, or lingered in the vicinity of, certain waggons and drays, from which were dispensed refreshments that were enjoyed with a zest which the bracing air of the day could alone create.*

There may well have been talk of a show at the dinner that followed the 1855 ploughing match when nearly two hundred locals sat down 'to a handsomely supplied dinner at the Bush Inn' in Willunga. A meeting of interested persons took place a few months later, again at the Bush Inn. After a few more months of efficient organisation, the first show was held on Thursday 20 March 1856 and a detailed description appeared in the *Register* two days later:

*The day was exceedingly fine; but the heat did not affect the attendance, for early in the morning small groups of persons were to be seen wending their way towards the site of the Exhibition, near the Bush Inn. There was a large and commodious booth erected for the display of produce, and its surrounding enclosure contained a very good collection of agricultural implements, while, adjoining, were the refreshment booths and the stock yards devoted expressly for the use of horses, cattle and pigs. Towards 12 o'clock, when the busy care of the exhibitors had arranged the produce for the inspection of the judges and the public, the scene became exceedingly animated – the presence of two or three thousand persons, including a fair proportion of ladies, all in holiday attire, promenading to the strains of a very good band brought from Adelaide expressly for the occasion, enhanced the picturesque character of the spot ...*

As if to emphasise the show's relevance to the whole region, the following year it moved to McLaren Vale. A block of land behind the Devonshire Hotel was the site. This change, however, must have inspired inter-town rivalry. Following differences of opinion about its planning and location, the show was discontinued after 1857 and only resuscitated in 1866 after the formation of the Willunga Agricultural and Horticultural Society.

Prizes were keenly contested at the ploughing matches and shows. In the early shows prizes were awarded for the best grain, livestock, dairy produce (butter and cheese, bacon and ham), vegetables and fruits; poultry and wine sections were introduced in the second show. Fruits exhibited at the first show included wine and table grapes, apples and pears and melons. The prize for the best collection of melons went to Mr Giles for his watermelons – other exhibitors having entered pie melons! Sometimes a section would attract no entries, at other times a single entry was deemed worthy of only second prize. In 1866 the 'Best 10 lbs potted butter' was won by Mr Waters, the judges commenting that it was 'not very good'. With more practice standards must have improved, and six years later this class attracted eight entries.

The Willunga Show prospered in tune with the fortunes of farming in the district, in 1876 moving to a permanent site at the Willunga Recreation Reserve, purchased through public subscription. Merry-go-rounds and sideshows appeared in the 1880s, around the same time as the Church of

England parishioners introduced their charity stall. In 1891 the Willunga Agricultural Hall – the same hall used today to prepare community lunches during the Almond Blossom Festival – was officially opened, in conjunction with the 36th show. E.H. Hallack happened to be in Willunga for the 1892 show, and described the event for the city press:

*Arriving at the township the evening before the Show, the approaches to the hall and exhibition grounds presented a healthy state of activity, sheep, cattle, pigs and carts laden with produce of different kinds being frequently met with thereabouts. There was a good attendance at the Show, visitors from Adelaide and from all parts of the surrounding districts mustering in force, and the exhibits of stock, vegetables, fruit, and fodder were in some instances brought from localities many miles distant.*

Until 1907 the show had always taken place in March. In that year it moved to October, to accord with other shows in the district, and remained a spring show. Cookery was not embraced until the 1920s, though sections for butter and cheese, bacon and ham, had been included since the early days. In 1926 show day changed from Thursday to Saturday. The opening of the railway in 1915 enabled many more people to attend, and in the 1920s special trains were scheduled so that visitors from the city could spend a day at the Willunga show. Some of them picnicked in the grounds beneath the shady red gums, others enjoyed the luncheon prepared and served by Willunga ladies.

Meanwhile, the McLaren Flat show had been instituted, in response to a suggestion from the president, Geo. Connor, and secretary, Mr Cyril Robertson, of the local Agricultural Bureau. A 'moonlight revel' on McLaren Vale Recreation Ground, attended by around two hundred locals, helped raise money for the first show, held on 30 October 1926. In the beginning it was an indoor show, concentrating on flowers, produce, crafts, and cookery; tables and boxes to display entries were borrowed from the Willunga show committee. Gradually, through donations, working bees and fund-raising dances, the McLaren Flat Horticultural and Floricultural Society improved facilities, increased prizemoney and offered trophies for the highest aggregate points in each section.

Like the Willunga show, the McLaren Flat show has always been a true community event. In its early days it included children's sports, and the climax was the Show Ball in the evening. A section for pets was introduced in 1933 and is still a feature of the show, pets ranging from cats and dogs to hens and guinea pigs, with even a blue-tongue lizard in 1997. A feature of the 1936 show was the prize offered by Sir William Sowden, former editor and part-proprietor of the *Register*, for a black-and-white sketch of McLaren Vale as it would appear in fifty years time.

Shows were suspended during the second world war, resuming with new enthusiasm in 1946. Two years later, the McLaren Flat show society became

affiliated with the Southern Country Shows Association, and from 1949 the show was more like the usual country show with sections for horses, cattle, sheep and poultry, the winners taking part in a Grand Parade around the ground.

Both Willunga and McLaren Flat shows thrived in the 1950s. A new poultry shed and additional sheep pens were constructed at McLaren Flat, the sheep section was expanded and a new section for milking goats added. Sheaf tossing was included in the ring programs, and a special section for Rural Youth exhibits introduced. The cookery section of the McLaren Flat show attracted over 200 entries, dairy produce and fruit around 100 entries each. Dulcie Sparrow consistently won the trophy for the highest aggregate points in the cookery section, which included classes for fruit cake, sultana cake, currant cake, plum pudding, sponge sandwich, sponge roll, cinnamon sponge, scones and lamingtons. There was also a class for summer pudding, but this seems to have been very different to the traditional bread-and-berry dessert of England. According to Elva Dyer, summer pudding McLaren Vale-style was a layered dessert, with a layer of green jelly at the base, then white blancmange, then red jelly. Elva remembers how her piped cream decoration won her the first prize.

Dulcie Sparrow was also a Royal Adelaide Show champion. Connor Sparrow described his wife's preparations:

*we only had wood stoves and I had to do the wood chopping about which she was very fussy. It had to be cut small and even and be of good quality so that the fire could be kept at an even temperature. There was a lot more skill in cooking in those days ... It made a long day as she would be cooking most of the night and the entries had to be displayed before 8 o'clock ready for judging.*

Though the Willunga show ceased in 1968, the McLaren Flat show continued to prosper. The preserves section attracted 141 entries in 1965, when Elva Dyer, yet again, won the Geo. Connor Memorial Trophy for the highest aggregate points. In 1970 there were more than 700 entries in both dog and horse sections. That same year saw the introduction of the Miss Showgirl contest. New clubrooms were completed in 1979 when, for the first time in many years, the sideshows were deemed to have been 'most satisfactory'. The McLaren Flat show was rated the Best Agricultural Dog Show in South Australia in 1983. It hosted the Fruit Cake Championship in 1985; and the Meadows Rural Youth Group had a hay-stacking competition in 1987.

Competition from new events in the 1990s, however, saw gate-takings decline, together with entries in many sections. New sections were added (for cavies), and the Miss Show Girl contest was enlarged to cater for all ages from five years to Grannies and Grand Dads. In the 1997 Aussi Ute competition, prizes were offered for the most original ute, best custom ute, best business ute and best farm ute, the winners joining the horses and cattle in the Grand Parade.

The McLaren Flat show still attracts large numbers of competitors in the ring events, where the riders are mostly girls, confidently composed as they trot and canter, impeccably dressed in creamy-coloured jodhpurs, tweedy jackets and riding helmets. Horses, too, in sizes proportional to their riders, are sleekly groomed, their manes neatly plaited and tied in tiny tufts, tails trimmed to an even bob.

But it is still the cookery and preserves, crafts and flower arrangements that draw the biggest crowds. Even before the judges have finished, a little after midday, exhibitors – and especially children and parents and grand-parents – are anxiously waiting for the doors to open. Whose honey crackles have won first prize? Whose decorated cup cakes? Which boy or girl has created the best animal from fruits and vegetables? Whose arrangement in an egg cup has been honoured?

The children's cookery section is exuberantly colourful; alongside it, the sedate sponges and orange cakes, scones and jubilee cakes, suggest a much more serious intent. In size, shape and general appearance there often seems little to distinguish the cakes but when cut, differences are immediately apparent – fruit unevenly distributed, texture too coarse, too thick a layer of jam in the sponge sandwich. There are far fewer cakes today than in the 1950s and 1960s, when tables would be laden with huge fruit cakes, sultana cakes, currant cakes and plum puddings, a reminder of the years when the region was known for its currants and raisins, apricots and prunes.

In the adjoining room preserves and eggs are on show – plates of fresh eggs, in shades from soft white through palest green to speckled and milk coffee brown, and decorated eggs, including intricately carved and painted emu eggs in the open section and gaudy, imaginative creations in the under-8, under-12 and under-16 years sections. There are lots of Humpty Dumptys, unusual animals or birds, eggs decorated to a Christmas theme in a way that reflects the area or the show itself. This is where the children linger, eager to show off their own artistry or bask in the glory of friends' successes.

McLaren Flat Show, 1997

# ELVA DYER, SHOW CHAMPION

In 1931, at the age of fifteen, Elva entered a posy of flowers in the McLaren Flat show and won first prize. From then on she exhibited at every show, winning prizes and trophies for her orchids, cut flowers, flower arrangements, pot plants, ferns, cakes and preserves, finally retiring when she turned 70.

Elva's mother set a precedent by winning a handsome trophy for her dried prunes at the second McLaren Flat show in 1927; her plum puddings were always show winners. Following in her footsteps, Elva entered in all the local shows – McLaren Flat, Willunga, Strathalbyn, Happy Valley and even the Royal Adelaide Show – but most consistently at McLaren Flat, where for 23 years she won the trophy for the most successful exhibitor in the preserves section.

'It's all looks!' Elva exclaims as she explains some of her tricks – such as displaying jellies in tall, slender jars to maximise their colour impact, or using a

skewer to gently manoeuvre shreds of peel into jars of strained marmalade. One year she made an unorthodox jelly from prunus plums, its deep, intense crimson colour rewarded with the Champion Certificate for the most outstanding exhibit in that section. Her notebooks record her recipes, and the dates she made her jams: peach jam on 1 February 1967; Orleans plum, damson plum and egg plum on 6 January, 18 February and 21 February of the same year; blackberry jam on 7 February 1976. Cake recipes are annotated: 'should use Golden Crust flour' is added next to the recipe for Small honey cakes, while the tried-and-tested recipe for cockles includes the definitive 'use half butter & half marg'.

# WILLUNGA
## ALMOND BLOSSOM FESTIVAL

The first blossoms open in July, not long after the winter solstice – some almost pure white, others modestly blushed with delicate centres of fairy floss pink, their appearance a welcome reassurance that warmer weather will eventually return. It is the season for Willunga's Almond Blossom Festival, traditionally held during the last week of July. Throughout the week busloads of visitors tour the district, at this time of year refreshed by winter rain and at its softest and most appealing. From the heights above Willunga, symmetric smudges of pale pinky grey identify the almond groves in a variegated green landscape.

The inaugural Willunga Almond Blossom Festival of 1970, intended 'for the people of Willunga as well as tourists', attracted thousands of visitors and raised $2900. It began with a variety concert in the Willunga Hall, followed by a 'Drama Night' in the same venue, and included during the nine days an art and antique exhibition, archives display, a demonstration on almond cracking and another on cooking with almonds, and a ball at which Miss Almond Blossom was announced – the contest, open to girls 17 years and older, was initially decided by popular vote, votes counted as cash! The Saturday procession, headed by marching girls, finished at the Recreation Park where Scottish and Serbian dancing groups performed, radio-controlled model aircraft buzzed the children, and men competed in the log-chopping contest. Throughout the week buses took visitors on blossom-viewing tours, and barbecue lunches (only 60 cents! with Seaview wine an optional extra) were offered at the Recreation Park.

Even before the first festival, however, the winter budburst had been celebrated in the 1950s by an Almond Blossom Ball to raise money for the proposed new town hall, and in the 1960s a Southern Districts Blossom Festival was held. In all its years, only minimal changes have been made to the pattern established by the first Willunga Almond Blossom Festival. In the 1990s the barbecue gave way to a roast turkey lunch – Aldinga Table Turkeys is the festival's main sponsor – and since 1993 the ball has been moved from the opening weekend to become the festival finale on the final Saturday night – which means that the crowned Miss Almond Blossom no longer opens the festival at the official ceremony. In addition to Miss Almond Blossom, judged on personality, knowledge, poise and confidence, the title of Miss Community is awarded to the girl who raises the most money.

The festival still runs from one weekend to the next, starting on a Saturday with side shows and amusements at the oval, a band and fireworks at night, with the street procession and fair now on the following day. Since 1991 the Lions Auction, traditionally held on the last Saturday of each month, has been included as a festival attraction – either at its start or end, depending on the calendar – together with the Willunga Lions Quarry Market, which shifts from its habitual second-Saturday-in-the-month to coincide with the festival.

Each year has had particular attractions, such as the veteran car rally of 1971. At the 1972 festival a booklet on cooking with almonds, compiled by members of the local Anglican parish, was launched. A Fun Run from McLaren Vale to Willunga oval, still a feature of the festival program, started in 1977, the first year that local businesses and services entered floats in the procession. The Sunday Fair Day that follows the procession is the festival's main event, attracting about 10,000 people. Local pipe bands, jazz groups and school orchestras provide entertainment, sack races and football kicking competitions are organised, and almond and olive products are available for tasting. The program includes displays of old farm machinery, historic cars and model railways, horseshoeing and sheep shearing, and demonstrations by the local pony club and dog obedience club.

In the early years the variety concert was enthusiastically embraced by local amateurs. Among the acts performed at the 1972 concert was a sketch from the Table Tennis Club, songs by Willunga Primary School students and the choir of Mount Compass Area School, and a Gilbert and Sullivan selection from Willunga High School students, the concert concluding with the theme song of the Willunga Almond Blossom Festival. The variety

Willunga Almond Blossom Festival parade, 1991

concert is no more, but students from local schools provide entertainment in the Recreation Centre on the day of the fair and during the subsequent week, when local women cater for tourists and town residents with morning and afternoon teas and lunches. The hall, festooned with banners of local sporting and social clubs, is set with trestle tables and long benches, while against the walls stallholders sell pottery and other crafts, homemade cakes and preserves, in aid of local churches and charities. As many as 200 dinners are served daily, students from the nearby high school helping with the cooking, clearing and serving. The lunch menu ($10 for three courses) might include a choice of soup – creamy almond or pumpkin – followed by roast turkey or vegetable quiche, then apple crumble or bread-and-butter pudding for dessert.

This involvement of the whole community in the festival won for the Almond Blossom Festival the 1992 South Australian 'Community Event of the Year' award. Local residents act as volunteer guides to tour groups booking lunches at the hall, showing them around the historic town and the almond-cracking sheds. Until recently, an ecumenical 'Blessing of the Crops' service was part of the festival, first held in the ruins of the old Free Presbyterian church on the Aldinga Road and later incorporated into the official opening ceremony.

By 1987 the festival had raised the impressive amount of $500,000 and by the end of the century proceeds should reach $1 million. This money has been returned to the community, most noticeably in the form of the community-owned Recreation Centre, opened in 1978 and finally paid off in 1993.

Procession of winemakers, McLaren Vale Wine Bushing Festival

# THE McLAREN VALE WINE BUSHING FESTIVAL

In retrospect, it seems as though a beautiful princess must have landed among the McLaren Vale wineries in the 1960s and, kissing all the wine-makers, woken them from a slumberous routine. Or perhaps it was the cherubic Bacchus, newly installed in the region as patron of a wine-and-food club. All at once the district came to life: new wineries opened, bottled wine replaced bulk sales, and the district wanted to celebrate. What eventuated was the McLaren Vale Wine Bushing Festival.

In 1972 Greg Trott, Tony Brooks and fellow members of the Spontaneous Events Society organised, as one of a series of events with unlikely themes, an Elizabethan Feast. Food was served on homemade pine platters, drinks in tumblers shaped from (imported) beer bottles and costume was obligatory. Fires illuminated the Kuitpo Hall, mead and mulled wine were served from huge cauldrons, local bakeries baked large loaves, winemakers offered extra-ordinary wines, and everyone rated it 'the best party ever'. Clearly, it had to be repeated.

At the same time David Hardy was putting forward ideas for a local wine festival with an Elizabethan theme. Other regions, such as the Barossa, had a vintage festival, but the McLaren Vale winemakers wanted a different kind of event to promote their region. For several years the district's annual wine show had taken place in October, with trophies awarded to the best shiraz, cabernet sauvignon and dry white wines. This competition had developed from an informal showing of wines initiated in 1965 by the Southern Vales Cooperative and from 1968 organised by the newly-formed McLaren Vale Winemakers' Committee. Since the purpose of a festival was to present new wines to the trade and public, it seemed logical to combine the wine show with the cele-bratory feast, and to continue the Elizabethan theme by crowning the maker of the champion wine of the show Bushing King or Queen.

The term 'bushing' derives from the old English custom of hanging a branch of ivy outside the tavern, as a sign that it sold wine. 'Women's beauty is like unto an Ivy bush, that cals men to the tavern, but hangs itself withoute to winde and wether,' wrote John Florio in 1591. Similarly in medieval France, households with more wine than they could use in a year would fix a spray of ivy over the door to indicate that they had wine for sale. For centuries ivy had been symbolically associated with wine, being sacred to Dionysus (Bacchus); in ancient times banquet guests would place wreaths of ivy (and other plants) on their heads or around their cups, believing that this would counteract the effects of the wine. The branch of ivy could also signal the arrival of new wine and so the tradition was tailor-made for McLaren Vale, where many of the new whites are released towards the end of the year. One important detail was changed: the bush displayed at each winery was not a spray of ivy but an olive branch, in late spring covered in clusters of tiny buds and pale creamy flowers. In this way, the Festival Committee honoured the pioneers of the wine industry in the region, who had developed the custom of planting olives in association with vines.

For the first Bushing Festival in 1973, the Elizabethan Feast moved to the vast cask hall of the old Tatachilla winery. Word of mouth had spread its reputation, and over 600 guests gathered from near and far to be welcomed by flaring bonfires and the sizzle of spit-roasts. At a given signal the doors were opened and the costumed diners invited into the hall – and magically transposed to another era. The space was lit by candles in massive iron candelabras made for the occasion, the floor strewn with straw. Huge platters of food were borne in on litters and whole baked pumpkins set on the tables; wine flowed, brass quintets played and *a capella* singers sang. Guests might have arrived not knowing what to expect, but they left with a clear idea of McLaren Vale food, wine and hospitality. Wine industry elder Len Evans proclaimed it one of the greatest spectacles he had attended.

The enthusiastic response to the first festival stimulated local winemakers to make it bigger and better. In 1974 it extended over ten days, starting with the Friday Winemakers' Luncheon at which the Bushing King and Queen were announced, and including a street procession and fair. A team of twelve

Clydesdales, controlled by old teamsters 'Tuffy' Rayner and Fred Margitich and drawing a five-tonne wagon, led the procession through McLaren Vale, where in a newly-proclaimed 'Wine Square' Robyn Archer performed as an 'Elizabethan ballad singer'. Wineries such as Seaview, Ryecroft, Hardys, Amery and St Francis advertised their 'cellar parties': a five-course meal plus wine for $10 per person.

The 'cellar party' was a feature of Bushing Festivals throughout the 1970s and 1980s. Individual wineries would host lunches, dinners and banquets amid casks and fermenting vats to present their new releases.

Bill and Merilyn Hardy, Bushing King and Queen 1988

These were public events, though invitations were extended to friends and loyal customers; such invitations were prized, and there was always the possibility of a visit from the Bushing King and Queen, asserting their royal prerogative and insisting on a respectful welcome. One memorable sovereign was Dr Hugh Lloyd, a founding partner in Coriole vineyards and Bushing King in 1974, who played the role with great aplomb, commandeering the services of one of the pipers to herald his entries as he toured the district. His wife, Mollie Lloyd, described the excitement of the occasion in her diary:

*Friday October 25 [after being told Coriole had won both red wine trophies]. It was terrific – Everyone welcomed us, kissed me & the good will was wonderful, had lunch, too excited to eat, stayed until about 3.30 . . .*

*Saturday October 26. King and Queen – weather perfect – up early and a photographer came out from the* News. *Down to Coriole and then to*

*Institute. We were thrilled, all the children were there – Rode with Hardy's, Don Dunstan on wagon with 11 Clydesdale horses to oval where they had magnificent 2 day fair, hot air balloons, sky divers in red and blue para-chutes ... [In the evening] we were piped in at Seaview where we ate ... Fabulous day ...*

*Wednesday October 30. Dressed and went to Seaview to cellar party. Piped in by 3 handsome pipers. Lovely evening ... Good food and terrific dancing all out in Seaview entrance, first time they have done it but really good music ... we left at 12.15*

Traditions developed as the Wine Bushing Festival cemented its place in the local calendar – such as the singing of the Bushing Wassail by a group of colour-fully cloaked winemakers at the start of the first official event of the festival, the Winemakers' Lunch – always held on the last Friday of October. Arts and crafts have been associated with the Bushing Festival since its early days, many wineries exhibiting the works of local artists. The popular Craft Market at Kay's Amery Vineyards, where wine-tasting almost takes second billing after family entertainment, celebrates its 25th anniversary in 1998. For children there are hay rides on a Clydesdale-drawn dray, jingling Morris dancers and chocolate frogs in white, pink, green and blue. Inside the winery local craftspeople, many of them regulars at the market since its inception, set up stalls to show their jewellery and lead lighting, home-made pickles and preserves, pottery and hand-turned wooden rolling pins.

Other traditions of the 1980s include the barbecue at d'Arenberg's tin sheds with music

---

# The Bushing Wassail

'Tis for love of wine we sing

Glory to the Bushing King

And the joys good wine doth bring

Glory to the Bushing King.

On your feet now, to the beat now.

Off your arses, raise your glasses.

Let us make the rafters sing ...

Glory to the Bushing King.

---

from Dick Frankel and his Jazz Disciples, the Women Potters' exhibition at Seaview winery, and Hardy's champagne breakfast. The street procession and Bushing Fair have been a feature of most festivals, the Bushing Fair moving to Middlebrook winery when the procession was discontinued for six years from 1983. In the early years it was a real pageant, with prizes awarded to the best floats and best decorated bicycles. In 1976 first prize went to the McLaren Vale Primary School, which was celebrating its centenary, though the Ingoldby/Wirra Wirra entry – a donkey laden with wine casks that replenished grateful

Winemakers singing the Bushing Wassail

glasses along the route with dry red wine – was deemed 'original'. There were also competitions at the Fair – wood chopping, tractor driving, wine barrel rolling, in 1979 a vineyard scarecrow competition. In 1977 a media bottling competition was introduced, in which teams of two from radio, television and print media try to fill and cork as many bottles as possible in the allotted time, siphoning the wine from casks. Starting in 1980, the National Amateur Wine and Beer Show has also been held in conjunction with the Bushing Festival.

When it extended over ten days, the McLaren Flat show was sometimes part of the festival, as were Melbourne Cup lunches on the first Tuesday of November. Since the late 1980s, however, the Bushing Festival has been a three-day weekend. The street procession has been restored, brass and pipe bands alternating with 1940s trucks from local wineries, battered and bruised racing cars carried on trailers, Country Fire Service volunteers on an old-fashioned fire engine, a family of camels and a Richard Hamilton dray pulled by four handsome draughthorses. As in earlier festivals, it involves the wider community: the Aldinga Surf Life Saving Club with its surf boat; sheepish stars of the McLaren Vale Football Club; and McLaren Flat Primary School girls in long frocks practising for the Mini Debutante Ball.

The Bushing Fair which follows the procession has had several venues, most recently McLaren's on the Lake. After 25 years the Fair has seen many changes, but it seems to be returning to its original intent, a family day bringing together townspeople and the wine industry. The sideshow atmosphere has been subdued as wineries take a more prominent role, many choosing this occasion to offer their new releases, accompanied by simple finger foods – such as grilled marinated chicken in Turkish pide bread, provided by the Star of Greece cafe. Entertainments are varied, from popular pub bands to Punch and Judy shows and storytelling sessions for children, while contests include woodchopping and the exuberant Celebrity Media Bottling.

New events have been introduced to the Bushing program. Scarpantoni Estate has, for the past two years, presented a Saturday evening classical concert with food and wine, in the tradition of the 'cellar party'. From 1997, Not the Winemakers' Lunch, a fun alternative to the formal Winemakers' Luncheon, with its own alternative 'king', has been held at Wirilda Creek winery. At the heart of the festival, however, is the tasting of the newly-released wines at the individual wineries, many of which offer added attractions of music and art exhibitions during the Bushing weekend. This blend of wine and food, art and music, hospitality and festivity has characterised the Bushing Festival since its inception and continues to draw people to the region – not only for the Bushing but also for the Continuous Picnic and the Sea & Vines celebrations.

The almost forgotten antecedent to the Bushing Festival was Hardy's Vintage Fete, celebrated in McLaren Vale at the end of vintage for about forty years from 1890. Initiated by Thomas Hardy, it was initially held at his Bankside cellars and transferred to McLaren Vale when city gatecrashers became too much of a problem. The Vintage Fete continued the old English tradition of 'Harvest Home', a day of feasting and merriment for farm workers offered by landowners at the end of the harvest season.

Known locally as the 'vintage sports', it was McLaren Vale's annual festivity and a local holiday, attracting 'residents and settlers from a considerable distance'. There were sports for men and children, from handicap races and hurdles to novelty events such as catching the greasy pig, an egg-and-spoon race, a water-carrying handicap and a cask race. Results and a full description of the day were published in city newspapers. The tug-of-war between the vintage hands and anyone else seemed always to be won by the vintage hands: 'The vintage hands and their friends entered into the affair with much enthusiasm, and gave the spectators some very creditable exhibitions of athletics', reported the *Register* in 1897. Later in the afternoon 'a tea was provided … A very large number sat at the tables, and afterwards the hall was cleared for dancing, which was kept up by the young folks and several elderly couples till considerably past midnight'.

At the Vintage Fetes, Thomas Hardy appears as a benevolent *paterfamilias*. In 1899 the *Register* described him as like 'the father of a huge family [who] moved about the wives and children, discussed the prospects of the coming season with the former, laughed and played with the latter, and entered with quite youthful spirits into the fun of the festival'.

# THE McLAREN VALE
# CONTINUOUS PICNIC

The innovation of the 'gourmet weekend' in the Clare Valley in May 1985 changed the style of festivities in South Australian wine areas. The progressive dinner concept, with emphasis on the quality of the food and wine – at bargain prices compared with restaurants – was an instant hit, and has since been adopted by other wine regions. In later years, live music has enhanced the conviviality of the occasion, and this formula of good food, wine and music – B.Y.O. joie de vivre – has been a huge success in terms of tourism and sociability and also in terms of cellar door sales. The event attracts all age groups, from fun-loving yuppies to families with young children and comfortably superannuated retirees.

McLaren Vale wineries first experimented with the idea on a small scale with a Sip 'n' Savour day in September 1985, when a number of wineries teamed up with local and Adelaide restaurants. In 1992 it was extended to a two-day weekend and retitled 'The Continuous Picnic', in reference to Michael Symons' history of Australian eating, *One Continuous Picnic*. Under this name the festival has flourished, attracting more than 10,000 visitors over the weekend, while the number of participating wineries has increased from 23 to 30. Always held during the first weekend in October, and since 1993 on the Sunday and holiday Monday of that weekend, its timing is perfect; typically the weather is warm and sunny and the countryside looks idyllic. Ribbons of soft green dance down vineyard slopes and at the ends of rows bloom red and pink roses. An air of carefree pleasure prevails.

Programs for The Continuous Picnic illustrate the passing parade of Australian food fashions. A potpourri of Chilean, Spanish, Thai, Cajun, Korean and Mediterranean food was presented in 1992, but since 1994 such national affiliations have faded and eclectic Mod Oz reigns. Increasingly, wineries offer a choice of dishes – six of the 30 participating wineries in 1997 advertised a vegetarian alternative – together with a choice of desserts and proper coffee. Prices have remained pleasingly low, the cost of a glass of wine

increasing from $2.50 in 1992 to $3.00 in 1997, while a serve of food cost $6.00 in 1992 and $8.00 in 1997.

The enthusiasm for The Continuous Picnic has spilled over to the Sea & Vines festival, since 1997 held during the long weekend at the start of June – when again, the weather is usually benign. In that year, too, the McLaren Vale Winemakers Incorporated took control of the festival from the Southern Development Board, which had originally conceived the event as a promotion for specific products: oysters from South Australia's west coast in 1992, farmed barramundi in 1993 and farmed yabbies in 1994. With the focus firmly on seafood, the McLaren Vale Sea & Vines label was affixed in 1995,

and the weekend has become established in the regional calendar as an opportunity to feast on prawns, oysters, calamari, tuna, mussels, King George whiting, barbecued octopus and yabbies – all kinds of seafood, char-grilled or deep-fried, with pasta or in risotto, as satay or salad, and all with the best of McLaren Vale wines and lively music.

For the time being, at least, this combination seems set to continue as the prime means of enticing visitors and their dollars to the region. Individual wineries have adapted the formula; since 1989 Woodstock has presented an annual Easter Art Affair where wine, food, music, art and crafts come together in a week-long festival. The Australian String Quartet has given a post-dinner performance in the 'Vintage Shed' of the new Tatachilla winery in McLaren Vale, while jazz concerts have been staged in the natural auditorium of Wirra Wirra's cask-lined cellars, Salopian Inn supplying platters of local foods –

olives and tapenade, locally cured and smoked meats, garfish and tommy ruffs, chicken cooked with olive oil and dukkah.

To date, these festivities have typically been on a relatively small scale, but the closing event of the 1998 Adelaide Festival, Womad in the Vales, brought around 5,000 people to the McLaren Vale Oval. A younger sibling of the biennial Womadelaide – an Adelaide celebration of the World of Music Arts & Dance – the 12-hour concert featured singers and musicians from Australia, Africa, Scotland, central Asia and eastern Europe, together with the amazingly flexible acrobats of Circus Ethiopia. Cartwheeling, flying, diving, sleight-of-hand juggling and human pyramids immediately became an irresistible challenge for the more daring of the young males in the audience. Larger-than-life puppets and buxom ballerinas on stilts wandered among the audience giving impromptu performances.

In this ideal setting – behind a low, scrubby hill, with vineyards to the east and west – and in perfect weather, Womad epitomised the relaxed conviviality so characteristic of McLaren Vale, and of South Australia in general. Children frolicked in spontaneous groups, adults sampled a range of McLaren Vale wines and everyone enjoyed a diversity of food, from Middle Eastern platters to Russell Jeavons' pizzas. Evening arrived with a full moon silhouetted over vineyard rows; the darkened oval was resonant with bonhomie and waves of music faded into the distance. As the finale to an already acclaimed festival, it was an unqualified success.

Womad in the Vales was backed by the City of Onkaparinga and McLaren Vale Winemakers; both would happily support a second concert as part of the next Adelaide Festival. These public events are popular, well-publicised and well-patronised, and raise the district's profile – especially its wine profile. At the same time, however, the truly local festivals, which are just as dependent on behind-the-scenes cooperation and volunteer energy – such as the Strawberry Fair for the Madge Sexton Kindergarten, the February Multicultural Festival and the Port Noarlunga street fair – should also be recognised for their contributions to the region's culture, cohesiveness and community spirit.

# CHAPTER
# COMMUNITY

'No man is an Island, entire of itself,' wrote John Donne. It is the community that breathes life into a region and creates its sense of identity; it is the community that promotes this identity, through cooperation and collaboration and interaction.

The shared interests that bring people together include the church, sport, learning and the welfare of the region and its community. The early years of settlement in the McLaren Vale region saw a reliance on imported institutions – in particular, religion – to provide a focus for the community, but before long there were locally representative cricket and football teams and clubs, their competitiveness introducing the first hints of identity.

From the mid-nineteenth century the Institutes provided culture in the form of library services, uplifting lectures and lively soirees. As the population became more self-reliant it responded directly to the needs of the region, lobbying for roads and transport services and establishing the district hospital. Still more recently, people have united to protect and preserve their physical and cultural environment.

# SEVEN

Festivals such as the Willunga Almond Blossom Festival and the Port Noarlunga street fair, the monthly markets at Aldinga and Willunga and the McLaren Flat show all depend on community involvement; without the efforts of volunteers they would not have begun, nor could they continue. At the same time they provide a focus for the community and benefit the region in a material way, all profits being returned to the community. This healthy interdependence is a key to the region's vigour and self-confidence.

In a shining example of community spirit, typically characterised by a willingness to subordinate individual interests to the greater good, McLaren Vale winemakers have begun to promote their wines collectively at national and international exhibitions. The benefits of this flow on to each winery and indirectly to the region's restaurants and Main Streets, gradually filtering through to the entire community.

Other community groups work towards the preservation of the region's natural and cultural heritage, acting not simply out of self interest – looking after their own backyards – but with the interests of visitors also at heart.

# PEOPLE

Emigrants to South Australia were predominantly English, and from the southern counties in particular. William Colton and Charles Thomas Hewett, pioneers of McLaren Vale, both came from Devonshire; families who settled in the Kangarilla area in the 1840s and 1850s typically came from Somerset, Hampshire, Berkshire, Kent, Warwickshire, Northamptonshire and Suffolk. Willunga and its slate quarries attracted the Cornish, as the persistence of names such as Pethick, Kernick and Pengilly testify. By 1850, about half of the population of the Willunga district was from either Cornwall or Devon. Nevertheless, there were also a few Scottish and Irish among the first settlers – James McLeod came from Scotland, George Hepenstal from Ireland.

From the late 1840s and early 1850s assisted emigration from Ireland increased greatly; potato blight had hit Ireland in 1845, and the succeeding years were ones of famine. Poor Irish families would often make sacrifices to send one family member, whose efforts later helped finance the voyage of others. Among the record number of 11,871 assisted immigrants in 1855, more than 5000 were Irish, and some would undoubtedly have been passengers on the ill-fated *Nashwauk*, wrecked off Moana in 1855. Orphan Irish girls were also brought out, the first arriving in 1849. Around 5500 were sent from Ireland to South Australia in 1854 and 1855, some probably to the Willunga 'depot' for single girls where they rebelled against the self-righteous discipline of Thomas Kell.

For the first five years assisted emigrants to South Australia outnumbered those who paid their own way but for the next five years the trend was reversed. Proportions were approximately equal in 1846, but in the next few years assisted emigrants were again in the majority. Many were sponsored or persuaded to emigrate by the reports they received from friends and relations already settled in the colony. At the end of 1857, the English-born still constituted a majority (39 per cent) of the South Australian population, but 35 per cent of the colony's inhabitants were born in Australia. Ten per cent were born in Ireland, seven per cent in Germany and six per cent in Scotland. The

McLaren Vale region was predominantly British. It had virtually no residents of German origin, and few immigrants from other colonies.

The uniformity of the population in terms of birthplace did not preclude class differences. As *Quiz* commented in 1893:

*Society is somewhat exclusive. There are, as is usual in country towns, little cliques. Tea drinking is a favourite occupation, and there is a good deal of scandal to every square yard of conversation. Yet there are some earnest Democratic souls down South who don't care a dump for birth so long as it is unaccompanied by intelligence and worth.*

Locals acknowledged social and role differences between the main towns in the nineteenth and early twentieth century. McLaren Flat was seen as democratic, egalitarian and, with its Women's Bureau and Country Women's Association, more community-oriented. In the earlier-established McLaren Vale, where old families such as the Pridmores and the Trotts employed household servants, class distinctions were more precious. Willunga, at the head of the railway, was the business and administrative centre while (Old) Noarlunga serviced the needs of the district farmers.

The population of the region is still relatively homogeneous and over-whelmingly Anglo-Australian, with nine out of every ten people living in the Willunga Local Government Area born in Australia or the United Kingdom. The 1996 census shows that nearly three-quarters of the population of the Willunga Local Government Area were born in Australia, and of these over 70 per cent had mothers and fathers also born in Australia. An additional 16 per cent of the area's population was born in the United Kingdom while less than one per cent of the population was of Greek or Italian background, compared to three per cent in the state. There were virtually no Vietnam-born residents in this area, compared to nearly one per cent in the whole state.

A number of Italians settled in the Blewitt Springs area in the 1930s, among them the Brunato, Cassetta and Franceschini families. At the same time as clearing their own blocks, the men worked in nearby vineyards; Giovanni Franceschini and Egidio ('Gid') Brunato both won state championships in pruning competitions. Italians and Greeks have since contributed much to the region's contemporary life and culture, way out of proportion to their actual presence in the population. Vince Scarfo and Emmanuel Giakoumis sustained the local olive industry, while the Scarpantoni and Maglieri families have won acclaim for their wines.

Emmanuel Giakoumis with Mark Lloyd (left)

# EMMANUEL GIAKOUMIS

Emmanuel has many 'firsts' to his name: first in Australia with crushed green olives; first to harvest olives mechanically in 1974; first to produce extra virgin olive oil in McLaren Vale.

This is a beautiful country, says Emmanuel, so long as you've got a brain and muscles! He arrived in South Australia in 1955 with only a couple of shillings to his name, but by 1956 he was leasing the McLaren Vale olive grove originally planted by Thomas Hardy, which he then purchased in 1972. At first olives were a weekend interest, but in 1959 he left his job as electrician and motor mechanic to work with olives and almonds full-time. Soon he began to prepare crushed green olives in the same way as his mother had done on the Greek island of Samos, using only water and salt. These olives could beat the imported ones in both price and quality, and for many years Emmanuel produced 20 tonnes or more annually. He maintains that there's a critical time for harvesting the olives, and that instinct and experience are the most important ingredients in the process. At the same time he was also producing quality olive oil, using modern machinery imported from Italy, and had no trouble selling as many as 1500 tins, each of 18 litres.

Having planted kalamata olive trees in 1980, he was able to start pickling kalamatas in 1985 and now prepares about five tonnes each year, his own harvest supplemented by local purchases. Kalamata olives traditionally have a shallow slit near the pointy end of the olive and Emmanuel developed machines to do this, treating about 200 kilos per hour. Around 1987, however, he decided to cut costs by eliminating this process and discovered that the olives were better, less likely to become soft. Most South Australian kalamatas are now left whole, though imported Greek ones are slit!

Even though he sold the olive grove in 1984, Emmanuel is still involved in the industry, assisting with the blending of oils for Coriole. A mixture of Mission and Verdale is his ideal, and his favourite way of appreciating the fresh oil is to drizzle it on toast then sprinkle with a little salt and lemon juice.

# DOMENICO SCARPANTONI AND STEVE MAGLIERI

The low arches and vine-covered arcades of the Scarpantoni and Maglieri wineries are immediately reminiscent of an Italian country farmhouse. By no means out of place in this environment, they emphasise the Mediterranean empathies recognised by some of the colony's earliest annalists.

Steve Maglieri has twice been Bushing King and has won countless awards for his shiraz and other red and white wines, but it is the Italian-inspired Lambrusco that has ensured popular success. Maglieri was the first to make this light, fruity, red sparkling wine in Australia, and is the largest producer of Lambrusco in the country. It is made entirely from McLaren Vale grapes, as are the premium wines under the Steve Maglieri label.

Steve Maglieri arrived in Australia in 1964 in the footsteps of his father, who had come to McLaren Vale in 1958 and worked for ten years on Pirramimma vineyard. Domenico (Dom) Scarpantoni had arrived in 1952 and, after grape-picking along the Murray and cane-cutting in Queensland, settled in the region as a farm manager for David Hardy.

Dom's first purchase of land was in the low-lying area just east of McLaren Vale, where Colton and Hewett began more than a century earlier, but in 1968 he exchanged this for 20 hectares of scrub and orchard on a rise to the south of McLaren Flat. Instinct told him that this was a good position, and so it has proved; two years later he bought an additional 12 hectares next door. The winery was built in 1979 with the help of his two winemaker sons, Michael and Filippo, all wines being made exclusively from grapes grown on the property. Today it is very much a family business, with two generations of Scarpantonis looking after all operations from pruning to marketing to organising festivities. The Scarpantoni's traditional Italian banquets were a feature of Bushing Festivals in the 1980s.

As he sits on the front lawn of the winery, surveying rows of vines descending into the township and resuming again on the slopes on the other side, Dom confides that this is 'the most beautiful place in the world'.

# CHURCHES

Adelaide has been called the 'city of churches', but this area to the south of the city is a region of churches. Fifty years after the first British settlements there were about twenty churches and chapels from (Old) Noarlunga to Sellick's Hill – in Clarendon, Kangarilla, McLaren Flat and Vale, Willunga and Aldinga and all minor settlements in between – serving a population, in 1890, of just over one thousand.

While emigrants in the early decades came mainly from the southern counties of England, they were also predominantly Protestant 'dissenters', meaning that they belonged to non-conformist (non-Anglican) denominations, the principal ones of which were Wesleyan Methodist, Congregationalist and Baptist. Most Cornish immigrants, for example, were Methodists. Indeed, religion was a motive for emigration, since dissenters in England in the 1830s had inferior legal standing, being excluded from

McLaren Vale Congregational Church, c. 1860s

universities, for example. Among South Australia's founding fathers were some notable dissenters; Robert Gouger was a Congregationalist.

In the very early days church services were held in private homes or in the open; at McLaren Vale people assembled beneath the giant gum tree beside the well on Charles Hewett's Oxenberry Farm. The first McLaren Vale Church was in fact an non-denominational chapel, 'The House of The Lord', which was used by Congregationalists, Methodists, Baptists and various others. Its foundation stone was laid at a Harvest Thanksgiving in February 1844, on land donated by John Morphett. Nine months later the building itself was opened. Entirely funded by public subscription, it was a simple, homely building: four walls, a door at one end and a window in each of the adjacent walls. This plain, whitewashed barn still stands, almost apologetically, behind the loftier (former) Congregationalist church that displaced it in 1861. The honour of the first church in the region, however, probably goes to the Wesleyan Methodist church at Willunga, which also opened in 1844. Four years later the original structure had to be extended and in 1856–57 another larger church was built, this in turn being dismantled in 1895 and rebuilt as the present church, now the Willunga Uniting church. Since early this century the bell from the 1857 church has been suspended in a massive old red gum in vacant land – the 'bell paddock' – opposite the church and is rung before morning service every Sunday.

One of the aims of the South Australian Association, which in 1834 urged the British government to found a colony in South Australia, was to establish a colony without any established church and without any state-supported religion. In the end neither of these was realised exactly as intended, but in matters of religion South Australia was different to the other colonies. Its strongest religious voice was Methodist rather than Anglican, and its church-going population seems to have been proportionately greater than in the other states.

The number of churches in the district gives some idea of the importance of religion in the early years. In Willunga in 1851, when the township was barely ten years old, attendance at the Wesleyan Sunday School at Willunga averaged 55 during the year. For the size of the population, fundraising efforts were remarkable. At the tiny settlement of Eyre's Flat [Kangarilla], a bazaar held in 1869 to mark the anniversary of the opening of the Bible Christian chapel raised over £40 and at Willunga, a bazaar on the day of the agricultural show in 1869 raised £90.

Sunbeam Circle Sunday School, Willunga, c. 1900

In June 1846 Governor Robe decided to introduce a system of state aid, making no discrimination between the Church of England and other religions and offering grants in proportion to both the amounts of money contributed locally and the numbers of regular church-goers. Many of the 'dissenting' religions – including the Bible Christians, Congregationalists, Primitive Methodists and Baptists – rejected such grants as being unscriptural, unnecessary and corrupting and campaigned for their abolition, while Anglican,

Catholic, Wesleyan Methodist and Lutheran faiths accepted them, claiming that such state aid was divinely authorised in the Old Testament. The Anglican churches at Willunga (1848) and (Old) Noarlunga (1850) were among the first to benefit from the scheme, which came to an end after 'voluntarists' gained a majority in the Legislative Council at the 1851 election and defeated a bill to continue church funding. South Australia was the first of the colonies to break the traditional connection between church and state.

A combined Sunday school picnic, c. 1923

In almost every settlement in South Australia Methodists were the first to hold regular services, thereby attracting families who might have arrived with a different brand of faith. Within Methodism, however, were several different denominations – Wesleyans, Primitive Methodists, Bible Christians. Willunga had its Wesleyan church, a Bible Christian chapel (1855) and Primitive Methodist chapel (1868). In addition there was a large Roman Catholic church (1850) accommodating 200 worshippers; an Anglican one (first church 1848, St Stephen's 1884); and in High Street a Church of Christ

(1860s). Attendance at church was a social ritual, as *Quiz's Tourists' Guide* made clear in 1893:

*There are five churches and five public-houses in Willunga. On Sundays the population turn out in their best attire – plug hats, black coats and pants, new bonnets, bright skirts and all the rest of it. In the afternoon some of them drive or walk to Port Willunga, or they journey to Sellick's Hill, or climb some other precipitous height in search of wild flowers.*

Before the various groups came together in 1900, the Wesleyans had churches at Willunga, McLaren Vale, Noarlunga, Sellick's Hill, Aldinga, Bethany and Kangarilla; Primitive Methodists at Willunga and at Binney Road (the Strout cemetery); and Bible Christians at McLaren Flat, Kangarilla and Seaview. One consequence of the Methodist union was a surplus of church buildings, some of which were simply demolished. Others were sold and used for commercial purposes, and already in 1892 the Primitive Methodist chapel at Willunga was being used as a wine store – it is now Vanessa's Restaurant. The chapel at Seaview was taken over by the Education Department and became a school. 'The school we went to first was the old chapel up here near Seaview, which is now Chapel Hill winery,' recalls 'Cud' Kay, born in 1914.

On Strout Road, just off McMurtrie Road, is the tiny Bethany chapel – so-named because it was about the same distance from McLaren Vale as the biblical Bethany from Jerusalem. The chapel celebrated its centenary in 1954, and although it closed in 1967 the modest little building still stands. Cement render now covers the original clay, straw and rubble, while alongside, dwarfed by an overgrown olive tree and tall gum, is the old supper room of galvanised iron. Members of the McMurtrie family are buried behind the chapel, while opposite is a paddock that once belonged to the Trott's, who called it the Church Block – though it should have been Chapel Block, says Greg Trott, who remembers using a horse-drawn plough in 1953 to cultivate between the vines as well as between the rows. In 1972 this paddock supplied grenache grapes for a red wine which, to avoid using 'grenache' on the label, was called Wirra Wirra Church Block. The label remains but the Church Block connection has long disappeared, and since 1983 the wine has been a blend of cabernet, shiraz and merlot.

McLaren Vale had a strong Congregationalist following. 'The House of the Lord' became a Congregationalist chapel in 1850, and the solid slate-roofed church alongside, officially opened in 1862, became the centre of community life for the Gloucester end of the township. In 1909 it founded a 'cause' in Port Noarlunga, and soon afterward the town's first church – now an antiques gallery – was built, using local limestone. With diminishing attendances, the McLaren Vale Congregational Church closed in 1966. For several years from 1974 it was home to the organisers of the McLaren Vale Wine Bushing Festival, its significance officially recognised in the historical plaque unveiled at the first Bushing Festival in 1973. It later served as the McLaren Vale Arts Centre, which Jerry Elder opened with an exhibition of superb photographs taken around the turn of the century by Ernest Lewis Fidge. Now, under folksinger Dave Clark, it has become the Singing Gallery, a venue for concerts and art exhibitions.

With the exception of those in the old-established towns of (Old) Noarlunga and Willunga, Anglican churches came relatively late. At Kangarilla the Church of England, built on donated land by volunteer labour, opened in 1904; St Margaret's Church of England in McLaren Vale opened in 1911. For about thirteen years until 1981 the popular Anglican minister for the whole region was Canon George Cameron, and more often than not the communion wine was port from Pirramimma's barrels – the same port sold to the locals in flagons. In a parish where wine was almost the lifeblood it was difficult not to be converted, and Canon Cameron even established a tiny vineyard on his property near Willunga.

Lutheranism has been long established in many parts of South Australia, but is a recent arrival in the McLaren Vale region. From 1933 visiting pastors conducted services at Mount Compass and other southern centres, and a

Lutheran church was built at Mount Compass in 1961. St. Paul's, at McLaren Vale, opened in 1963 and other churches were later established at Aldinga and Seaford. In 1955 a Lutheran college was established on part of the old Tatachilla vineyard, which had been purchased by the Lutheran church in 1964. With an enrolment of about 300, it attracts boys and girls from nearby

Thanksgiving display, Congregational Church, McLaren Vale, c.1930s

areas and as far afield as Happy Valley and Victor Harbor. By 1999 it will be a complete secondary school with a special interest in agriculture. Agricultural subjects are gradually being incorporated into the curriculum, and a poultry yard, wetlands area and vineyard are being established.

# THE INSTITUTES

In the nineteenth century virtually all South Australian country townships had their Institutes – non-political, non-sectarian community centres offering library services to the local population, their halls hosting concerts, lectures and dances.

The Institutes – sometimes called Mechanics' Institutes – were modelled on the Mechanics' Institutes that began to proliferate in England in the early nineteenth century. The first in South Australia was the Hindmarsh and Bowden Institute, in what is now suburban Adelaide; Clarendon Institute, established in 1853, was the eighth in the state and Willunga the ninth, in 1854.

Many institutes owned their own premises, the Willunga Mechanics' Institute being an exception – though this seemed no hindrance to its operations. Its reading room and library opened about February 1854, the reading room being supplied with four colonial papers – the *Government Gazette*, [Adelaide] *Times*, *Register*, and *Observer* – and many numbers of the *London*

Outside the McLaren Vale Institute, Australia Day, c. 1920s

*Illustrated News*. By the time of its first annual meeting the Willunga Institute had more than 350 books and 72 members, each of whom had paid one guinea subscription. Regret was expressed, however, that:

*the portion of the library more especially of an improving and instructive character, namely books of history and those which give an insight into the elements of the arts and sciences, has been nearly altogether unused.*

The philosophy of the institutes emphasised self-improvement; non-working time should be spent acquiring useful knowledge. Strongly opposed to gambling – an alternative leisure pursuit – they forbade card playing in their halls. Their aims were educational, and institutes realised these by offering opportunities for learning through library services and lectures, which were often on themes of literature or travel in other countries.

Through a pooling of community resources, some institutes were able to offer self-education classes. By 1869 the Aldinga Institute, established nine years previously, offered classes in reading, debating and singing, and in 1872 purchased a piano. Though interest and membership dwindled to almost nothing over the next ten years, the singing class was revived in 1886 and a literary society formed in 1893. The Institute must have continued to thrive, for in 1935 the foundation stone was laid for a handsome new building, the opening of which was celebrated with a concert given by the Austral Philharmonic Society.

Providing a library service was the most important of the institutes' functions. From 1859 the South Australian Institute offered a 'travelling box library', the boxes to be swapped between institutes every three or four months. Disregarding official policy, many institutes – including the one at Willunga – expressed a preference for 'light literature' such as biography, travel and novels over more edifying tomes on history or philosophy. Gradually, fiction came to dominate in many of the libraries. When inventories were prepared in 1900, more than 90 per cent of the Clarendon Institute collection was classified as fiction.

At (Old) Noarlunga an institute operated for many years before its building was completed in 1881. At McLaren Vale, too, the library operated from the town's first church before the McLaren Vale Institute opened in 1893, having been built by volunteer labour on land donated by Sir John Colton. The hall also served as the venue for the dance on the occasion of the Vintage Fete. The original building was demolished and replaced by the present building, officially opened by the Governor, Sir Alexander Hore-Ruthven, on 1 July 1933. Kangarilla Soldiers' Memorial Institute took over what had been the Temperance Hall, built in 1875 and used for public and social gatherings. The Port Noarlunga Institute dates from 1914, when a residents' committee was formed to raise funds for an institute and library. The site was purchased in 1920 and the institute opened in 1924, the next-door library in 1929.

In the early twentieth century the institute halls were less a focus of intellectual life than the centre of community social activities such as school concerts, public meetings, films and dances. The new McLaren Vale Institute was designed to seat about 500 people and to be suitable for showing the new moving pictures, as well as to house an extensive library. Until the 1970s, when local councils began to take responsibility, institutes still provided library services with the aid of travelling boxes. The Willunga council established a mobile library service in 1979 and permanent libraries at Willunga and Aldinga in 1986 and 1992 respectively.

Many institute buildings still serve a community purpose. The Noarlunga Community Arts Centre, which occupies the Port Noarlunga Institute, provides workshop spaces for local art groups, runs classes in art and dance and arranges regular exhibitions, concerts and performances. The Aldinga Institute is now meeting place for the Almond Grove Family Church and the site of the monthly Aldinga market (first Saturday of the month), while the McLaren Vale Institute hosts a monthly arts-and-craft market (last Saturday of each month).

# SPORTS

Cricket was the first organised, or semi-organised, sport in the colony. In country areas, a day of cricket was always a social occasion, with games and activities organised for children as well. Geoffrey Manning, in *Hope Farm Chronicle*, records Boxing Day 1853 as the date of the first cricket match in the district. The following February a team from Willunga challenged the Morphett Vale team:

*the match lasted until nearly sundown, when the parties adjourned to the Bush Inn, and partook of an excellent dinner, and the day's amusement was concluded with the greatest harmony.*

The pioneering clubs in the southern area were apparently Morphett Vale and Aldinga (in 1854), the Willunga club being formed soon after. Noarlunga's cricket team dates from 1862, but the club lapsed and had to be revived several times in the next ten years. The Clarendon cricket club began in 1865, Kangarilla in 1870. In the early twentieth century there was even a Seaview team. The Southern Cricket Association was formed in 1889. Rivalry between the neighbouring villages was keen and once, after a free-for-all fight, contests between Aldinga and Willunga were abandoned for some time.

In the beginning, equipment was distinctly primitive, bats and stumps being made locally from sheoak wood, the bats all in one piece without any spring. Balls were somehow 'knitted with string'. Country pitches were generally rough and ready, some using slate in the nineteenth century.

In the early twentieth century cricket was the dominant summer sport in the district. Social games would be played at Port Noarlunga during the holiday season. The Rayner family included enough cricketers to form its own team, which in the 1920s would enjoy an annual post-Christmas picnic game against McLaren Vale. In the days of large families, assembling a team was not too difficult. In the 1890s the Threadgold family in Kangarilla challenged the Kangarilla side to a match, but lost; the Smart family did the same in 1930, and won.

# THE SHIRAZ ASHES

In the tradition of country cricket, and in the spirit of the legendary Ashes, fiercely contested between Australia and England, comes another cricketing trophy: the Shiraz Ashes – gathered after setting fire to a pile of vine cuttings (ostensibly shiraz, apparently grenache). The inaugural match took place at Port Willunga in 1996, after a lavish picnic barbecue lunch offered by McLaren Vale winemakers to a group of English wine writers and buyers, the visitors happily accepting the locals' challenge. The pitch might have been soft and uneven, the boundaries watery and variable, the improvised rules somewhat arbitrary, the umpires (Geoff Merrill and Greg Trott) momentarily blind and deaf, the twelfth man too frequently renewed and the refreshments too tempting – but the English snatched victory by one run.

A repeat match against another English team took place on Port Willunga beach in February 1998 – this time with Geoff Merrill and Simon Hackett as umpires. Again, the Salopian Inn presented a superb feast of barbecued seafood and McLaren Vale winemakers a dazzling array of wines. Oddly enough, the English team again managed to win by one run.

The McLaren Vale team is keen to show its true colours on an English ground, and hopes 1999 will see the winemakers return triumphant with the Shiraz Ashes, now held in a funerary urn in the trophy cabinet of Australia House in London.

Football was played in the Adelaide region in the 1860s but real interest in the game began in the 1870s, with Willunga one of the first teams playing. The Willunga Football Club was formed in 1874, at a time when the rules of the game were erratic. It was not until 1877, when the South Australian Football Association was established, that the Melbourne rules were generally adopted.

Willunga was said to have a very powerful team. Around 1880 Willunga apparently defeated a combined South Australian team that had previously beaten a Victorian side. 'Everyone in those days [1890s] was wildly enthusiastic about football,' recalled Mary Maud Aldam, 'and the games would be wildly exciting'. Just before the first world war Willunga was temporarily banned from the Southern Football Association because it was said to be too strong for the other teams, which included McLaren Flat, McLaren Vale, Aldinga, Morphett Vale, Mount Compass and Myponga.

The Willunga Football Club, 1890

Grand final at Willunga in the 1920s

The football club at McLaren Vale dates from 1880, at Kangarilla from 1901. Aldinga had a team in the early twentieth century, one of the players being Charles Dickinson, the Sellicks Beach fisherman. The Port Noarlunga Football Club was initiated in 1935 as a way of maintaining contact during the off-season of the lifesaving club, since not all the lifesavers lived locally. According to Reg Hyde, formerly a driver for Briscoe's bus service:

*Football was pretty strong in the south [in the 1930s]. There was some mighty good footballers came from the south, and they all had good teams ... We played for the love of the game.*

# PETANQUE ON SAINT VINCENT'S DAY

The newest sport – and more game than sport – is pétanque, which can be played on any almost-level patch of ground. Mediterranean in origin, it seems happily at home in the McLaren Vale region, especially in association with wine and wineries. Since 1994, Kerry Flanagan has organised an annual pétanque competition at the Wirilda Creek 'boulodrome' on or close to Saint Vincent's day, 22 January. Teams play for the Vincent's Cup – actually a rusty old dipper, but suitably commemorative. In addition to the symbolic trophy, prizes include sets of boules and bottles of wine. The competition is run according to proper rules, the final always taking place on the regulation dolomite-surfaced pitch. Players come from local and Adelaide clubs, together with individual enthusiasts, including a good sprinkling of Francophones. It is a day of fun, wine and food, though games can be deadly serious. Tape measures, pieces of string and other verifying accessories are produced at the slightest provocation!

Patron saint of vignerons, Saint Vincent was a Spanish priest martyred by the Roman emperor Diocletian in the early fourth century. According to legend, his remains were discovered hundreds of years later and, accompanied by a flock of ravens, were taken to Cape St Vincent, the southwestern-most tip of Portugal. When his bones were later removed to Lisbon, where he is the patron saint, ravens again flew in escort. He was probably adopted by vinegrowers because of the resonance of his name.

In 1797 Cape St Vincent was the scene of a significant victory over a more powerful Spanish fleet by the English. In recognition of his success, Admiral John Jervis was created Earl St Vincent and appointed First Lord of the Admiralty. It was the Admiralty that commissioned Matthew Flinders to explore Australia's southern coastline and in 1802 he, in turn, honoured his patron in naming both Cape Jervis and Gulf St Vincent.

# FOR THE GOOD
## OF THE COMMUNITY

In the days when there were no bands for hire and no commercial caterers (except the local publican), people clubbed together and jobbed in. Anyone who could play a musical instrument entertained others at institute concerts or made toes tap at local dances; good cooks contributed their talents to suppers. In small communities everybody had a part to play. Eric Dungey, born in (Old) Noarlunga in 1915, recalls a past era:

*We played for a lot of dances. Father was a good pianist, and I finished up playing the violin . . . We used to go to Aldinga, McLaren Vale, over here, and played for the different dances. We raised quite a lot of money . . . 'cause you didn't get paid for it. I mean you did it for the benefit of the town more or less.*

Bethany Chapel

Local ladies would cater for lunches at the annual show, for church teas, for weddings and anniversaries and birthdays. Groups such as the Country Women's Association earned reputations for their magnificent baking skills, their cakes, tarts and sponges designed not only to please but to strengthen this reputation. For the wedding of Mary Strout and Clifford Floyd at the Bethany Chapel in May 1956, the women of the Bethany Ladies' Guild, famous across the district for their cooking, catered for the reception in the Supper Room with the following menu:

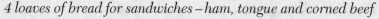

# MENU FOR WEDDING RECEPTION

*4 loaves of bread for sandwiches – ham, tongue and corned beef*

*6 dozen sausage rolls*

*3 dozen each pies and pasties*

*5 sponges, iced and trimmed in halves*

*2½ dozen each of macaroon tarts, chocolate crackles, cornflake kisses, brown lamingtons, pastel lamingtons, jelly cakes, small iced cakes, small cream cakes*

*5 dozen each cream puffs and cream lilies*

*1 box choc sticks*

*fruit salad and jelly with whipped cream*

*soft drinks, fruit punch and tea*

Events such as dances and strawberry fetes, sports' days and gala days, were entertainments in their own right as well as fundraisers; having fun contributed in a tangible way to the well-being of the community and also to the intangible community spirit. Lilian Gawley, who was born 1902 and moved to (Old) Noarlunga in 1929, was active in the organisation of children's sports' days where additional prizes were awarded for the best decorated bikes and prams, the best-dressed doll. 'It kept everybody together and it kept everybody doing something, working for something,' she commented.

In the nineteenth and early twentieth century people were typically working for sports or recreation facilities, a church or a community hall. Many of these began as community-owned facilities but gradually most have been taken over by local government. The Port Noarlunga Institute hall and library, for example, is now the property of the City of Onkaparinga and houses a community arts centre. One of the few facilities still owned by the community is the Willunga Recreation Park, including the hall and oval, which is administered by an elected group of citizens who act as trustees and report annually to residents. The initial impetus came from a group of civic-minded citizens in 1874 who proposed that an area of recreation land be set aside for local people. The land was purchased in 1875 and became the venue for the annual Willunga show, the solidly built Show Hall opening in 1891. Regulations for use of the area in 1885 included the prohibition of sport and games on Sundays, of cattle and horses, and of intoxicating liquor; further, no charge was to be made for admission to the ground without the consent of the trustees. The annual Almond Blossom Festival raises funds for the recreation complex and financed the adjoining Community Centre, which opened in 1979.

This community spirit is still alive and vigorous in the region, but the projects tend to be larger, benefiting a broader population – for example, the district hospital at McLaren Vale. The McLaren Flat Show, entirely organised by local volunteers, is strongly supported by local businesses and proceeds from the show are returned to the community in the form of new or improved public facilities. Service clubs such as Apex, Kiwanis, Lions, Rotary and Zonta have taken over the roles and functions of many of the old informal community groups and work for the public good at the same time as they promote business and professional interests.

## THE LIONS AUCTION

On the last Saturday of the month, even early in the morning, hundreds of cars, utes and trailers are parked along Binney Road, Willunga, for the monthly Lions auction. Some people have brought goods for sale, others have come to be part of the crowd and perhaps to snaffle a bargain. It is like a giant trash-and-treasure market where everything finds its price – and by the end of the morning just about everything has disappeared.

Four auctioneers, all voluntary, work in individual sections, progressing through the lots displayed any-old-how in roped-off rows. They range from gum boots to garden gnomes, bicycles to barbecues, and include old tyres and tools, timber and building materials, yellowed paperbacks, farm equipment, rolls of wire mesh and obsolete computers. Bargains abound – an air cooler for $5, a tin of assorted fishing reels for $6, a stack of plastic buckets for $12. One little girl scores a collection of Barbie dolls; someone else gets half a dozen boxes of antique bottles, saucepans and assorted kitchenware and a sturdy sharpening steel for just a dollar.

The auctioneer keeps up a lively banter with the audience. When an exercise machine fails to attract a bid, it is lumped in with a plastic jerry can, a chair with sagging springs and various parts of a golf buggy, and the whole lot sells for two dollars. For the next item there's even some competition, the cobra garden ornament fetching $4. In the poultry shed another auctioneer rapidly disposes of dozens of eggs – $5 for a box of three dozen guinea fowl eggs – before reaching the live birds: laying hens, roosters and chicks of all sizes; silky bantams and khaki campbell ducks; geese neatly bundled into chook feed bags; budgerigars and pigeons.

People come from as far as the northern suburbs of Adelaide and Tailem Bend to attend these auctions, which were initiated soon after the Willunga Lions Club was formed in 1969. (The name is an acronym: Liberty Intelligence Our Nation's Safety; the movement began in America in 1917 and is now international). Most of the auction goods are sold on a 15 per cent commission basis, and to date nearly $300,000 has been raised. The canteen staffed by the ladies' auxiliary – tea, coffee and cold drinks, with homemade cakes and scones and hot pies – has itself generated over $75,000.

All funds go back to the community. The Lions clubs of Willunga and McLaren Districts support the Almond Blossom and Bushing Festivals, establish and maintain parklands and reserves and purchase sporting equipment for local schools. In addition, the Willunga club each year donates $1000 to Willunga High School for a series of awards announced at the annual speech night.

# FOR THE GOOD
## OF THE ENVIRONMENT

One of the first projects of the Port Noarlunga Vigilance Committee, formed at a meeting of residents and ratepayers in 1914, was to plant marram grass and small trees on the sandhills, stabilising them and preventing their drift into the river. It also built retaining walls and planted pines along the seafront. Fifteen years later the Christies Beach Progressive Association set about improving its foreshore and providing amenities such as tables and benches for picnickers, swings and see-saws for children, and a shelter-shed.

Since then, and especially in the last 25 years, similar associations have been established throughout the region. The early incarnations were typically called Progress Associations. Today the groups most often call themselves Residents' Associations, their object being the promotion of the general interests of residents and ratepayers. The change of name hints of a shift in interest and intent away from the construction of new facilities and buildings – which typically represent Progress – toward protection and preservation of the present and the past and safeguarding of the future.

A number of conservation groups are active in the region, their concerns including revegetation and water management. The Community Landcare Centre in Willunga's High Street is home to several landcare and other local groups, such as Friends of Willunga Basin. At Port Willunga, the landcare group organises working parties to collect seeds and cuttings from the fragile dunes and propagate the plants from this important patch of original vegetation. The group also grows other local species and distributes them to residents for footpath plantings, reasoning that native plants will compete with weeds and check their growth, thus reducing the need for herbicide sprayings. In 1986 Maslin Beach residents formed a Greening Committee to revegetate their reserve as a sesquicentenary project. It is now known as the Frank Hilton Reserve in honour of the retired science teacher who planned and organised the project, and is planted with saltbush, native daisy, emu bush and groundcover species including native myrtle and warrigal greens.

The Friends of the Aldinga Scrub maintain and revegetate this environmentally important locale. Members of Trees for Life are replanting the gullies of the Willunga hills, first 'damming' them with stacks of old newspapers that allow water to filter through and promote soil build-up behind them. They have also established 'Willunga Wirra', a plantation of native shrubs and grasses on the edge of the Willunga golf course.

As much concerned with culture as nature, Friends of Willunga Basin is a community association dedicated to the preservation of the natural character of the region, its rural landscapes and heritage assets, and the promotion of planning initiatives and legislation that support this. It began in the late 1980s as a spontaneous protest movement in opposition to the proposed Sellicks Marina, which would have seen massive coastal development as well as construction of tourism and leisure facilities. Earlier proposals, such as the development of a boating harbour at Port Willunga in 1977, had not proceeded, but with Council support the Sellicks plan appeared to have every likelihood of success. The concerted actions of residents, alarmed by the effects it might have on local ecosystems and by the possibility of sand displacement along the beach, eventually led to government intervention and the abandonment of the plan in 1989. The association now is a permanent institution in the community and its activities have been influential in shaping local and state government policy regarding the future of the Willunga Basin. In 1995 the group sponsored an Eco-Festival 'to celebrate the regreening of the Willunga Basin and the harmony of people with nature'.

# FIGHTING FIRE

Controlled burning was one of the tools used by the Kaurna people to manage their environment, but when Europeans began to discipline the environment fire came to be seen as a threat, settlers soon realising its devastating potential. After bushfires in 1874 caused thousands of pounds of damage to property and fencing and roused 100 men to fight them for two weeks, a public meeting was called in Willunga to discuss prevention measures. Property owners recognised the need for firebreaks and volunteered to clear individual sections, while they asked the District Councils of Willunga and Myponga to clear Range Road, which runs along the top of the ridge.

From 1935 designated councils were required to keep fire-fighting appliances on hand, but it took many more fires and disasters, culminating in a big fire in the Mount Bold area in January 1939, before coordinated action was taken. The 1939 bushfires were the worst in Australian history – but then came the war, and thoughts turned to the possibility of air raids. Volunteer fire-fighters were instructed on extinguishing the various types of fire to be expected in air raids.

After the war these trained recruits formed brigades to fight bushfires and the EFS – Emergency Fire Service – was born. Training was standardised, and common procedures for fighting fires established. The Government offered grants for the purchase of fire fighting equipment; with a few modifications, ex-army vehicles proved suitable. Instruction courses were run for fire officers, and gradually the movement spread. By 1949 there were nearly 650 volunteer firemen in 97 units in seven EFS districts throughout the state. The Emergency Fire Service became the Country Fire Services in 1977.

The early brigades were a bit like Dad's Army, their equipment makeshift and improvised and, by today's standards, extraordinarily primitive. Fires were fought with water, wet bags and branches from trees; whatever equipment could be mobilised was called into service. In the mid-1950s the Port Noarlunga unit converted a 'Diamond T' bus donated by Mr Briscoe into a fire tender. The Willunga EFS, formed in 1957, rebuilt an ex-army blitz wireless van as a fire-fighting unit. Volunteers built fire stations, often with donated materials, and all the usual fund-raising schemes were put into practice – including an art exhibition organised by Sellicks CFS in 1984 that attracted entries from 150 artists and sold $13,500 worth of paintings.

Women have traditionally served as auxiliary members, supplying meals and refreshments and selling tickets in the giant Christmas stocking raffle, but in 1980 a group of Aldinga women formed the first female CFS crew in the state. On call during the day when many men were working, they were ready to drop what they were doing and assemble at the fire station, leaving their children in the capable hands of volunteers from the local CWA.

Fighting fires is serious, but there is also a fun side to the CFS. There are competitions between brigades and state championships in operations such as the hose reel drill and pump drill. These are part of the basic training for all volunteers, additional training being available at specialised centres.

Between them, the Willunga, Happy Valley and Noarlunga CFS groups today have fifteen local units and around 600 members. Individual brigades still raise funds in order to improve their fire-fighting capabilities – which often means installing improved communications systems – but they can now rely on local councils and the CFS organisation to fund purchases of new equipment and cover the maintenance and running costs of appliances and buildings.

## ⁓ REMEMBRANCES ⁓

Many of the pioneer families of the region are remembered in the names of roads – Johnston, McMurtrie and Oliver Roads near McLaren Vale; Binney, Colville and Giles Roads near Willunga; Jared Road at Port Noarlunga and Norman Road at Sellicks. Local identities and people who made notable contributions to the community are similarly recognised, their names given to parks and reserves such as the Gemmel Tassie reserve in McLaren Vale (Dr Tassie was a caring and respected doctor in the district for many years from

1943); the Herbert Allen Memorial Park at Willunga; the Dolph Waye and Clarrie Eatts Reserves at Silver Sands Beach.

Servicemen who fought in the various wars are also memorialised. After the first world war pines were planted along St Andrew's Terrace, Willunga, and along Main Road, McLaren Flat, to honour men who enlisted; similarly at Port Willunga, an avenue of pines beginning at the seafront and later continued along Port Road recognised those who fell in the war. In McLaren Vale the plantings in the Recreation Ground were made soon after the departures of those who enlisted, as Fred Low recorded in his diary:

*Sat. Sep. 9th, 1916. In the afternoon the Vale people planted some Oak trees in honour of the soldiers that went to the front, they planted them in the Recreation Ground and on the road I planted a Oak tree for Reg it was the third tree starting from the northend of the row by the east fence on the top side in the Recreation Ground.*

## SOUTHERN DISTRICTS WAR MEMORIAL HOSPITAL INCORPORATED

After the second world war community sentiment again strongly favoured a memorial to honour those who had lost their lives, and the suggestion from the local Returned Servicemen's League that a hospital would be a fitting tribute was unanimously approved. In September 1945 the McLaren Vale Progress Association called a public meeting to consider the need for a hospital service, at the same time hoping to persuade people that the only logical and economic solution was one central hospital serving the whole district.

The issue was canvassed at public meetings in other parts of the district over the next few months. Residents endorsed the need for a hospital and, despite a few half-hearted protests, it was accepted that the hospital should be based at McLaren Vale, the largest town in the region, and named the

Southern Districts War Memorial Hospital. In December of that same year the state government agreed to subsidise it, matching dollar-for-dollar money raised locally.

Over the next five years residents threw themselves into fundraising with 'Queen' contests and competitions such as guessing the weight of a bag of wool. The CWA and Red Cross lent their support, and local winemakers contributed $6600. Among those donating the $1000 that gave them the right to name a hospital bed in perpetuity were Thomas Hardy & Sons Ltd, Stephen Smith & Co Ltd, The Emu Wine Company Pty Ltd, Penfolds Wines Pty Ltd, both the Kay and Johnston families, the McLaren Vale Football Club and Southern Football Association.

The hospital committee acquired the old Congregational manse and six acres of land, and Mrs Katherine Hall, sister of Frederick and Herbert Kay, transferred at valuation her property 'Tsong Gyiaou', once a private school in the town; this building became the nurses' quarters. Two acres of land adjoining this were donated by the Reeves family, local blacksmiths since the 1880s. In April 1950 the foundation stone was laid, and a year later the hospital opened, virtually free of debt.

New wings were added in 1965 and 1971 to expand the initial capacity of 14 beds. Groups such as the Women's Hospital Auxiliary and the Southern Districts Lions Club made possible the purchase of improvements such as air-conditioning units and an electrocardiograph. The 42 per cent cut in government funding in 1992, however, obliged the hospital to make many changes, and it is now a private hospital with public facilities. Community support is still vital, and for the purchase of new medical equipment the hospital still relies on the efforts of an extraordinarily large contingent of volunteers, about 100 in total, who run the hospital shop and raise money for the hospital through stalls and raffles.

# CHAPTER
# THE COAST

The sea glimmers tantalisingly from unexpected vantage points – the crest of a rise, the corner window of a hilltop house, the end of a sweep of vines. It intrudes gently into the landscape but never dominates, appearing more as a prolongation of the plains in a seamless vista where green becomes blue.

As the western boundary of the McLaren Vale region, the coast links with the hills to the south and east. It helps frame the region and shape its culture.

In no other major vineyard region in South Australia is the sea so close, so influential. It tempers summer's fierce heat and induces cooling winds in the evenings; in winter it moderates temperatures and reduces the risk of frost. The vines and their fruit take full benefit, a long ripening period favouring development of the rich fruit flavours that characterise McLaren Vale wines. Almond and olive groves and fruit orchards are similarly blessed.

The coastal settlements of Port Noarlunga and Port Willunga began life

# EIGHT

as working ports, bringing essential goods to pioneer farmers and, more importantly, taking farm harvests to markets where their value could be realised. Before too long, however, an Australian beach culture had been implanted, and by the early twentieth century the coast was firmly associated with summer holidays.

First came the picnics by the sea on special holidays such as Christmas Day and New Year's Day. As early as 1861 Christmas was celebrated at the beach, and it became a standard ritual for many families. The beach was also the choice for school picnics and the annual Sunday school picnics.

In the twentieth century the coast represents leisure and pleasure, but 150 years ago people had different perceptions. The coast was synonymous with ports, shipping and trade, both legal and illegal; it was a place of work rather than relaxation, with attendant risks and dangers – as shown by the history of shipwrecks.

# SHIPWRECKS

'The coast between these two Points is rocky and the ground is not fit for any Ships to anchor in,' wrote Colonel Light of the shore between Sellicks Beach and Witton Bluff.

Along this stretch of the gulf there are no real harbours where ships can be properly sheltered from the prevailing winds, especially the winter southerlies, and the combination of shallow reefs and south-westerly gales, together with inadequate warning systems, proved treacherous to shipping in the nineteenth century.

One of the first ships to run aground was the *David Witton*, shipwrecked off Port Noarlunga in 1839 and today remembered in the name Witton Bluff, the point between Christies Beach and the Port Noarlunga jetty. An anchor believed to be from the *David Witton* was discovered in 1969 and is now displayed outside the Witton Centre at Port Noarlunga.

Probably most of the disasters could be attributed to storms, with perhaps a contribution of human error, but vaguely suspicious circumstances surround the wreck of the *Tigress* in 1848 near the mouth of the Onkaparinga, and the *Nashwauk* in 1855 off Moana. In both instances it seems that a light on shore had been mistaken for an anticipated navigational light, the captains believing they were in safer waters further north. This deceptive light they saw was apparently one kept burning in an upstairs room of Dalkeith, a large house owned by Andrew Harriott above present-day Moana beach. There were rumours that Harriott was involved in smuggling, some people also implicating Richard Bosworth of Prior Court, slightly east of Dalkeith. Harriott certainly had an opportunity to profit from the mishap, purchasing at the subsequent auction the *Nashwauk* wreck and its remaining cargo, along with the rights to whatever else might be washed ashore.

Two people were lost from the *Tigress*, but all crew and passengers on the *Nashwauk* – including 130 single Irish girls among the 300 mostly Irish emigrants – were landed ashore and taken in care by local residents. Surprisingly, despite the frequency of wreckings and strandings – at least seven ships wrecked near Aldinga reef before the *Star of Greece* in 1888, and at least an equal number off the coast around Port Noarlunga – casualties were few, and often a good deal of the cargo could be salvaged and later auctioned, as were the wrecks themselves. Against this background the *Star of Greece* shipwreck, in which one-third of the crew drowned, represents the extreme of misfortune. The *Advertiser's* account of the wreck on 14 July 1888 depicts the scale of the calamity:

*The ill-fated* Star of Greece, *which left the Semaphore on Thursday after-noon, now lies a total wreck about 500 yards from the shore, and one mile north of the little jetty at Port Willunga. The storm which raged during the night was severely felt in Adelaide, but it is along the south coast that its fury appears to have been most experienced. All the circumstances surrounding this almost unprecedented disaster in the shipping records of the colony will require searching enquiry, for from first to last the blows of fate seem to have been only too well seconded by human carelessness and want of forethought … With the first break of dawn several of the residents in the neighbourhood of Port Willunga were upon the beach …. There was no lack of individual heroism in rescuing the few sailors who came alive through the tremendous breakers which rolled upon the sandy beach, but the arrival of the rocket apparatus or of a rescuing steamer from Port Adelaide was waited for all day in vain. Three or four years ago rockets were kept at Port Willunga in readi-ness for a shipping disaster along the coast, but the desire for economy is said to have induced the authorities to take them away. Is it any wonder that indignation was loudly expressed at this lamentable state of things by those who during Friday saw their fellow creatures perishing for want of a rocket or lifeboat?*

The tragedy of the *Star of Greece* shipwreck is that it happened so close to shore that the desperate sailors could be clearly seen on the broken wreckage by people on the beach who, powerless to rescue them, could only watch them die. Pounding surf hindered attempts to reach those in the water and prevented any vessel putting to sea. Of the 28 men on board, 17 drowned and 11 reached the shore, one owing his life to the tireless efforts of Mounted Constable Stephen Tuohy from the Willunga Police Station, later awarded a medal for his bravery. An official enquiry was held almost immediately to investigate the cause of the disaster and reasons for delays in the arrival of assistance. While no blame was assigned, the chairman of the enquiry made a number of recommendations to ensure that the circumstances surrounding this event would not be repeated.

As usual, goods salvaged from the wreck were auctioned. The ship's bell was bought by local farmer Thomas Pengilly and has remained in the family's possession, while the figurehead for many years decorated the portal of a Port Willunga house. Together with a few other relics the figurehead is on display in the South Australian Maritime Museum in Port Adelaide. The spar from the *Star of Greece* mast was erected above the beach as a local memorial but in 1975 was transferred, together with the marble plaque at its base, to the stables of the Willunga courthouse. A commemorative plaque, unveiled on the centenary of the wreck in 1988, now stands at the top of the cliffs at Port Willunga.

The remains of the wreck, off Lion Point, can still be seen at very low tides; it is one of four wrecks included in the South Australian Underwater Maritime Heritage Trails. Since the late 1940s, however, the name has been better known in connection with the Star of Greece kiosk-and-cafe at Port Willunga.

# BEACH PICNICS

Connor Sparrow recalled going to Port Noarlunga with neighbours on Christmas Day around 1915, taking food for the day and returning late at night. Sporting events were organised on the beach, stalls sold icecream and other treats, and it was clearly a memorable occasion. The Australian tradition of Christmas on the beach became established around the middle of the nineteenth century. In 1862 the *Advertiser* reported:

Port Noarlunga, c. 1920s

*Christmas-day was spent by most of the people in this quarter upon the sea-beach, at Port Noarlunga. ... Mine host, Mr Carrick, had a good supply of everything requisite for the enjoyment of the visitors, and tea and coffee were liberally indulged in, but we did not see more than one case of drunkenness out of about 500 people. All enjoyed themselves so well, it was the universal desire to repeat the same sort of treat next Christmas. The boats belonging to the fishermen and others were in great requisition with those who preferred sailing to riding and perambulating the seaside. On New Year's Day a number again visited the favourite spots, and amused themselves in various ways.*

Port Noarlunga, c. 1920s

Others remember Port Noarlunga as *the* place people went to on Christmas Day; on 28 December they gathered at Glenelg for another day of sports, while for New Year's Day revels Port Willunga was the place to be. People would promenade on the jetty, there would be races on the sand and 'tossing the sheaf'. In 1906, for the cost of one shilling, holidayers could take a pleasure cruise in gulf waters.

In the early decades of the twentieth century the McLaren Vale school would go to Byer's Beach (probably in the vicinity of Moana), Bethany Sunday

School to Port Willunga for the day. 'A local farmer would supply a four-wheeled trolley and a pair of horses ... We left the church about 9 o'clock and got home around the same time at night', reminisced Connor Sparrow.

At first it was the adventure of going somewhere different that drew people to the coast, the exhilaration of the salty air rather than the attraction of the sea itself. Men and women in formal suits and long dresses paraded up and down the beach and along the jetty. Children paddled, but rarely swam. Gradually, attitudes relaxed. The South Australian Amateur Swimming Association was formed in 1898, though the first (men only) swimming club dates from 1863. By the turn of the century safe swimming was assured in enclosed pools along the coast and more people were venturing into the water, although bathing regulations still segregated men from women. Mrs Constance Martin (née Dunstan), who grew up at Port Willunga in the early years of the twentieth century, recalled that, as 'one of six boys, I early became a boy and was allowed to bathe with them. Well old Mr Harry How was very much against that. He thought it was indecent for a girl to be bathing with the boys.'

By the 1920s the sensuality of sea and sun had worked their magic and the beach became synonymous with summer holidays.

## ⟞ PORT NOARLUNGA'S ⟝
## HEYDAY

The growing popularity of cars, the introduction of a train service to Willunga and the discovery of surfing on Australia's eastern coast transformed Port Noarlunga from a minor port and fishing village into South Australia's top beach resort. It was promoted as 'the Holiday Makers' Paradise' in a 1924 advertisement for blocks of land. Nearby Christie's Beach was extolled as 'the only beach within easy distance of the City where the "Surfer" can revel in the only form of bathing that he thinks worth while'.

When George Hepenstal took up land at Port Noarlunga in 1840 it was with the intention of establishing a whaling operation in the gulf. Unfortunately for him, whales were not plentiful, and French and American whaling ships were allowed to monopolise the waters. The nearest George came to a whale was one washed up on the beach. Hepenstal worked as a farmer and fisherman before returning to the family estate in Ireland in 1861. His well, sunk in 1841 near the corner of Gawler Street and Witton Road today, became known as the Whip Well and was much appreciated by horses and visitors until the 1920s.

Port Noarlunga, c. 1925

In the 1840s grain and flour, carried by barge from the mill upstream at Noarlunga, were shipped from the port. When the first jetty was completed in 1855 cargo was transported from the river by horsedrawn tram, a cutting through the sandhills giving access to the jetty (about 30 metres south of the present one). This jetty was extended in 1878 but after repeated storm damage it was condemned, and a new one built in 1920.

This new jetty signalled the start of Port Noarlunga's period of prosperity. The jetty extended right out to the reef, a set of steps enabling people to continue their exploratory promenades on the rocks and even to gather shellfish or go fishing. On the opening day in December 1921 the jetty was so crowded (attendance was estimated at over 2500) that after cutting the blue ribbon the Governor, Sir Archibald Weigall, climbed on a sandhill to address the crowd, remarking that he had 'never seen anything in the Mediterranean or the Riviera to equal the beautiful blue expanse of the sea that afternoon'.

In the 1920s the new train service from Adelaide to Willunga took passengers either to Morphett Vale or Noarlunga, from where it was a three- or four-mile journey to the beach – by horse and buggy in the early days, later by 'charabanc'. As car ownership expanded, so did the numbers of people travelling by car, and on Sundays as many as 100 cars could be counted at one time. Council even gave permission for a volunteer local to control the traffic in the summer months. Tom Harlow wore a special khaki uniform, provided by Council, and for many years was a local identity; he also took on the responsibility of warning holidaymakers returning from the beach that bathers were not allowed in the street! Perhaps this ruling was directed mainly at women, for whom the fashionable option was beach pyjamas.

From the late 1920s through the 1930s summer tourism was the mainstay of Port Noarlunga, supporting a kiosk and refreshment rooms and dozens of boarding houses, boarders booking from one year to the next. In 1933 the Port Noarlunga Hotel began operations (it had obtained the licence relinquished by the Horseshoe Hotel at Noarlunga) and provided additional accommodation. On the southern side of the Onkaparinga River was the weatherboard hall of the Norwood Cycling Club, where members could doss down for a weekend. Camping and caravaning became more popular in the 1940s, though for years previously parties of schoolboys would spend several weeks of the summer holidays camped near the river. Geo. C. Davies recollected the pleasures of those camps around 1914 – swimming every morning, fish for breakfast, visits to the ochre pits and carving lumps of ochre, fishing ('one morning three of us caught five dozen garfish') and rabbiting, and rowing six miles upstream to Noarlunga for the pleasure of the row and to telephone home.

Chrystabel Duell, who was born in (Old) Noarlunga in 1915, has described the exhilaration of the summer holiday period, with:

*cars, and horses, and buggies everywhere ... I remember they had a man in uniform directing the traffic. The beach was just full of tents and people that had brought their lunch for the day, and it was a lovely gala atmosphere. Of course the life savers were there too ... In those days they just went to the beach and stayed, and during holiday periods when Briscoe's buses were running, they would be just continually coming down with people's luggage because you know they would have booked into boarding houses. They were just full. It really was a very happy town. And of course at the pictures, you would have to book a week before or you'd never get a seat.*

From Christmas to Easter seems to have been one long carnival. 'Every Christmas used to be terrific at Port Noarlunga', reflected Lilian Gawley, a long-time resident of the district: 'It was really alive. They used to have sideshows down near the beach and everything. ... They had dances and turn-outs in the hall nearly every night. Yes, it was really a place.' There were boats for hire for excursions along the river, games of tennis and mini-golf, walks along the beach to the caves at the end. In 1925 a footbridge across the estuary (slightly east of the present footbridge) was constructed, giving access to the shallow reaches of the Onkaparinga estuary. From 1936 Australia Day was celebrated with a street procession followed by beach activities – sand races and water sports, a treasure hunt, sand castle competitions and the 'slippery pole', together with demonstrations by the local lifesavers.

Reporting on the New Year Day celebrations, the *Advertiser* of 2 January 1934 said:

Beach picnics, Port Noarlunga, 1927

*Large crowds thronged all the beaches again yesterday, Port Noarlunga experiencing a record attendance of more than 10,000 persons. Approximately 2000 motor cars visited the town, in addition to 40 charabancs and motor lorries. The beach was crowded with people all day, and was gay with coloured umbrellas and tents of all descriptions. The surf was at its best, and thousands of bathers were to be seen enjoying the breakers from early morning until late afternoon. An aeroplane taking passengers for short trips was well patronised.*

*The 'Gang' Camp has added greatly to the life of the town, and sports and other entertainments have been held each day. On Saturday afternoon members of the camp played a match against the local cricket club, and they gave another concert at night, which was well attended. The trophies won at the various sports contests were presented on Sunday evening. The camp was struck yesterday and members returned to the city.*

Balls and dances were held in the local institute. Organised by the Institute Committee, they would feature top bands from Adelaide – such as the Blue Diamond – proceeds being used to repay the building loan. The hall was also let to a Mr Freak who showed silent pictures and Mr Rowe, who showed 'talkies'.

Attracted to this thriving resort, Adelaide businessman Hugh Corpe built Fan Court, a large, imposing mansion that dominates the Port Noarlunga foreshore. A few years later, after the start of the war, there was talk of demolishing the structure because it was such a conspicuous landmark. The 1935 house, white with sea-blue trim and topped by an octagonal tower, is surrounded by massive white walls that were said to have cost £1500, more than an average house in 1935, and required the levelling of two sandhills. Both Hugh and his wife Frieda Corpe contributed to the local community, Hugh donating a surf boat to the Port Noarlunga Surf Life Saving Club on its establishment. Frieda Corpe started Port Noarlunga's first kindergarten in a caravan shed in her home; her help in establishing a permanent kindergarten is acknowledged in its name, the Frieda Corpe Community Kindergarten.

The Port Noarlunga Surf Life Saving Club was established in 1933. In winter months many of the lifesavers became footballers; since very few lived locally, a football club was a way of maintaining the social contact. The paucity of men during the war years inspired a group of local women in 1942 to form the Port Noarlunga Women's Life Saving Team, the first women's group in the state.

The popularity of Port Noarlunga seems to have stimulated the Christie's Beach Progressive Association (formed 1929) to develop neighbouring Christie's Beach into an equally vibrant resort. The beach, with no undertow, was said to be safe and one of the best between Semaphore and Victor Harbour. The first Christie's Beach subdivision was laid out in 1923, but for many years the town was only sparsely settled, its bakery not established until 1947. Holiday shacks were built with total disregard for any council regulations, often using timber washed up on the beach. The first sports day organised by the association in Easter 1929 was such a success that it was repeated the following Christmas, and became an annual Easter event. There were races over varying distances for boys and girls, for single and married ladies, the Christie's Beach Handicap plus numerous novelty events – bowling at the stump, wheeling a barrow blindfold, pinning the tail on the donkey and guessing the weight of the sucking pig.

Port Noarlunga was still a busy summer resort after the war, and at week-ends and on public holidays cars would be bumper-to-bumper on the old South Road, then the only road to the town. In winter, however, it was dead, according to Clive Whitrow, licensee of the Port Noarlunga Hotel and the town's unofficial mayor. Famous in Adelaide and along the coast for its beer garden, the first in the state, the Port Noarlunga Hotel was a popular meeting place. 'Everybody converged there, everyone met there between four and six in the afternoon' – this being still the era of six o'clock closing. Clive spent some of the war years in north Queensland where he came to appreciate its tropical outdoor bars and on his return to Adelaide decided to create some-thing similar, planting hundreds of frangipanni, banana palms and other semi-tropical plants. His beer garden opened in 1947 with seating for 100 people and within a few years was expanded to fit 400. Even then, he says, if you weren't there by four o'clock you wouldn't get a seat!

The boarding houses (or guest houses) remained popular throughout the 1950s and into the 1960s, but Port Noarlunga's heyday probably came to an end with the development of housing and industry on what used to be barley growing and dairying land to the north and east. Nearby Christie's Beach became a suburb of Adelaide, with its own shopping centre and hotel, and Port Noarlunga itself came to seem more like a beachside suburb than a holiday makers' paradise. Each summer, however, it still shows something of its carefree holiday character and its beach, reef and river attract surfers and swimmers, scuba divers and sailboarders, canoeists and fishermen.

# AQUATICS AT PORT NOARLUNGA

On any weekday from October to December, and again between February and April, clusters of schoolchildren gather on the foreshore at Port Noarlunga, while outside the Surf Life Saving Clubhouse others zip themselves into colourful wetsuits. All are participants in the water activities offered by the Port Noarlunga Primary School and Aquatics Centre, under manager Andy Tyler.

The Centre started with learn-to-swim programs in the mid-1970s and now offers a full menu of water sports – sailing, sailboarding, snorkelling, canoeing, fishing, surfing, as well as swimming – with an emphasis on water safety and environmental awareness. The Centre was instrumental in the establishment of the underwater reef trail at Port Noarlunga.

One of only two such centres in metropolitan Adelaide, it attracts each year around 15,000 primary and secondary school students, and during school holidays often welcomes children from the School of the Air and Aboriginal outback schools.

Port Noarlunga is uniquely advantaged for water activities. 'Where else in the world can you find beach, reef, estuary and wetlands, all within one square kilometre and close to the city?' asks Andy Tyler.

# MOANA BEACH

From Port Noarlunga's southern headland, a clifftop walk follows the coast-line all the way to Moana. Its starting point looks down over the beginner's surf of Southport Beach, near the tip of the sand spit that almost closes off the mouth of the Onkaparinga. Here the river, a mere shadow of its earlier self, seeps towards the sea past cliffs banded in shades of cream, ochre and pinkish red.

Along the way to Moana are magnificent vistas of sea and land as far south as Rapid Bay, and at the end a typical Australian surfing beach, a wide arc of clean sand facing white-edged breakers. The surf might not be as vigorous or as challenging as at ocean beaches around the coast of Australia, but Moana is generally rated the best surfing beach close to Adelaide.

Just a few years after blocks had been offered for sale at Christie's Beach and Port Noarlunga, the Lakes Beach Estate company opened a subdivision at the next beach south, and announced a competition to name the beach. Over 2000 entries were received, the winner being 'Boon Boona Beach', a name supposedly meaning 'sea beach' in an Aboriginal (but not Kaurna) language. In 1928, however, preference was given to 'Moana', a Maori word meaning 'blue water'.

Moana was promoted by developers as the Manly of South Australia, its 'Premier Surfing Beach' with a 'magnificent sweep of clean sandy hard beach. Its surface is ideal for riding, walking, and is a glorious playground for children. All beach sports are played there in safety ... Bathing is safe at any point, and cars can be parked right on the beach' – as they are today, south of the Surf Lifesaving Clubhouse.

One of the advantages of Moana was proximity to the railway; the stopping place (there was no platform in the early days) was only 1.5 km from the beach. As at the earlier subdivisions, however, settlement was slow, and even at the end of the 1930s there were no more than ten houses. A boarding house operated for a few years from about 1927, but Moana did not become a holiday resort in the same way as Port Noarlunga. Nevertheless, crowds of people – and cars – would converge on the beach on summer Sundays and buy refreshments from the octagonal kiosk, now the Blue Water cafe.

Just beyond the kiosk Pedler Creek runs through sandhills to the sea in an area now known as Moana Sands Conservation Park. For over 6000 years these dunes were successive homes to Kaurna people, whose imprint on the land remained in their middens, stone hearths and relics of campsites. Remains of animals, fish, shellfish and emu eggs have been found on the sites, along with stone artefacts. Together these represent a rich source of information on prehistoric diet. Because of its Aboriginal significance, the Moana Sites Area was registered as part of the National Estate in 1978 and remains a protected area that also provides a sanctuary for many water birds.

# SURFING

Along the Australian coast, surfing grew into a kind of cult in the early 1960s. In South Australia it may not have had the following it had on the eastern coast, but there have been surfing clubs and competitions in this state for around thirty years, many at beaches from Christie's south to Aldinga. Clubs enabled novice surfers to learn the manners of the sport as well as techniques. They were more like informal assemblies, groups congregating at agreed locations – a beachside kiosk, a boat ramp – and rarely had clubhouses.

Surfboard technology has changed enormously in the past thirty years, but with the new lightweight longboards and malibus, not to mention boogie boards, the 1990s is witnessing a new wave of popularity for surfing. (Jeweller and artist Gerry Wedd, who grew up in the area and founded the Oceanside surfing club at Christies Beach in the early 1970s, calls boogie-boarding the 'punk rock' of surfing.) Most of the Adelaide-region clubs are based around Seaford-Moana, as is the South Australian Surfing Association. There are clubs for longboarders (including a group of malibu enthusiasts who call themselves the Maladjusteds), for children under 16 (the Micro Groms) and, for about the last ten years, a girl's club, the Booner Bamis.

Moana Beach, 1929

# MASLIN BEACH

In appearance the most dramatic of Adelaide's southern beaches, Maslin Beach is also, perhaps, the most notorious: Australia's first official unclad beach. It is named after Thomas Maslin, who arrived from Berkshire in 1836 and took up land along Maslin Creek in 1850. Farming land still surrounds the small enclave, one of the most recent of the district's coastal settlements. Blocks of land were first sold in 1958, when Gulf Parade was still a dirt track; by 1975 only 68 houses had been built.

The unclad section is the southern end, where sheer cliffs, eroded by time, drop to the water's edge. Their colours are muted, as if put through the wash too many times, but the horizontal bands of mustard and pink are still distinct. These sandstone and limestone layers were laid down sequentially around 60 million years ago, to be tilted and exposed when an earthquake later split the land to form the gulf. Sea erosion at the southern headland, Blanche Point, has isolated Gull Rock, a miniature version of the famed 'Table Rock' of Port Noarlunga, which was gradually eroded by rough seas and completely gone by 1918. Just separated from the mainland, Gull Rock looks like a wilful toddler trying to escape a parent's grasp. To the north is Ochre Point with its black volcanic boulders, and inland the gully where Kaurna people scraped coloured ochres for body decorations and for trading.

Maslin Beach (Robert Hannaford)

# AUSTRALIA'S FIRST OFFICIAL UNCLAD BEACH

In the 1930s Moana was the first beach in South Australia to allow men to bathe topless. In February 1975 neighbouring Maslin Beach became the first Australian beach to allow men, women and children to swim naked.

For years previously, people had swum in the nude at Maslin Beach – and at other Adelaide beaches – very discreetly. Early in 1975, however, arrests of a number of people bathing nude at Maslin Beach made front-page news. Magistrate Kelly fined one man $50, warning that the maximum penalty was three months imprisonment. 'There are certain evil consequences flowing from it [bathing without clothes] at Maslin Beach,' he said. Meanwhile, a policeman (in shorts) and policewoman (in dress and hat) patrolled the beach, keeping in radio contact with a concealed patrol car.

Aware of this somewhat farcical situation, Premier Don Dunstan made an announcement that nude bathing at Maslin Beach would be legal from 14 February 1975, and police would be instructed not to prosecute for 'indecent exposure in respect of nudity'. He explained that, since the entire beach from Maslin to Port Willunga was a government reserve that had been in the care of the Council from the early 1960s, the government had simply taken back a section and put it under the control of the Coast Protection Board.

Some locals protested – not against nudism *per se*, but on the grounds that streets would be filled with cars and that some people would be deprived of access to the cliffs. 'It is rather frightening to see naked people playing volleyball and cricket on a beach that was a quiet family place until recently,' said one resident. 'It is not nice having to pick your way through perhaps 100 naked people or being approached by some man asking the time.'

In the event, none of these fears was justified. Today car parks easily accommodate all the cars, and the scattered groups of naked swimmers could hardly be considered intimidating. Maslin Beach is big enough to be shared by all beachlovers.

Port Willunga land sale, 1921

# SUMMER AT PORT WILLUNGA

In 1899 English visitor Maisie Smith spent a holiday in a rented cottage at Port Willunga. In a letter to her mother she wrote:

*Laura [Maisie's aunt] and the kids are all going to the seaside next week – Port Willunga – and it occurred to her that I might as well go too. They are taking a cottage for a fortnight or so . . . there is no railway, so there will be no trippers . . . they say it is a lovely place and has exquisite shells.*

Port Willunga jetty and bay, c. 1910

Like Port Noarlunga, Port Willunga was originally seen as a safe and convenient harbour for ships loading wheat and flour from the nearby mills at Willunga and Aldinga, as well as slate quarried from the enclosing hills. It seems that smugglers also considered it a safe haven, and one of the reasons for a police presence at Willunga was to curtail suspected smuggling. During the gold-rush period a number of Ballarat-bound Chinese adventurers came ashore at Port Willunga; forbidden to land at Port Adelaide, they had hired a boat that was going to smuggle them into Victoria but instead was wrecked at Port Willunga. Undaunted, they hired bullock drays for their luggage then walked to the diggings – all but one, who died and was buried at Willunga.

In 1851 the township had been partly laid out and several buildings completed, while at least twenty more were said to be in planning stages. Its first jetty, completed in 1854, was ingloriously impractical, even after it was extended to almost double its original length in 1855. During a storm the following year the jetty was accidentally shortened when two schooners broke from their moorings and smashed into it. Another, even longer, extension was added in 1857 but a few years later it was finally conceded that the jetty was unworkable and in the wrong place.

The 1868 jetty, its old piles still protruding from the sand, was positioned about 400 metres south of the first. Unbelievably, it, too, was too short, and five years after its opening requests were made for an extension. In 1892 when E.H. Hallack visited the area, agriculture was in the doldrums, demand for slate had shrunk, and Port Willunga 'like many others on the southern coast, is awaiting a turn of the tide, both inland and seaward', he reported. 'There are the rusty iron rails of the jetty, and the stores with their splendidly built walls remain intact, but the roofs, floors, doors, and windows are emblems of the past.' Near the base of the old jetty, beneath the sand, is one of the Tjilbruke springs, and a rough stone monument opposite the Star of Greece kiosk recalls Kaurna ancestor Tjilbruki's sad trail along the coast.

At the turn of the century Port Willunga was relatively isolated. Though her younger cousins travelled by coach, Maisie Smith and her aunt and uncle set off for their holiday by bicycle, leaving Adelaide about five in the morning and reaching the cottage at half-past two in the afternoon. Luggage came separately – horse-drawn coach to Aldinga then smaller dray for the final stage. Hardly a township, Port Willunga's scattering of houses included the old Pier Hotel or Uncle Tom's Cabin, home to the Martin family; the other Martin home, known as the Harbourmaster's Cottage; the Seaview Temperance Hotel, formerly the Lewis Arms; and a dairy. The Alton Guest House on the corner of Port Road, once the summer residence of the Dunstan family, was not built until 1907. According to Maisie, there were 'nearly a dozen houses in the place, but never a shop. The butcher calls occasionally and also the baker and grocer. We have tested the greengrocer and find that he has potatoes and now and then a plum or two and that he has the cheek to call himself a "fruiterer and greengrocer"'.

Aldinga was just over a mile away, and Maisie called there daily for her letters. In 1892 E.H. Hallack thought this town rather lacklustre, but the 1909 *Cyclopedia of South Australia* described it as having 'a thriving appearance, [with] a butter factory, machinists' and other shops, and several stores'. It also had two churches, a hotel and a temperance hotel. The Aldinga Temperance Hotel operated for over fifty years until 1920, many of its guests attracted by 'the picturesque beach of Port Willunga, where holiday-makers may enjoy bathing, fishing and other sea-side pursuits'.

Maisie was delighted by the beach:

*The sea is very pretty and quite safe … we had a lovely bathe this morning … The sea is glorious and we are positively the only people down here … We had another lovely bathe this morning. We stay quite close and fool about in the waves because of the children. Will goes fishing and sometimes brings us some lovely fish for tea. Fancy, the first day a great six foot long shark took hold of his hook and broke his line, nearly pulled him into the sea. There are heaps about and come into quite shallow water.*

But even Maisie's cheerfulness could be challenged by a week of heatwave weather, and she wrote to her mother: 'I think I am a weeny bit tired of a tiny cottage with rooms up to 100 deg. and sandhills infested with snakes, scorpions and a sea full of stinging jelly-fish, crabs and sharks.'

The sea was Port Willunga's chief attraction. 'Its magnificent, broad, sandy beaches offer unbounded opportunities for safe sea bathing, and for surfing it is not easily surpassed', extolled the promoters of a land auction in 1921. 'It appeals because of its free and easy life and unrestricted formalities and of its quiet rest and comfort.' The proximity of stores, churches and school at Aldinga were cited as an inducement to would-be residents, though more important was the image of Port Willunga as 'an ideal retreat from the cares of business and the stress and worry of the City'. Land sales notwithstanding, Port Willunga remained reclusive; in the 1930s it had only twenty or so houses, plus a few nearby at Aldinga Beach, according to local fisherman Jeff How who used to deliver milk in summer.

The How family has been associated with Port Willunga since its beginning. Jeff's great grandfather William arrived in 1853 with his wife and two children, one of whom, Amelia, married Thomas Martin of the Pier Hotel – and died soon after, aged 20. Thomas became licensee of the Seaview Hotel, initially known as the Lewis Arms and licensed from 1856 to 1894, when it became a temperance hotel. Jeff's grandfather grew up in the Lewis Arms; his grandmother, Fanny How, who was working at the Pier Hotel at the time, was the first to see the masts of the shipwrecked *Star of Greece*. Jeff's father Bill How, together with some of his brothers, were the first commercial fishermen at Port Willunga and in turn taught Jeff, who carries on the family tradition. And it was Bill How who initiated the tunnels or 'dugouts' at the base of the cliff, near the site of the second jetty.

Bill was a recruit in the South Australian Tunnelling Company during the first world war and helped construct underground dugouts for hospitals in the battlefields of France. Returning to Australia and suffering from shell shock, he sometimes needed to find quiet and shelter, especially during thunderstorms, and used his expertise to hollow a retreat in the soft stone of the cliffs. This first tunnel was used for storing nets, and later for keeping the catch cool. One of Bill's brothers dug the next one, and camped there for holidays. Two of the other dugouts were used as changerooms and the remaining tunnels for storing boats.

New Year's Day festivities at Port Willunga continued through the early 1900s, when stalls sold sweets and drinks on the jetty and the local publican set up a bar. In 1915, however, a big storm ripped out a section of the jetty near its end, and though local fishermen constructed a makeshift connection people could no longer stroll its length. After years of accumulated storm damage, the jetty was finally demolished by the army during the second world war, and soon after the council stopped use of the road to the beach.

Port Willunga – Port Willy to habitués – still has its holiday houses together with a growing population of permanent residents attracted by the very same advantages touted in 1924: a pristine beach and relaxed lifestyle. As residents, they are concerned to preserve its character and environment.

## WILLUNGA CREEK LINEAR PARK

The Willunga Creek flows from the slopes behind Willunga township through rich farming land, past the oft-sketched Pengilly's farm and the cluster of dwellings that once formed the settlement of White's Valley, then through the old Martin's farm to the northern end of Port Willunga beach. In this latter section, the District Council of Willunga developed a Linear Park, incorporating the old stone ruins that probably used to be the stable or dairy of Martin's farm.

The impetus for this park came from the Port Willunga Landcare Group, instigated by the Willunga Council in 1994. Residents were concerned by the pollution of the creek and the development of stagnant ponds in winter. Council, sharing these concerns, investigated the possibility of a wetlands scheme. Land between Bowering Road and the coast was acquired in 1995 and 1996, using grants from the South Australian government's Metropolitan Open Space Scheme. A plan for a nine-pond wetland was agreed in principle, but in 1996 Council postponed a final decision on the scheme and the valley became simply a natural park. Since amalgamation of the three local councils to form the City of Onkaparinga, however, the plan has been reconsidered and is likely to be realised.

The boardwalk that extends from the beach over low dunes and leads to the ruins of the Harbourmaster's cottage was also funded by MOSS, as was the cliff walk to the top of the bluff off which the *Star of Greece* met its fate.

# ALDINGA AND
## SELLICKS BEACHES

Where Ports Noarlunga and Willunga had boarding houses and organised summer entertainment, the more isolated and later settled Aldinga and Sellicks beaches had holiday shacks. Recalling earlier times, Mary Maud Aldam wrote in the 1950s:

*It was a very isolated stretch of beach from Pt. Willunga to Sellicks years ago. Now the Motor Age has brought People out & weekend Cottages have been erected Along the cliffs. It's a wonderful stretch of sand along the beach . . .*

Holiday shacks, Aldinga Beach, c. 1950s

As a holiday destination, Aldinga and Sellicks Beaches attracted families and fishermen. Family groups from McLaren Vale used to camp near Sellicks at Christmas and Easter in the 1930s, and people would go netting for whiting at night. From the beach people caught mullet and tommy ruff, using beach worms as bait. Aldinga Bay was known locally as Boat Harbour, and in summer boats would be moored inside the reef. In the 1940s 'the boats brought in good catches of salmon, snapper, trevally, mackerel, gummy shark, mullet, whiting, gar and snook,' wrote Nancy Weisbrodt. After spending many summer holidays camping near the beach, in 1940 her family bought a block at Aldinga Beach that had previously been farming and grazing land owned by Tom Aldam, Mary Maud's brother.

In the 1920s there were about a dozen dwellings at Aldinga Beach, including the Harley Davidson club house. Some were simple beach shacks while others were more substantial, such as the large stone house built by McLaren Vale grape grower Les Stock and later owned by almond grower Dick Strout. The first land subdivisions in the area took place in the 1930s, and more land was opened up in the early 1940s. According to Nancy Weisbrodt, it was illegal during the war years to spend more than £25 on a building that was not to be a permanent residence, but for that sum – and after marking out the ground plan with sheep bones – her father built an asbestos and wooden room on timber foundations. Found materials, such as planks washed up on the beach, often served to extend the original buildings; it is the nature of shacks to grow almost organically, budding like seaweed. One or two original shacks with their galvanised iron tanks can still be seen along the Esplanade, but more often the structures fall into the real estate agents' category of 'luxury beach houses'.

A sense of freedom and of wonderment at the marvels of nature underlies the stories of people who spent their summer holidays or grew up at Aldinga or Sellicks Beach, and for whom going to Aldinga for groceries (and for the children, a packet of Minties) was an adventure. Nostalgic memories of a carefree childhood colour their tales of exploration on the reef and discovery of its fascinating marine life – starfish, multi-hued fish and crabs, living cowries and blue-ring octopus. They talk of shell-collecting walks along the beach; cubbies in the sandhills surrounded by eloquent bird life; spider orchids and ferns in the scrub. And, of course, the rabbits.

For holidaying families in the pre-myxamatosis 1950s, rabbits represented dinner as well as a recreational activity for energy-rich children. Foxes living in the dunes were also trapped and shot – but not eaten.

According to Nancy Weisbrodt:

*We practically lived off fish and rabbits which were in plentiful supply. The cliffs were honeycombed with rabbit burrows and we trapped, snared and shot them for food and skins.*

Motorcycle races on Sellicks Beach

A regular summer highlight was the annual Sellicks Beach speed trials, motorcycle races on the wide band of hard, level sand that extended for three kilometres or more along Aldinga and Sellicks Beaches. The beach was firm enough to serve as a runway, and in the 1930s visitors could even take joyflights, the planes taking off and landing on the beach.

The motorcycle event began in the early 1900s as a hill-climb up Sellicks Hill, but when Council decided against closing the main road south on a holiday weekend the races moved to the beach in 1913. They were always held in summer, but over forty years the dates varied. Some years the races took place on the Australia Day long weekend in January, in others just after Christmas, but on almost any summer weekend there were motorcycles on the beach, club members testing their machines to see just what they could do. Connor Sparrow had clear memories of summers at Sellicks Beach, when:

*they had motor cycles racing on the beach [and] there were nearly four kilometres of beautiful level clean solid sand and it stayed that way for several months. This race meeting was held annually on the public holiday at the end of January. The only buildings on the Esplanade were a Harley Davidson Club House which was a large galvanised iron shed [slightly south of the present day junction of Esplanade and Aldinga Beach Road] and another dwelling that still stands ...*

Helen Fisher, who spent holidays at Aldinga Beach in the 1930s, remembered the Club House and:

*the motor bikes roaring across the paddocks, usually on a Friday night. We were always thrilled to see them arrive because the family sometimes visited the 'Club'. It was fun – they had an old gramophone and they would dance and sing and we would have supper. Then each year they would have the motor bike races on Sellicks Beach. That was the only time the place came to life. People came from everywhere for the races.*

There were both speed trials, with competitors continually attempting to set new records over a mile or a half-mile (the 100 mph barrier was broken in 1916) and events for motorcycles in different classes, with and without

sidecars. Most of the bikes had no front brakes, so for a half-mile race an additional half-mile of sand was needed for the bikes to slow down. In 1924 they raced over ten miles, but a few years later the distances had been increased to 20 and 100 miles. In 1932 Jack Cantlon won the 100 mile handicap (on a 2¾ Rudge) with an average speed of 66.9 mph (107 kilometres per hour), breaking the previous record set in 1929. These speeds were obviously considered dangerous enough for the riders to warrant some protection, and in 1924 the South Australian Motor Cycle Club made it compulsory to wear crash helmets during the races. As these were expensive, the club bought crash helmets, which could be hired for one shilling for one event. Ross Haynes, who used to race in the early 1930s, says they were made of compressed fibre and known as 'pudding basins'. Some of the early riders wore protective leggings; later ones had leather pants and jackets.

'If the sand was wet you could go like hell … you could go a hundred miles an hour,' enthuses Ross, but sometimes this meant waiting hours for the tide to go out. Racing on firm, damp sand was like racing on a speedway track, except when riders chopped corners. Accidents were rare, and never serious, and if cars became bogged in the drier sand there were always mates to help push them out. As many as fifteen or more cycles would line up for the races, which were enormously popular and attracted many onlookers and supporters. There was a picnic atmosphere, recalls Ross Haynes, but when it came to the races, and who was racing whom, it was deadly serious!

The races continued until 1953 and were re-enacted for the South Australian Sesquicentenary in 1986. Even after official racing ceased, people used the long stretch of sand as a speedway. The potential danger to children that this represented led government to place a police motorcycle officer on beach duty in 1975. Two 'traffic-free' areas were declared in 1979 between the Aldinga and Sellicks ramps to prevent through-traffic on weekends and public holidays, and later the whole beach was classed as a road, drivers subjected to normal road rules and a speed limit.

Sellicks Beach is the southernmost end of Aldinga Bay or, as Light named it, Deception Bay. It takes its name from William Sellick, who bought land in the region in 1854. On a clear day the view extends as far north as Mount Lofty, as Colonel Light would have seen it. Looping over the hills to the south are huge pipes bringing water from Myponga Reservoir. Near the point, where the hills fall into the sea, hang-gliders launch themselves from the cliffs and float away, suspended beneath billowing, multi-coloured kites.

Beyond the high water mark the sand is covered with masses of small, smooth, irregularly shaped stones in tones of grey, mauve and pink. These are the 'pebbles' once collected by Sellicks' pebble-picker James Heathersay, who for about ten years from 1912 supplied mining companies at Broken Hill with selected stones, always uniform in size, for use in their ore processing operations. Once his pebbles were shipped as far as Queensland, but eventually they were replaced by stainless steel balls.

Sellicks' pebbles have been valued for their decorative effects. Small stones form a simple geometric pattern in shades of grey and beige on the M.C. Lovelock Memorial Gates at the Aldinga oval, erected in 1946. (The Lovelocks were pioneers in the district; M.C. Lovelock was a local sportsman and past chairman of Willunga District Council.) The most original example of their use is a house on the Esplanade at Sellicks Beach. Pebble Gallery, with its mock-Norman facade, has had several owners since the first pebbles were placed in the early 1920s. A black-and-white hound – a replica of the real one guarding the house – looks out from high, stone-studded battlements. The pediment of the garage, added later, displays the Bicentennial logo and the year 1988 picked out in deep grey pebbles. Even the letter box, a miniature of the house itself, is covered with pebbles.

# FISHING

Shack-dwelling families may have lived on fish during the summer, yet the resources of the sea seem not to have been exploited until the coast came to be valued as a holiday destination. E.H. Hallack commented in 1892 that 'one is led to think that there are good fishing grounds in the neighbourhood, although fish as an article of diet is almost an unknown quantity, both at Aldinga and Willunga'. The How brothers began fishing at Port Willunga around 1910, a few years after May Vivienne commended the 'splendid fishing' there, the best period being November to March.

The Kaurna people had a deep understanding of the sea and coast. They knew when fish made their annual migrations up and down Gulf St Vincent, which species could be eaten and when they were at their prime. At the turn of the century Mary Maud Aldam would see them 'on their Walkabout from the Lakes on their way to Adelaide. Spearing the Mutton Fish [abalone] and collecting the Shellfish from the Reef was a great pastime for them.' Thomas Martin (grandson of the first Thomas Martin) remembers Aborigines at Port Willunga standing in the shallows to stalk and spear mulloway, some as big as 25 kilos, using a long, three-barbed spear. At some sites the elders would camp on the cliffs watching for fish migrating along the coastline.

Professional fishermen at Port Noarlunga, Port Willunga, Aldinga Beach and Sellick's Beach may have observed Aboriginal ways and adopted them, since Aboriginal people were still visiting Port Willunga when the How brothers were young. In the 1930s, Dolph (Adolphus) Waye 'had a huge tower on the beach by Silver Sands ramp where he would sit for hours if necessary watching for schools of fish', Helen Fisher recorded. At Port Noarlunga too, the professional fishermen would sit in the sandhills looking for the telltale shadows. November to May were the mulloway months while mullet, salmon and whiting could be caught all year.

In the old days the fishermen had only rowing boats, and netting seems to have been the most common technique. At Aldinga the How brothers netted the reef, at high tide setting nets to cover a wide area; in the morning the nets

How brothers and helpers with a catch of salmon, Port Willunga, late 1960s

were brought in and dried on poles near the beach. Small mesh nets were used for mullet, larger mesh for salmon and mulloway. Catches could be as great as one tonne – then horses could barely walk under the load and fishermen would travel all night to get their catch to the fish market by early morning. In the summer months fish was also sold directly from the boats, on the beach or near the jetty at Port Noarlunga; in the 1920s mullet and salmon were threepence each or six for one shilling.

Professional net fishermen continued to operate along the coast until around the 1970s, fish stocks gradually dwindling at the same time as restrictions on commercial fishing began to be introduced. Most of the catch would be taken to market, but in the 1950s and 1960s people were still able to buy fish on the beach or in front of the hotels, where the fishermen would stand with their baskets of mixed fish.

The recreational fishermen and women were equally canny, recognising four main fishing grounds at Aldinga Beach. According to Helen Fisher, these were 'the Point or Snapper Point, the Boat Harbour Ground, the Club House Ground and the Sandhills Ground. They were reached by lining up various landmarks with one another.' Snapper were abundant; in one morning in 1947 Marjorie and Ken Hay (parents of Nancy Weisbrodt) caught nearly 100 kilos of snapper, and fish of 10 kilos were not uncommon. People used nets as well as lines. Helen Fisher wrote:

'When the tide was out my dad would knock sticks into the ground to show where the rocks were and when the tide came in we would net within those poles. Garfish and even snook at times were netted in large quantities. Whoever caught lots of fish in those days shared with everyone on the "block" as we called the shack area.'

Professional fishing at Port Willunga began with the How brothers around 1910 – Bert, Tom, Stan and Bill. Tom seems to have been the instigator; it was Tom who left home and went to Melbourne, where he fished in Port Phillip Bay and learnt how to make nets before returning home.

For the last 20 years Jeff How has been the Port Willunga fisherman, having eventually taken over the commercial fishing licence from his father, Bill, and his uncles. Bill was renowned for his skill in sighting schools of fish, scanning the seas from his lookout on the cliffs above the dugouts. From the shadows over the sandy bottom he could tell what the fish were, how many there were and where they were heading. Even in his eighties he was still looking for fish and shouting instructions to the team below. Jeff uses the same spotting techniques as his father, the only difference being that his father's generation had rowing boats where he uses an outboard motor, and where they pulled in the nets by hand he can use engine power.

Sea salmon, mullet, mulloway, whiting and squid form the bulk of his catches, salmon being the most prolific. Jeff knows the seasonal migration patterns of the different species; some, such as mulloway, travel northwards from about October to January, southwards from January to May – by which time Jeff himself has migrated to fish from Balgowan, on Spencer Gulf. His biggest catch was a school of salmon, which he first spied from inside the Star of Greece cafe and then again off Maslin Beach. 'We started at ten in the morning, finished at 4.20 am the next day – 20 tonnes of salmon netted, and we had to get it all to the fish market.'

The mulloway he used to catch could sometimes reach nearly 50 kilos – and the bigger they are the better for eating, says Jeff. It's only in the last ten years or so that whiting have been plentiful, and only in the last twenty have squid been considered edible. His favourite for eating is the salmon, which he fillets and cooks in the microwave with seasoning, a squeeze of orange or lemon juice, and a dab of butter.

# AQUATIC RESERVES

When the new Port Noarlunga jetty was built in 1920, it extended right to the reef, with steps allowing immediate and easy access. Early photographs show summer crowds on the reef – men in dark suits and hats, women in long white dresses holding parasols. Washed away in the 1930s, the steps were replaced by a precipitous ladder that in turn disappeared when the end of the jetty was destroyed by a storm in 1987. Ten years later, a new stairway was affixed to the end of the jetty – but finishing 20 metres short of the reef, so that anyone who wants to investigate it has to swim the final stretch.

The Moana middens provide ample evidence of the Kaurna people feasting on the rich resources of fish and shellfish of the reef environment, and it seems that the new settlers also appreciated them. As early as 1866 it was reported that 'there are plenty of shell-fish on the rocks near Noarlunga, which are eaten by numbers of people'. After the opening of the new jetty, exploring the reef at low tide was one of the standard summer holiday adventures. In the 1960s exploration took an underwater approach, and the impact of spear fishermen led to a decimation of the the fish population around the reefs. Restrictions against spearfishing were introduced in 1965, and both the Port Noarlunga and Aldinga Reefs were declared Aquatic Reserves in 1971, two of thirteen in the state. It is illegal to remove any marine organisms, whether seaweed, shells or swimming fish.

The Aldinga Reef is a flat, shallow, rocky platform that officially extends for about three kilometres from just south of the old Port Willunga jetty. It is centred on Snapper Point, beyond which is the 'drop-off', a spectacular underwater cliff about 10 metres in height with associated caves, fissures and pinnacles. A favoured diving location, it shelters sponges and soft gorgonian corals (*Melithaea* species). Among reef fish is the locally endangered blue groper (*Achoerodus gouldii*) which, despite its popular name, is not the same species as its illustrious namesake of warmer waters. Slow-moving and slow-maturing, the groper feeds mainly on shellfish and molluscs of the reef environment. It proved an easy target for early spearfishermen, but off the reef spearfishermen themselves are easy, if occasional, targets for white pointers.

The Aldinga Reef, its intertidal zone beginning at the base of the beach-side cliffs, has always been more accessible than the Port Noarlunga reef, which shares many of the same features. The latter is part of a larger reserve encompassing the Onkaparinga estuary (Port Noarlunga Reef and Onkaparinga Estuary Aquatic Reserve). The estuary extends almost to the township of (Old) Noarlunga, but since 1985 has been combined with the Onkaparinga Gorge as the Onkaparinga River Recreation Park, under the administration of the National Parks and Wildlife Service. As well as providing recreational space and preserving the natural environment, the park acts as a buffer between surburban development and rural land to the south.

Port Noarlunga jetty and reef, c. 1930

There are several different habitats within the estuary, including the biologically rich floodplain between the bridge and the oval that contains a significant area of samphire. Eelgrass grows on the muddy banks of the lower estuary, providing food and shelter for the various species of fish and other marine fauna (crabs, prawns) living in this environment. A variety of birdlife inhabits the region – herons, egrets, spoonbills and strawnecked ibis in low-lying wetlands, swans and pelicans in areas of shallow water and samphire banks, and cormorants, divers and ducks on the river. Since the early 1990s wetlands have been developed in the estuary in an attempt to improve the quality of water in the river and encourage more fish and bird life.

The estuary is particularly important as a breeding and nursery area for jumping mullet, yellow-eye mullet and black bream, and many other fish species migrate in and out. Old residents recall the Onkaparinga as 'teeming with fish' earlier this century. Between July and November the bream were at their prime, 'fat and vigorous' according to Cliff England, who came to Port Noarlunga in 1929 and eventually bought a shop next to the Institute. 'We caught plenty of these fish, weighing up to six pound. Most of us used wooden reels and homemade rods.' He also caught plenty of the migratory salmon:

*My father and I frequently went fishing in the river, down just south of the footbridge, shortly after dark. Using mostly whitebait we caught large salmon weighing up to three and a half pounds. Some nights we caught up to fifty fish!*

Recreational fishermen still cast their lines into the river, but during the day the lower reaches of the estuary are more often used by canoeists and kayak paddlers, who launch their craft just below the road bridge where the Onkaparinga Canoe Club has its headquarters. Nearby the old 1890s homestead of the pioneering Sauerbier family is being developed as an interpretive centre for the whole Recreation Park.

# PORT NOARLUNGA REEF
## UNDERWATER TRAIL

Opened in March 1994 and one of only a few such projects in Australia, the trail guides underwater explorers along 800 metres of temperate reef system. Twelve plaques at depths ranging from six to ten metres, on both the shore and sea edges of the reef, describe the reef ecosystem, the physical processes that make the reef work, or particular marine flora or fauna. These include kelp and chitons, mussels, starfish, blue-ringed octopus, cuttlefish, poisonous toadfish, banded sweep, leatherjackets, scaly fin, old wife, horned blenny, magpie perch and a species which, while not exactly unique to this particular reef, is nevertheless is named after it: *Trachinops noarlungae*.

*Trachinops noarlungae* is a small fish less than 15 centimetres in length, modestly sporting a grey body with yellow fins and blue eyes. It often lives with several hundred of its mates in schools, and likes reef environments with large caves. It has no common name, though most *Trachinops* species are known as hulafish, and seems to have no commercial value.

The gap between the northern and southern sections of the reef, which allows boats to enter and anchor in sheltered waters, was once a gorge through which the Onkaparinga flowed out to sea 6000 years ago.

# CHAPTER
# REFLECTING

For over 150 years European artists have been depicting the landscape and environment of the McLaren Vale region, from the coast to the hills. Surveyors such as William Light and E.C. Frome, in the earliest years of settlement, attempted to document what they saw and experienced but were sometimes awkward in their translations of an unfamiliar landscape in a European idiom. This uneasiness helps convey to the present-day viewer some of the difficulties of adapting to a strange new land.

In the 1840s, S.T. Gill and George French Angas recorded the landscape, together with its flora and fauna and inhabitants, in a more romantic way and from an artist's perspective. Arriving in Adelaide in 1839, Gill set to drawing almost immediately. Among his sketches are a view of the Onkaparinga River above 'Horseshoe Township', dated around 1848, and an earlier one of Aborigines rubbing the stem of the grass tree on another piece of wood to start their fire. A few of his sketches were 'borrowed' by Angas and reproduced in *South Australia Illustrated*, a magnificent collection of sixty lithographed plates, mostly by Angas, published in London in 1847. Some of

# NINE
# THE REGION

the scenes may be idealised, but Angas's views of the coastal scrub near Rapid Bay, with Aborigines camped on the edge of the beach and net-fishing in the shallows, are an invaluable record of a culture that was rapidly disappearing.

Until the early twentieth century, landscapes of the region were mostly the work of enthusiastic amateurs who sketched and coloured and painted as their travels took them. Sarah Kay, grandmother of 'Cud' Kay, produced several books of delicately detailed paintings of local wildflowers in the 1890s. Around the turn of the century H.P. Gill, then Director of the Adelaide School of Design and later the first Honorary Curator of the Art Gallery of South Australia, painted views along the coast from the mouth of the Onkaparinga to Sellicks Hill. From the 1930s, however, artists were increasingly drawn to an area that offers views of such extraordinary diversity. From Hans Heysen to Ivor Hele, from Dorrit Black to Jeffrey Smart, a complete Who's Who of South Australian artists has, at one time or another, painted views of its beaches and barns, vineyards and hills.

# FASCINATION
## OF THE FLEURIEU

Painter David Dridan is fond of repeating Hans Heysen's remark that of all the hills he has painted, the Willunga hills are the most difficult to capture. Not all artists would agree, but for some their changing moods and expressions are a continual challenge. Softly dimpled in the early morning light, they are starkly flattened by noonday glare and shamelessly sensual at sunset; they can be sombre grey beneath a halo of cloud, hauntingly purple in twilight's haze.

So many artists have returned so often to this region, painting and repainting the same scenes. In the opinion of Daniel Thomas, Director of the Art Gallery of South Australia from 1984 to 1990, it is as important to South Australian art as Heidelberg to Melbourne's, or Barbizon to French impressionism. The words 'magical' and 'seductive' have been used to describe the quality of the landscape, its variety, its perennial yet ever-changing charm. It is tempting to attribute this to something spiritual, as Aboriginal peoples do, but for the artists of the 1930s, 1940s and 1950s who kept returning, pragmatic motives were also present; this southern region is close to Adelaide, and even in the days when cars and petrol were scarce Briscoe's bus service delivered passengers to Aldinga, from where it was only a short hike to Port Willunga.

Aldinga and Port Willunga were a hub of artistic activity in the 1930s and 1940s, stimulated by Kathleen Sauerbier's interest from the late 1920s. As niece of George Sauerbier, who had a homestead overlooking the Onkaparinga at Port Noarlunga, Kathleen may already have been familiar with the southern coast. In 1932 she purchased a house at Port Willunga locally known as the 'Residential Cafe', a dwelling that from 1856 had a history as a licensed hotel, the Lewis Arms. It became a temperance hotel 40 years later and during Kathleen's time was colloquially called the 'Manor House'.

At the end of 1932 Kathleen invited a group of friends to spend Christmas by the beach. Among them was the painter Horace Trenerry, who had previously done a few paintings of the area and required little persuasion to move there from the Adelaide hills. Together they set to painting local scenes – the dramatic cliffs and beaches, homely haystacks and barns.

Evening, mouth of the Onkaparinga (H.P. Gill)

Others attracted to the area included Marjorie Gwynne, whose paintings included impressionistic landscapes with farm houses, and Nora Burden, who had a cottage at Port Willunga. Dora Chapman and Geoffrey Shedley were also part of the coterie. David Dallwitz, then fresh out of art school, remembers spending a week or so with friends at Aldinga or Port Willunga over several summers in the mid-1930s, painting from the top of the cliffs, wandering along the deserted beach and swimming naked in the crystal clear water. They were aware of the Sauerbier–Trenerry group but, out of respect or reticence, hesitated to join them.

Kathleen Sauerbier married and moved to Melbourne in the mid-1930s, though she still made annual summer visits to Port Willunga; one of her fabric designs based on sea shells was inspired by walks along the beach. While she often favoured bold reds and ochres in her paintings, it was her use of soft blues and purples which influenced Trenerry, whose best work was done in this Port Willunga period. Even in the early 1930s he was acknowledged as one of the leading artists in the state. He was 'a cut above us' admits Dallwitz, who regards 'Tren', together with Margaret Preston, as South Australia's greatest painters.

Many others share this assessment, admiring Trenerry's intuitive understanding of South Australian landscape. Hugo Shaw, another artist who has focused on the Port Willunga area, sees him as a 'pure poet in paint' who expresses 'all the feeling, all the essence of the landscape'. As an individual, he is usually described as a loner and an eccentric, moving from one address to another and camping in abandoned houses – including the old Uncle Tom's Cabin – exchanging paintings for food, drink and art materials. In the 1940s he was diagnosed as suffering from Huntington's chorea, a debilitating hereditary disease that gradually restricted his activities and resulted in his death in 1958.

Trenerry captured this region, sometimes called 'Trenerry country', as no one else has. Rarely moving from Port Willunga and Aldinga, he painted what he saw around him – stooks of hay stacked in the mown paddocks, toppling haystacks with hens rummaging among the loose straw, the cliffs and sea, the beach with the blackened stumps of the old jetty and fishing boats. Often he painted the same subject more than once, returning to particular views time after time. Trenerry seems to have been especially attracted to roads – or rather, to the Old Coach Road, and to a span of that road between Aldinga and Maslin Beach. He depicted it from different angles, at different times of the year, sometimes revealing a triangular glimpse of sea; but it is always recognisably the same road which, in its wave-like rhythm, extends into the space in front of the canvas and meanders on behind.

Ivor Hele was also painting around Aldinga and Port Willunga in the 1930s, having bought the old Hotel Aldinga on the corner of Adey and Little Roads in 1937. One of Australia's most distinguished portrait painters – five times winner of the Archibald Prize between 1951 and 1957 – and knighted in 1983, Hele also painted coastal scenes around Port Willunga in the 1950s and 1960s. He often swam at Port Willunga, and from the top of the cliffs sketched the fishing activities and the farm horses being exercised on the beach. Hele's coast has a wild, untamed, almost primitive quality; the bare, weatherworn cliffs are depicted as muscled and sinewy, like the naked riders plunging into the sea in his painting *Riding School* (1963). His sea, less summery than that painted by his contemporaries, swirls and masses around the feet of the fishermen launching their boat in *Fish Sighted* (1965). One of Australia's war artists, Hele was sent to the Middle East and New Guinea but after the war settled in the renovated coaching inn and from then led the life of a recluse, his portrait subjects having to visit him for sittings.

As a teacher at the South Australian School of Arts and Crafts until 1940, and in private lessons, Ivor Hele had an enormous influence on a younger generation of artists who also painted this region, among them David Dallwitz, Hugo Shaw and Robert Hannaford. Jeffrey Smart described him as a dynamic, gifted and inspiring teacher of life drawing. But there was another teacher, also one of the Port Willunga group, who was similarly influential for Smart and fellow student Jacqueline Hick: Dorrit Black, who taught them composition or, in Jeffrey Smart's words, 'taught them to make pictures'.

Dorrit Black was a modernist who studied in London and Paris, established the Modern Art Centre in Sydney in 1932 and on her return to Adelaide in 1942 became vice-chairman of the South Australian branch of the Contemporary Art Society of Australia, with David Dallwitz as chairman. As a pioneer in the field of modern art in South Australia she found support from such sympathisers as Marjorie Gwynne, Horace Trenerry and Jeffrey Smart, all of whom absorbed and later reflected some of her ideas. While she encouraged all non-traditional styles of art – abstract, cubist, surrealist – her own approach owed much to cubism: bold, sculptural forms and colours. Dorrit Black often painted in the area around Port Willunga, her emphasis on strong, solid shapes perhaps best expressed in a 1942 painting of the newly-cut road above the Aldinga cliffs.

During the 1940s and 1950s many other well-known South Australian artists – John Dowie, Stewart Game, Ruth Tuck, Lawrence Howie, Clive Stoward, Max Ragless, Ivor Francis, David Dridan, Geoff Wilson, Jacqueline Hick – exhibited works reflecting views along the coast as well as the farming area inland. For the most part, they were rather conservative landscapes though Jeffrey Smart, in his painting entitled *Aldinga Barns* (1947), was already moving away from this tradition. One artist who focused particularly on the coast was Anton Riebe, whose summery scenes of the beach and headland of Port Willunga are quintessentially Australian.

Dora Chapman had contact with the Port Willunga coterie in the early 1940s and after her return to settle in Adelaide in 1957 she and her husband, James Cant, bought and restored a stone-and-slate cottage, 'Somerset', on St Peters Terrace, Willunga. This region was the inspiration for Cant's 1958–60 series of closely observed landscapes with their bleached grass and dried branches, often painted in washed-out ochres, greys and greens. While at Willunga Dora approached the National Trust to have the old courthouse turned into a gallery for local art, and though this never happened her initial request seems to have had the effect of drawing the Trust's attention to the historic value of the building.

The same qualities of landscape that attracted the innovative modern artists of the 1930s to the southern coastal district continue to draw artists to this region: its folds and forms, colours and light, and its ever-changing appearance from hour to hour, day to day, season to season. Among contemporary painters, Robert Hannaford – like Ivor Hele, a leading portraitist – has done a series of works on Maslin Beach, capturing its beauty and magic in different lights, from different aspects. This broad sweep of beach with its clear, turquoise water and intricate limestone formations has an innate appeal, but Hannaford is additionally fascinated by the way the various shades of the nude bodies reflect the colours of the cliffs, pinks and browns and sandy whites. Ivor Hele, who had a strong influence on Hannaford, also recognised this correspondence in some of his paintings, the golden tones of sand and cliffs echoing the glow of summer-tanned skin. Hannaford has painted Maslin Beach from the top of the headland, looking toward the sea, and looking back at the cliffs from the water, but perhaps his best-known view features a single, solitary nude figure – strongly built, feet firmly apart, and motionless – almost at the centre of the work, his eyes fixed on the horizon. This 1996 painting, a finalist in the 1997 Wynne landscape prize, effectively duplicates an earlier painting of 1980; it is, says Hannaford, the only time he has painted exactly the same subject twice.

Mandy Martin is another South Australian artist who has frequently found inspiration in the southern coast. Her painting of Ochre Cove, which decorates the Main Committee Room of Parliament House in Canberra, depicts this section of coast on a vast scale. Its dimensions (2.8 m x 12.1 m) made it, at the time, the largest painting commissioned in Australia. Like some of Hele's work, it hints at malevolent forces within the landscape, the sea motionless and darkly opaque, the light from the setting sun enhancing the coppery-bronze tones of the sheer cliff faces.

Among present-day artists of the McLaren Vale region Dee Jones has a singular place. Her style and subjects have since changed, but in the 1970s her inspiration came from her immediate environment. Dee's primitive style, simple but rich in detail, was particularly attuned to the rhythms of agricultural life, her paintings depicting scenes of olives and the olive harvest, vegetable gardens and orchards, and the symmetry of the ever-present vineyards.

# STROUT FARM SCHOOL

'The Strout Farm School' is a name casually given to a loose knot of artists who, while only once coming together to paint the same scene, have a long and close relationship and a strong attraction for the landscape of the McLaren Vale region. Like the members of the earlier Port Willunga coterie, all share a predilection for the open air – while admitting that 'plein air' painting has its drawbacks in the form of cold winds, scorching sun, persistent flies and mosquitoes, and the risk of disruption of the scene before them as the farmer shifts the tractor.

That one communal occasion was in winter 1994, a rare succession of sixteen rainless Thursdays when the old farm on Strout Road, McLaren Vale, hosted six easels, six folding chairs, six artists: David Dallwitz, David Dridan, Christine Lawrence, Lesley Redgate, Hugo Shaw and Geoff Wilson. All had been painting in the region for a long time and had a strong affinity with it, and all were united by art. For more than 15 years Wilson, Dallwitz and Dridan had camped and painted together in outback locations; Wilson, Dallwitz and Shaw teamed up at weekends; Christine Lawrence and Lesley Redgate had been taught by Dallwitz and Wilson at art school.

The idea and choice of venue were David Dridan's. The farm was one of the last in the district where hay was cut, stooked and stacked into old-fashioned, lopsided haystacks. These, together with the farm's dilapidated wooden barns, red-roofed galvanised iron sheds, rusting implements and spreading trees offered variety enough to suit all sympathies. From this one site each artist produced an individual series of paintings differing in colour, texture and composition yet at the same time complementary, together forming an extraordinarily rich evocation of place.

Without consciously trying, each of these painters has managed to capture some of the essence of the region, despite their very different visions and perspectives. While David Dridan aims to softly capture the personality and texture of a landscape, David Dallwitz describes himself as a realist painter who chooses his subjects because of their visual attraction. Dallwitz likes run-down buildings and machinery, with simple yet powerful forms; like Horace Trenerry, he is also attracted to roads, as is Geoff Wilson. Another realist painter, Wilson favours the pattern of built forms and roads within a landscape. Together with Dallwitz, and over many years, he has repeatedly painted the cluster of buildings of Pengilly farm on Bayliss Road, from different angles, different heights, different aspects, looking westwards towards the sea and south towards the tantalising hills. Hugo Shaw has a strong empathy for the colours and patterns of the coast. As a child, he spent many holidays at Port Willunga and, having rambled all over the beach and dunes and cliffs, feels himself part of the landscape. He believes the challenge for the artist is to express these sentiments through colour and to reproduce the colours of the environment – colours that are infinitely subtle, infinitely variable, and extraordinarily difficult to mix.

Not only did Horace Trenerry leave his mark on the landscape, he seems to have impressed his vision on succeeding generations of artists. David Dallwitz and Geoff Wilson both acknowledge the importance of strong lines, and Lesley Redgate deliberately uses lines – whether streaks of clouds in the sky, furrows in the soil, lines of fences or trees, or the lines in a paddock of wheat after harvesting – to give dynamic direction and colour differentiation to her paintings.

Redgate, who cites Geoff Wilson as her most influential teacher and mentor, is another to have painted Pengilly farm. Rural landscapes have always been her preference, but she feels particularly drawn to this region and finds in it unlimited inspiration. Her views sometimes juxtapose nature and culture, the soft contours and sensual colours of the natural landscape contrasting with the brittle edges of man-made objects such as tractors and wheat bins. She often chooses to frame her views with a distant backdrop of hills.

The challenge of the hills and their ever-changing colours has led Lesley to reproduce the same scene in different seasons, showing a transformation from the reds and oranges of summer to hints of green and then full green in winter, with wispy mist hanging over the top. These hills are also a strong motive in Christine Lawrence's work, her fascination with this landscape beginning in childhood after Sunday drives in the country with her parents. Imagining the hills as bodies asleep on the land, she invests them with life, playing with light and colour to highlight their folds and creases.

Hugo Shaw painting at Strout Farm

In many of the works by this group of artists there are clear hints of Mediterranean affinities. The silhouettes of vines and olive trees are common to both, the quality of the light is similar and the stone of old farm ruins around Willunga and Aldinga, while more self-consciously new than the weathered blocks of ancient ramparts and castles and squat romanesque churches, has a similar warmth and texture. Lesley Redgate admits to the influence of van Gogh and Cézanne, and her paintings, with their van Gogh colours of green and purple, yellow and blue, powerfully express this Mediterranean quality. Her intense blue is usually in the sky, especially in summer, but sometimes it is a slender finger of sea stealthily infiltrating a green landscape. Tones of mauve, lavender and purple are almost always present in her work, whether as shadings between harvest rows, shadows on trees, gradings of depth in the gullies of the hills or as the vibrant colour of a patch of Salvation Jane.

David Dridan probably speaks for the whole group when he gives his reasons for liking this region. One is the unspoiled nature of much of the landscape, which still contains pockets of bush that represent the traditional landscape as Light might have seen it in 1836. Second, he values the variety of subject matter it offers to painters, its agricultural diversity – from vineyards to orchards to olive groves to hayfields. Lastly, he cites its colour, its silence and its bird life. For Hugo Shaw the diversity is also present in terms of light, the different qualities of light throughout the day and the seasons.

Perhaps, finally, it is the elusiveness of the landscape that draws artists to this region and continually inspires them to try to capture its essence.

## JOHN OLSEN'S CLARENDON YEARS

John Olsen is one of Australia's most acclaimed artists,. His exuberant expressionist landscapes are underscored by his belief that 'to read an environment is the beginning of understanding and feeling for it'. While still recognisably Australian, they are completely unlike those of the Strout Farm School. For Olsen, landscape is not static; it is a living process that has to be felt as well as seen. His paintings, with their rich, glowing colours and frenetic movement, express this dynamic interaction.

John Olsen came to Clarendon in 1981 at the suggestion of David Dridan and rates the eight years he spent there, living in the Old Rectory and painting in his studio in the old Institute, as his best and most creative period. At Clarendon he experienced a totally different landscape to the flat inland country he had depicted previously and found inspiration in the extraordinary hills enclosing the township, made 'by God on one of his creative days'. Of the view, Olsen has remarked 'No bloody artist can paint it!', but between 1983 and 1986 he completed the Clarendon Season series of paintings. *A Road to Clarendon: Autumn*, won the Wynne landscape prize in 1985.

# ART IN THE COMMUNITY

In 1987 Barbara Powell-Weise, a professional artist then living in one of Adelaide's southern coastal suburbs, dreamed of an artists' village, a place where a community of artists – painters, musicians, weavers, potters, writers, sculptors, illustrators – could live and work together. Finding artists responsive to the idea was easy compared to finding the right location – ideally, somewhere south of Adelaide, in a rural setting, with appropriate zoning – but eventually a site at Aldinga, between Old Coach Road and Port Road, was selected. Situated in a picturesque environment adjacent to an historically interesting village, its natural advantages were self-evident: proximity to beaches, farmland and wineries, accessibility of established services such as libraries, shops, banks, hospital and medical services.

The South Australian government, as owner of this section of land fronting the Willunga Creek, conducted a feasibility study in 1997 and approved further development of a plan for the first artists' village in Australia, designed by artists and for artists. In this Village for the Living Arts residents would own their own land and buildings, with facilities such as workshops, exhibition areas, teaching rooms and workshops being communally owned. The village would be environmentally sympathetic, local materials being used as much as possible, and permaculture gardens would supply residents with fresh fruit, vegetables and herbs. Performances, exhibitions and teaching would encourage interaction with the wider community.

The response to this vision is an indication of the interest in art, and the arts in general, in the region. Art exhibitions are a feature of Bushing and Almond Blossom Festivals, while local artists' works are regularly displayed in local galleries, wineries such as Woodstock and restaurants such as The Barn and Limeburner's at McLaren Vale. Awards such as the annual Ryecroft Prize, offered by Ingoldby Winery in the 1970s, have encouraged local artists, and groups such as the Wine Coast Artists and Willunga Hill Art Group organise collective exhibitions. Members benefit from the opportunity to

Art and wine at The Barn

hang their works for public viewing, as well as learning from one another, painting together and participating in workshops.

The Willunga Hill Art Group is an informal collective of around 30 painters whose work covers an enormous diversity of styles from water-colours to acrylics, still lifes to collage. It originated from the group of students Rosemary Gartelmann had been teaching in her hilltop studio for two years; wanting to show their works together, they saw the approaching Almond Blossom Festival as an appropriate occasion. A venue was found at the Alma Hotel in Willunga, and other Fleurieu artists were invited to con-tribute to the exhibition which, with over 80 paintings hung and a good pro-portion sold, was judged a resounding success. The annual exhibition became a much-anticipated event at subsequent Almond Blossom festivals, each year adopting a specific theme such as 'Life in the Vales' and 'Regional Heritage', and gradually came to represent exclusively members of the group. Until recently, the group's main exhibition coincided with the Almond Blossom Festival, but in 1997 it took place during the Bushing Festival, while a smaller Christmas exhibition was held in December.

# NOARLUNGA COMMUNITY ARTS CENTRE

One of only three community gallery spaces in the Fleurieu Peninsula, the Noarlunga Community Arts Centre provides exhibition spaces for local artists and craftspeople, workshops, a performance space for dances, concerts and theatrical events, and a fully equipped soundproof music studio. More importantly, however, its programs encourage the whole community to participate in activities from classes in dance, painting and children's art to playwriting projects, film screenings and folk music concerts. It also serves as a resource centre and maintains a register of local artists, craftspeople and cultural activities in general.

The Centre opened in 1993 and since then has usually managed to arrange over twenty different exhibitions annually in the two exhibition spaces. The exhibitions often highlight work by young artists, together with contemporary and experimental art and mixed media creations that the more traditional venues tend to overlook. Each summer the the gallery organises a display of surfing art, which might include painted surfboards, sculpture, paintings representing surf culture, and jewellery with marine motifs. Included in the 1998 exhibition were a series of ceramic mermaids; 'History of Surfing' posters and other works by Gerry Wedd, one of the original 'Mambo' surfing gear designers; and a bright, sleek, miniature glass surfboard by Willunga glass artist Glenn Howlett.

Promotion of youth culture extends to music, many local bands being also part of the surfing scene, and to theatre; three of the four theatre groups based in the centre are made up of young people. For schoolchildren, storytelling is combined with explorations inside giant inflatable fish or on climbing webs representing underwater reefs.

The City of Onkaparinga plans to develop the Community Arts Centre at Port Noarlunga as a heritage and cultural centre, to be linked, via the Onkaparinga River, with a corresponding centre at (Old) Noarlunga in the old Horseshoe Hotel.

# REGIONAL CRAFTS

Hanging above the stairs to the cellar in the Salopian Inn is a strikingly original embroidered and appliqué friendship quilt made for proprietor Pip Forrester's mother by members of the McLaren Vale Patchworkers. Its centre square repeats the logo of the Salopian, a bottle of 1851 vintage red wine pouring into the chimney, while the surrounding 16 squares each reflect a restaurant-and-cooking theme – glasses and bottles of wine, bowls of fruit, a whole orange pumpkin filled with pumpkin soup, a slice of mulberry pie, strawberries, cakes and other desserts. Borders of red- and blue-checked teatowels are a gentle reminder of dishwashing chores to follow. Dominating the dining room of the Salopian, the quilt aptly epitomises the tone of the restaurant: good food and wine in a welcoming, homely atmosphere.

McLaren Vale Patchworkers is one of several thriving patchwork and quilting groups in the region, with a combined membership of around 70. For most members the craft is a hobby, though the McLaren Vale group has held exhibitions every two years since 1988. Often quilters and embroiderers work together on a large piece, which might then be donated to the community or other worthy causes. Quilt raffles organised by the Willunga and Aldinga groups have raised money for schools and CFS groups, and quilts have been donated to the local hospital, retirement homes and in 1994 to the New South Wales bushfire appeal.

The predecessor of the Patchworkers was the McLaren Vale Weavers and Spinners. This group was active in the 1980s, its main project – for the South Australian Sesquicentenary in 1986 – being a series of embroidered panels recounting the history of the region. Using wool that was hand-spun by members of the group and hand-dyed in natural dyes, the tapestry focuses on three eras of transport. The first panel shows bullocks with a wagon-load of huge logs resting at what is now The Barn restaurant; the second a steam train at the McLaren Vale railway station during the grape harvest; while in the final panel a wine tanker climbs the hill out of McLaren Vale against a backdrop of vineyards and farmland, deep blue sea and ochre cliffs.

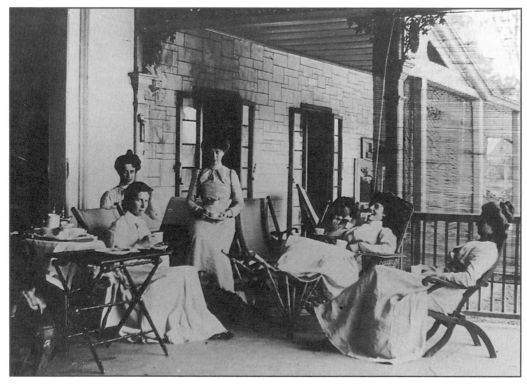
Taking afternoon tea at the old Reynell homestead, c. 1896; Gladys Reynell on left

The Sesquicentenary and the Australian Bicentenary in 1988 stimulated other community craft projects in the region. In 1985/86 the Seaford Spinners and Weavers wove a Jubilee Tapestry of the Onkaparinga River, based on an aerial view extending from the Port Noarlunga bridge to the ocean. It, too, was made with hand-spun, vegetable-dyed wool that harmoniously translated the subtle gradations of colour in the natural environment. The tapestry, which took six weavers nearly ten months to complete, was partly subsidised by the council and now hangs in the City of Onkaparinga library at Noarlunga Centre.

Willunga Quilters chose to commemorate the Bicentenary with a pictorial appliqué quilt, on display in the Willunga library. Decorating its sixteen squares are simplistic illustrations of some of the town's historic buildings – Willunga House, Morton's old cottage, the courthouse and the old railway station – together with the Delabole slate quarry and an idealised *Star of Greece* in full sail near the head of the Port Willunga jetty.

Regular arts and crafts markets testify to a lively interest in hand-made articles. The region's best crafts, however, are found at the Old Bank Artel and the Dridan Fine Arts Fleurieu Showcase, both at McLaren Vale. These galleries display and sell selected works with a very high standard of crafts-manship and a particular affinity to the area.

The Artel occupies the former premises of the ES&A bank in McLaren Vale's Main Street. It was born in 1992 when potter Dee Kurauskas and ceramic artist Margo Kellett, looking for an alternative to individual stalls at markets as a way of displaying and selling their products, floated the idea of a cooperative. Fourteen local craftspeople became the first members, and numbers since have fluctuated between eleven and thirteen. Crafts exhibited at the gallery include pottery, glass, jewellery, textiles, furniture, patchwork, woodwork and leather work – together with locally made chutneys and pre-serves, including a glowing grenache jelly. While the cooperative has always followed a conscious policy of maintaining diversity, pottery is always strongly represented.

The McLaren Vale region has an historic association with pottery through Gladys Reynell, grand-daughter of wine pioneer John Reynell and one of Australia's first studio potters. On her return to Australia after the first world war she established a pottery at Reynella, experimenting with various clays until she eventually found a suitable one from McLaren Vale. Later she worked with a white clay which, when glazed with cobalt oxide, turned a rich, deep blue after firing. Gladys often gave pottery pieces to her friend, Margaret Preston, with whom she had studied in England – and Gladys Reynell pottery features in some of Margaret Preston's acclaimed paintings of Australian wildflowers.

The Artel range includes raku-fired pottery from the Port Willunga studio of Dee Kurauskas, Lenore Scott's bowls and platters with fish and crab designs and Margo Kellett's highly glazed tableware with motifs of vine leaves, grapes and olives in clear, bright colours of green, blue, yellow and purple. Douglas Bell contributes wooden bowls of varying sizes fashioned from sheoak, pine, red gum and other woods; Denise Gullidge has a range of hand-knitted jumpers, jackets and berets in mohair, hand-dyed in rich, sombre tones; and Glenn Howlett presents fused and slumped glass objects in pale aquamarine and cobalt blue. In addition, the gallery displays patch-work and embroidered hangings, sheer silk scarves with flashes of emerald and sapphire, sterling silver jewellery and scented candles and soaps.

Glen Howlett stained glass window at
d'Arenberg winery

Some of the same craftspeople are also exhibited at local wineries and at David Dridan's gallery, situated in the old flour mill bought by Thomas Hardy over a hundred years ago. One section of the gallery is devoted to frequently-changing exhibitions by well-regarded Australian artists, often local, such as Mark Pearse with his images of fish, Silvio Apponyi with his naturalistic bronze sculptures and miniatures of native animals, and David and Judy Hardy, whose glazed ceramic table-top tiles and platters feature clean, bold designs of olives, lemons, quinces and sunflowers.

The other section of the gallery specialises in locally-made crafts, among which are Karyn Bradford's luminous silk scarves and hand-painted woollen ties, Margaret Simmonds' appliqué leather bags, Margo Kellett's tableware and Shirley Clare's range of pottery, bowls and platters glazed with Willunga slate to give a soft, dull, charcoal-grey finish that is lightened by a delicate pattern in pure gold around the rim. Like Artel, the Dridan Showcase sells jams, mustards and chutneys together with local olive oil and the delectable

Medlow fruit gels, hand-made nearby at the former Middlebrook property. For several years marine-themed exhibitions have been organised to coincide with the annual McLaren Vale Sea & Vines Festival and a selection of articles from these has been retained, including Mark Pearse's bowls with a blue fish design and glass artist Glenn Howlett's oyster platters, together with his iridised fish plates showing flashes of gold, purple and blue and an amazing stained glass seascape in which a cheeky squid floats above wavering anemones and seaweed. Glenn's art is also on display at his studio in Willunga and in the Willunga Hotel, where a large stained glass panel highlights the historic importance of slate to the town.

The Dridan gallery also stocks a range of woollen products – individual hand-knits, fine woven wool scarves, and imaginative felt hats. Sheep have nowhere near the presence they had in the region earlier this century, but a few small properties in the McLaren Vale-Aldinga area specialise in coloured sheep of different breeds, their fleeces naturally coloured in soft browns and greys, a few almost black.

At Clarendon, Onka Studio specialises in natural fibre fabrics – wool, silk, cotton, mohair, cashmere – that have been woven, screen-printed, hand-painted or dyed by the four members of the cooperative and made into jackets, skirts, scarves and other garments of their own design. Many of the pieces take inspiration from the natural environment of the area; swirls of blue and turquoise on softly draped silk evoke patterns of the sea, while reds and browns repeat the colours of the Onkaparinga gorge.

Wineries have played an important role in promoting local crafts, especially through displays and sales in their tasting areas, and some craftmakers prefer such arrangements. Georgia Rydon's dukkah sets – a platter for the bread and small dishes for the oil and dukkah – are used by Russell Jeavons in his restaurant and are available from Coriole winery. Glazed white with a simple blue scroll around the edge, they can be matched with Georgia's elegant olive oil bottles, also white-glazed with a simple relief pattern.

# ART AND WINE

Art and wine are natural partners, insists David Dridan who introduced art into the Bushing Festival and, through his various galleries, has always encouraged their pairing. 'Winemaker and painter are both artists in their own right,' he says. Unusually, he straddles both domains; primarily a painter, he has also made wine, though more for his own enjoyment and for sharing with friends. His cellar is full of works of art – from the labels to the barrels. Since the early days of his Skottowe winery in 1975 he has persuaded artists such as Clifton Pugh, Charles Blackman, Ray Crooke, Jacqueline Hick and Barry Humphries to use barrel ends as their canvas. Many of the early works were destroyed when the barrels were dismantled, but since then Dridan has shrewdly had duplicate rounds of masonite cut to exactly barrel-end size. For years, too, he has honoured a small number of bottles from each vintage with labels reproducing his own paintings and those of his artist friends. His latest vintage, Tinshack Shiraz 1996, is distinguished by Dridan's own work, together with paintings by David Dallwitz, Lesley Redgate, Sandra Rose, Hugo Shaw and Geoff Wilson. 'You can't paint good pictures if you don't drink good wines,' he declares.

David Dridan's collection is just one of many examples of the art-wine symbiosis in the McLaren Vale region. Since 1989 Coriole's chenin blanc label has displayed Mary (Mollie) Lloyd's naif-style painting of the cottage and winery set in a gently curvaceous landscape and framed by the elong-ated silhouettes of cypress. The same image, reworked by artist Bridget

Coriole winery, by Bridget Ohlsson

Ohlsson in shades of grey, also appears on Coriole's olive oil and vinegars. And Pirramimma's petit verdot and semillon both feature finely detailed abstract designs by Louise Johnston, wife of winemaker Geoffrey Johnston.

Several other wineries have commissioned artists to produce original works of art that complement particular wines. For the Mount Hurtle range of wines, Russell Morrison has produced four paintings of water birds that not only reflect the immediate environment of the winery and its dam, home to wild ducks, Cape Barren geese and black swans, but also pick up the Mount Hurtle logo of three black ducks. Debora Valentine's label for the Mount Bold range from Maxwell's depicts a lone grey-green pine next to a body of water and a shadowy fish, while for the Shilo Park Shiraz from Dennis of McLaren Vale she has painted a landscape in sombre blues, mauves and greens, representing the view towards the hills from Kay's winery.

Within the wineries, too, art accompanies wine. At Seaview winery, bas-relief sculptures mounted on the ends of enormous vats illustrate the six ages of wine, from Culture through Harvest, Vintage, Science, Maturation and Appreciation, this last one showing a man holding a glass of wine to the light while on the table before him are a wedge of cheese and bottles of wine. Bold, strong and dignified, they were carved from West Australian jarrah by Paul Beadle, former director of the Adelaide School of Arts. Outside, in the middle of the lawn between the winery and the old house, is a fountain in the form of a gracefully trellised grape vine, created by Richard Howard in the early 1980s.

Glenn Howlett's richly-coloured stained-glass scene of winepress, barrels and vines complements d'Arenberg's tasting room, while at Hardy's Tintara winery a stained-glass window depicts a cheeky Bacchus astride a barrel of wine. Around him run the words *Wer nicht lieb Wein Weib und Gesang der bleibe ein Narrsein Lebenlang* – in other words, Whoever likes not wine, women and song remains a fool all life long.

Patronage of the arts by the wineries goes back at least as far as the 1950s. An exhibition at McLaren Vale in 1952 featured paintings by Sarah Kay and James Ingoldby (the Onkaparinga at Noarlunga and the garden at Ryecroft). Chateau Reynella organised a Springtime Art Exhibition in 1956, and accompanied it with a cold buffet and Reynella's full range of wines. Woodstock Winery presents an annual Easter Art Affair with art, craft and music. The most significant patronage, however, was announced early in 1998, three McLaren Vale wineries – Maglieri, Rosemount Estate and Wirra Wirra – jointly sponsoring the Fleurieu Prize, Australia's newest and richest landscape art award worth $50,000. Each winery will acquire one of the first three Fleurieu Prize-winning paintings. Concurrently, two additional awards for landscape painting, each worth $10,000, will be made: the Fleurieu Vistas prize, for a painting depicting the landscape of the Fleurieu Peninsula, and the McLaren Vale Prize for a landscape, anywhere in Australia, with a wine theme. In addition, 20 South Australian sculptors will be invited to compete for a $15,000 sculpture prize and an art scholarship will be offered to a young South Australian painter or student.

The first awards in this national biennial competition for Australian landscape painting will be made towards the end of 1998. Organisers expect over 5000 entries for the main prize, from which 100 finalists will be selected and exhibited in a number of different venues in the McLaren Vale area, including wineries. Unlike other competitions and exhibitions, winners will not be announced until a week or so after the exhibitions open. In that interval, a series of dinners and special events combining art, wine and food will allow the public to meet the finalists and view their paintings as artists talk about their works and critics engage in passionate debate. Visitors to the exhibitions will also have the opportunity to vote for a 'People's Choice' in each of the three main awards, the winning artists each receiving the equivalent of $3,333 in wine and cash.

The brainchild of David Dridan, Tony Parkinson and Greg Trott, the art prizes represent yet another way of bringing wine and art together, at the same time drawing attention to the wines and landscapes of an area David Dridan calls 'the most exciting in South Australia'. The generosity of the three wineries, however, extends beyond their local region to benefit Australian art and artists in general.

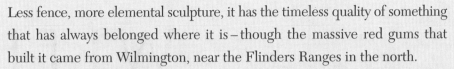

Less fence, more elemental sculpture, it has the timeless quality of something that has always belonged where it is – though the massive red gums that built it came from Wilmington, near the Flinders Ranges in the north.

The idea came from Greg Trott's imagination. In his version of the story, he was trying to explain it to others over a meal at the Salopian Inn and lamenting the difficulty of finding anyone to realise his fantasy when Russell Jeavons, then the restaurant's chef, made an offer to construct the fence. Russell's recollection is that he thought the idea preposterous and said so, but he kept his word and eventually interpreted Greg's vision, applying his own creativity plus a lot of technical skill and experience from his earlier logging days.

Essentially a plain post-and-rail fence as the early settlers used to erect, but on a Cyclopean scale, it was built over two vintages in the late 1980s, using nothing more sophisticated than a fork-lift and a chain-saw. The huge sections of red gum sit on the land, not in it; they are more than two metres in diameter, some weighing over three tonnes.

Symbolically very Australian, it is also, in Russell's view, very masculine, dominating the little valley in a here-I-am-look-at-me way. But its appeal lies in its simplicity and naturalness, and the statement it makes is one of quiet power and inner strength.

# EPILOGUE
## WITH

A year or so of travelling back and forth, between my sources of inspiration and information and my well-worn desk at home, has not only enhanced my knowledge and appreciation of the McLaren Vale region but made me think of it as 'my' region – the one I champion, as others support their favourite football team.

In the course of my work I have discovered new 'old' roads, new 'old' uses for slate, new vistas and new restaurants, and have had the opportunity to meet and talk to a great many fascinating people. Learning the stories of the newcomers who settled in the region one and a half centuries ago I have sympathised with their trials and tribulations, applauded their indomitable spirit and admired the way they adapted themselves and their institutions to a new environment.

Getting to know the region in this undercover and intimate way, from the perspective of an outside-insider, makes me see things differently. I notice changes in light and colour from day to day, from week to week, together with changes in the physical landscape, most commonly represented by yet

# RECIPES

another new vineyard. Where once were sheep, or strawberries, or almonds, are now regiments of permapine posts, at the base of each a life-support system in the form of a slender tube. The world wants wine, we hear, and the bandwagon is too attractive not to jump on board.

History may not always repeat itself, yet a backward glimpse would surely urge caution. Putting all one's eggs in a single basket – a basket full of wine for countries overseas – seems to me not only short-sighted but also, in the long term, potentially dangerous. Certainly, there are precedents for specialisation – in the Burgundy region of France, for example, one vast vineyard stretches from Dijon to Beaune. The wine-producing area is, however, strictly limited and on other terrains other forms of agriculture are practised. Diversity, not monoculture, is more likely to promote regional sustainability.

For most of its 150 years of European settlement the McLaren Vale region has been an area of mixed farming, especially after the 1840s and 1850s when the deterioration in wheat yields, as a result of repeated cropping, warned of the risks of over-specialisation. The district became reasonably self-sufficient, the land producing meat and milk, fruits and vegetables, and wine. Grain was milled locally; cheese and butter were produced on the farm or in local factories; fruits were dried and packed in the cooperative packing house. The clock cannot be turned back, but it is vital to acknowledge the importance to the region of producing at least some, and probably a significant proportion, of its own food needs. This has relevance to the present. As wine and food are natural partners, so a wine culture needs the complement of a food culture, which in turn must develop from a base of local resources, both ingredients and cooks.

In their primitive kitchens, early settlers seem to have been content to use local foods in familiar and traditional ways, their dishes being simple and sustaining. Special occasions would have called for a feast, which usually meant more in terms of quantity and variety though not necessarily different ways of preparation. Describing the dinner that followed the Willunga District Ploughing Match in 1851 the *Register* commented that it had been:

*provided by the worthy Host of the Bush Inn, with a profusion that evidently over-rated the proverbial capacity of ploughmen's appetites. Of the entertainment it might be said truly –*

> *'Here plenty reigns, and from her boundless hoard,*
> *Though not one jelly trembles on the board,*
> *Supplies the feast with all that sense can crave;*
> *With all that made our great forefathers brave,*
> *Ere the cloy'd palate countless flavours tried*
> *And cooks had nature's judgment set aside.'*

*It was, indeed, superior in viands, cookery, and attendance, to the generality of occasional dinners, and the Host, as if resolved to bring it within the means of every man and boy on the field, fixed the admission at the unremunerative price of 2s. each. As might have been expected, the room was filled with quite as many as it could accommodate.*

It would probably be wishful thinking to believe that the food offered on such occasions was particular to the region, though it may well have been typical and the ingredients of local origin. Nor could anyone today claim a distinctive cuisine for the McLaren Vale region. Similarly, of regional foods – local, distinctive ingredients of high quality – it now has very few apart from almonds, olives and olive oil, and fruit, especially summer stone fruit. Yet even the remnant fruit orchards are disappearing, victims of the cargo cult mentality that puts its faith in vineyards alone.

The continued presence of the orchards probably depends on their returning as much profit as vineyards, which in turn probably means value-adding. Value-adding has the opportunity to produce distinctly regional products which, ideally, would demonstrate a sense of belonging to the region, relating to and reflecting something of the region's past traditions.

In the old days seasonal gluts were turned into jams and chutneys and pickles. Visitors to the region today seek something different to take home, products which offer both individuality and superior quality. An alternative to jam might be intensely flavoured fruit 'spreads' with a high proportion of fruit and less sugar, while an alternative to chutneys, typically sweet, vinegary and hot (with either cayenne or chilli) could be a variant of the Italian mustard fruits, possibly with hot chillies taking the place of hot mustard oil. Other fruit products worth investigating might be luscious fruit pastes, similar to the jewel-like sugar-coated 'pâtes de fruits' that are a speciality of southern France, or brandied fruits, harking back to the days when Hardys, Horndale and others distilled spirit and made brandy.

Some of these products are already produced on a small scale. At Woodstock Coterie Kay Cazzolato has been making limited quantities of mustard fruits for the past six years, mainly to serve in the restaurant. Under the Fleurieu Fine Foods label Jill Chinner bottles spiced brandied figs and spiced brandied fruit. For the present, however, none of these products is sufficiently distinctive to be branded 'regional'.

An awareness of what a regional cuisine might mean is slowly developing, and two teams from the region – one led by Russell Jeavons and the other by Andrew Davies – presented menus in the Australian Regional Culinary Competition held in Adelaide in 1997. Along with this awareness is a realisation that the McLaren Vale region, with so few foods of its own, must extend its gathering arms to source ingredients from the southern Fleurieu, in much the same way as the Burgundy wine region relies on beef from the other side of the range for its celebrated boeuf bourguignon. Between Sellicks Hills Range and the southern coast is predominantly grazing land, producing beef, veal, lamb and pork as well as milk, cream and cheese – including goat cheese. These ingredients, as well as the harvest of the sea, can help form the basis of a regional cuisine, so long as producers and cooks work together, collaboratively and cooperatively.

Two points are absolutely vital. One is that a regional cuisine has to be a people's cuisine. Certainly, it should be offered in restaurants so that tourists can experience it, and restaurants might also give it a professional flourish, but it should also be accessible to domestic cooks who can prepare a special regional dish for a special day, or proudly offer visitors a dish that says, 'This is what we produce here and this is how we cook it.' Second, it must acknowledge the past, the resources and practices and traditions that are already there. The *terra nullius* principle must apply also in cuisine; no one can lay claim to a regional cuisine and invent it anew.

The following recipes from past and present will give some idea of the European gastronomic heritage of the region.

# KANGAROO STEAMER

James Hawker cooked and ate kangaroo steamer when surveying the region in 1838 and 1839. It was clearly a popular dish in all the colonies and probably the first authentically Australian (as opposed to Aboriginal) dish invented. Edward Abbott gave three recipes in his 1864 book *The English and Australian Cookery Book*, the simplest of which is as follows:

*Take the most tender part of the kangaroo, being careful to remove all the sinews. Chop it very fine, about the same quantity of smoked bacon (fat); season with finely powdered marjoram, pepper and a very little salt. Let it steam, or stew, for two hours …*

More sophisticated recipes added a glass of port or strongly-flavoured mushroom ketchup to the gravy and recommended serving the dish with rice.

# BERTHA PRIOR'S RECIPES

The following group of recipes, reproduced as they were written, come from a manuscript recipe book compiled by Willunga resident Bertha Prior over a period from the 1890s to around 1930. The book passed to Bertha's daughter Ethel, who for many years worked for Basil Dunstan when he was District Clerk at Willunga. It is now the property of the Willunga branch of the National Trust, having been bought at the Dunstan auction in the early 1970s. Since many of the recipes are attributed to various ladies of Willunga (Miss Goode the storekeeper, Mrs White of the Canberra Hotel, Mrs Culley and Mrs Jacobs), the book probably gives a fairly accurate, if partial, representation of food cooked and eaten in the district around the end of the nineteenth and early twentieth century.

## ALMOND FINGERS (B.M.D.)

½ lb S.R. flour • ¼ lb butter • 1 tablespoon sugar • ¼ lb almonds •
½ lb icing sugar

Rub butter into flour, add sugar, mix with yoke of one egg & a little milk.
Roll thin. Beat white of egg, mix in icing sugar, paste on top, sprinkle with
almonds.

## CONGRESS TARTS (Ty Kelly)

¼ lb ground almonds • 2 tablespoons caster sugar • 2 eggs • ¼ lb rasp jam
• a few drops essence almonds • sufficient pastry to line patty tins

Mix sugar and almonds beat eggs to a froth and stir in sugar and add
flavouring line tins with paste and put in each one 1 teaspoon raspberry
jam covering it with spoon mixture. Bake.

## NUT BREAD

2 cups flour self raising • ¾ cup milk • ½ cup sugar • 2 eggs • 2 ounces
butter • pinch salt • 4 oz chopped almonds • a few sultanas

Mix all together. Put in long cocoa tins. Bake ¾ hour.

## SWISS ROLL

Beat three eggs well add one teacup of sugar the same of flour 1 teaspoon of
cream tartar. Mix in flour ½ teaspoonful of c. soda dissolved in a very little
boiling water, mix well and bake in a quick oven.

## DIGGER BISCUITS (Florrie Lane)

1 cup plain flour • 2 cups of oatmeal or rolled oats • ½ cup of butter or
dripping • 1 cup sugar • 1½ tablespoon treacle • 3 tablespoon hot water •
½ teaspoon of carbonated soda

Make as biscuits.

## DIGGER NUTS

*1 cup plain flour • 1 cup sugar • 2 rolled oats and a few chopped armonds*

*Put ¾ cup butter 3 tablespoons of water 1½ tablespoons of treacle in a saucepan when boiling add 1 teaspoon carb soda have dry ingredients in a bowl pour boiling mixture over knead well & put on cold slide in little drops. Bake in a cool oven.*

## POOR MANS PUDDING

*¼ lb of suet • ¼ lb currants • ¼ raisins stoned • ½ cup sugar flour • breadcrumbs • 2 large tablesp treacle • 1 teasp soda • 2 eggs*

*Steam 4 hours.*

## QUINCE JELLY

*Let quinces be ripe and yellow. Wipe but do not peel. Cut them in slices. Put in a preserve pan, shake well or stir, barely cover with water. Let boil gently till soft. Turn them into jelly bag and let jelly drain from them.*

*Boil 15 minutes, take from fire, stir 2 oz sugar to one pint juice, boil again. Remove scum as it rises. Boil until it sets. Boil quickly or colour will not be good.*

## MELON MARMALADE (Mrs Taylor, School mistress)

*2 lbs melon • 3 lemons • 8 breakfast cups of water • 7 lbs sugar*

*Cut up melon and lemons and put the water over, let stand all night. Boil till tender then add sugar & boil until it jellies.*

## FIG CHUTNEY (Mrs White, Canberra Hotel)

*Cut up 4 lb figs • 1 lb cooking apples • 6 onions*

*Put all together in saucepan with a bottle brown vinegar and allow to boil for ½ hour. 1 teaspoon salt 1 tablespoon dry mustard ½ cup treacle 1 oz pepper corns boil ½ hour then put 1 lb sugar boil 2 hours.*

## WORCESTER SAUCE (Mother's recipe)

*½ gallon dark vinegar • 1 cup golden syrup • 1 cup Damson jam • ¼ lb garlic well bruised • ¼ lb whole ginger • 1 oz cloves • 1 oz cayenne pepper*

*Boil all together 2 hours not let it simmer but boil all the time. When cold strain through a colander and strainer. When cold bottle.*

## TOMATO SAUCE

*Boil 12 lb tomato until it is all disolved strain it add 3 pints vinegar • 8 ounces onions • 8 ounces salt • ½ ounce chillies • 2 ounces pepper ground • ½ ounce cloves • ½ ounce mace • ½ ounce ground allspice.*

*Burn little sugar to make look good couler & good taste. Boil well strain and cork tight.*

## PLUM SAUCE

*6 lbs plums • 2 lbs sugar • 3 pints vinegar • 3 teaspoonfuls salt • 2 teaspoonfuls black pepper • 1 teaspoonful cayenne pepper • 1 teaspoonful ground ginger • 1 oz cloves.*

*Boil together 2 hours, bottle when cold, cork & seal.*

## LEMON YEAST FOR BREAD

*juice of one lemon • 1 tablespoon flour • 1 dessert spoon sugar • 1 teaspoon salt • enough boiling water to make dough*

*Pour boiling water on lemon sugar when cold add sugar [probably should be flour] salt next day set your dough.*

# ELVA DYER'S RECIPES

Elva Dyer, a stalwart of the local show circuit, also has her handwritten notebooks of annotated recipes, a record of her prize-winning cakes and jams and jellies. The following represent a selection of her show champions, never before confided – let alone published!

The following three sauces were always entered in the show section for three different sauces, one bottle each.

## APRICOT SAUCE

*1 lb white sugar • 3 lbs ripe apricots • 1½ pints light malt vinegar • 3 teaspoons salt • ½ teaspoon cayenne pepper • 1 teaspoon ground ginger*

*Tie all these in a muslin bag: 1½ teaspoons cloves • 1 teaspoon whole allspice • 2 teaspoons whole peppercorns • 1 oz garlic cut up*

*Boil all together gently 2 hrs and strain, then heat up again and bottle.*

## PLUM SAUCE

*1 lb white sugar • 3 lbs ripe plums • 1½ pints light malt vinegar • 3 tsp salt • ½ teaspoon cayenne pepper • 1 teaspoon ground ginger*

*Tie these in muslin bag: 1½ teaspoon cloves • 1 teaspoon whole allspice • 2 teaspoon whole peppercorns • 1 oz garlic*

*Boil all together for 2 or 3 hours then strain. Heat up again and bottle.*

## TOMATO SAUCE

*12 lbs red ripe tomatoes • 3 oz salt • 2 onions (sliced) • 2 lbs sugar • 1 pt Anchor malt vinegar*

*Boil 2 hrs and strain then add spices in muslin bag: 1 oz whole allspice • 1 oz peppercorns • ½ oz cloves • 2 oz garlic chopped*

*Then add: 1 tspn ginger • 1½ teaspoons cayenne pepper*

*Boil for another 1½ hrs and bottle.*

## FRUIT CHUTNEY

1½ lb apples peeled & cut in slices • 1½ lb dark plums sliced • 1½ lbs ripe tomatoes, put boiling water over & skin them & slice • 2 lbs sugar • ½ lb seeded raisins • 1 quart malt vinegar • ½ tablespoon white pepper • ⅛ teaspoon cayenne pepper or ¼ tsp • ½ tablespoon ground ginger

Put in muslin bag: ¾ tablespoon whole cloves • ¾ tablespoon whole allspice • ½ tablespoon mace

Put all in pan and cook for 1½ hours & bottle.

## PLUM CHUTNEY

3 lbs red plums stoned and sliced • 1 large onion sliced • 2 oz garlic (sliced in bag) • 1 pint vinegar • 2 cups white sugar • 1 level dessertspoon ground ginger • 1 level dspoon ground cloves • 1 level dspoon salt • ¼ or ½ teaspoon cayenne pepper

Cook all together slowly 2 hrs & bottle.

## TOMATO CHUTNEY

3 lbs ripe tomatoes sliced • 2 large apples peeled & sliced • 1 small onion peeled & sliced • ½ lb sugar • ½ pt vinegar • ½ tsp cayenne pepper (level) • ½ level tablespoon salt

Tie in bag: ½ tsp cloves whole • ¼ oz whole ginger • 1 oz garlic chopped in bag

Boil for 1½ hours rapidly & bottle.

## APRICOT JAM

4 lbs apricots ripe, cut in halves • 5 lbs sugar • 1 cup hot water

Leave ½ hr with water on before cooking. Boil all together fast for 15 min & add 1 level teaspoon tartaric acid. Bottle jam hot.

## TOMATO & PINEAPPLE JAM

*2 lb sugar • 2 lb ripe tomatoes (skinned) • ½ tin strained crushed pineapple • 2 lemons juice only strained*

*Bring fruit to boil for a few mins, then add 2 lbs sugar & boil 30 mins. Bottle jam hot.*

## PLUM JELLY

*3 lbs firm slightly underripe red plums (Santa Rosa) • 1½ pts water • sugar*

*Wash & chop plums, add water & simmer slowly until tender 1 hr. Strain through muslin, add 1 cup juice to 1 cup sugar & juice of 1 lemon (strained). Boil rapidly for 15 mins. Bottle while hot.*

## BOILED PLUM PUDDING

This, says Elva, is a very important and much sought-after recipe, her mother's recipe which won her first prize everywhere.

*¼ lb bread crumbs • ¼ lb S.R. flour • ¼ lb butter • ¼ lb brown sugar • ¾ lb currants • ¼ lb raisins • ½ lb sultanas • ¼ lb mixed peel • ¼ teaspoon allspice • ¼ teaspoon cinnamon • 5 eggs • ¼ cup brandy • 2 oz almonds minced & rolled*

*Mix all the fruit & bread crumbs, with a little flour. Beat butter & sugar to a cream, add eggs, then all fruit, flour, etc. Put a pudding cloth in boiling water for 1 min & wring out & then sprinkle it with flour to stop sticking. Put mixture in cloth & tie tightly. Boil for 5 hrs & 1½ hrs second time.*

## SPONGE SANDWICH

*4 eggs* (they must be fresh, specifies Elva) • *½ cup sugar* • *¾ cup Nurse's corn flour* • *2 teaspoon plain flour* • *1 teaspoon cream tartar* • *½ teaspoon carb soda*

*Sift flour etc 3 times*
*1 tsp butter* • *1 tsp milk*

*Beat whites of eggs stiff, then add yolks & beat again till stiff, then add sugar & beat again then add sifted flour etc. Boil milk & butter, stir in quickly. Put into 2 x 8" baking tins. Then cook at 190° for 20 mins.*

## SPONGE ROLL (Elva's masterpiece)

*3 eggs* • *½ cup sugar* • *¾ cup Nurse's corn flour* • *2 teaspoon plain flour* • *1 teaspoon cream tartar* • *½ teaspoon carb soda* • *1 tsp butter & 1 milk melted*

*Beat white of eggs stiff then add yolks & beat stiff then sugar & beat again then gradually add sifted flour etc. Have a sponge roll tin lined with greaseproof paper. Pour mixture in & bake in oven 180° 10 mins. Have a damp towel ready to lay hot sponge on, spread quickly with rasp jam & roll up quickly & tight.*

# NANCY WEISBRODT,
## SUMMER AT ALDINGA BEACH

When Nancy Weisbrodt's family spent summer holidays at their shack at Aldinga Beach, the family lived on fish and rabbit. Her father, a passionate fisherman, had a paper maché boat – the only one of its kind, she says – which he would row out to just beyond the edge of the reef to fish for snapper and snook. Mullet and tommy ruffs were caught from the beach, salmon were netted. There were no facilities for freezing, so whatever was surplus to the family's requirements was given away or sold; on one supremely successful day in 1951 they sold 22 snapper weighing a total of 236 lb (107 kg).

Back at the shack, the filleted fish – or sliced as cutlets, if large – would be cooked in 'spitting hot' beef dripping in a heavy cast iron frying pan on a wood stove, and served with lemon wedges (the family always brought a load of their lemons to the beach), salt and pepper, bread and butter and mashed potato or, occasionally, chips cooked in beef dripping. The fish was rarely floured before frying, though fillets were sometimes coated in egg and breadcrumbs or a thick batter – probably to make them go further. Fish heads were boiled, the flesh taken off the bones and allowed to set; this 'jellied fish' was spread on bread to make fish sandwiches. As a variation, whole small snapper were steamed and served with a parsley sauce. Blue swimmer crabs were simply boiled.

Rabbit was eaten a couple of times a week. In Nancy's family the children used snares, though neighbouring children had ferrets; her father would shoot them, and the occasional hare. Hares would be hung for several days (her father, having grown up in England, liked to follow English custom) then gutted, skinned and jointed before being marinated in red wine and prepared as jugged hare. The pieces of hare would be floured then browned in dripping, water plus some of the marinade added together with onion, bacon and mixed herbs, and the dish cooked very slowly. It was very rich and very gamey in Nancy's memory, but her father loved it because it reminded him of England.

Rabbit was stewed or made into a pie, probably following a recipe very similar to the one following. It comes from *The School of Mines Cookery Book*, first published in Adelaide in 1930 and religiously followed by Nancy's mother.

RABBIT PIE
*1 rabbit • ¼ lb bacon • 1 teaspoon salt • ¼ teaspoon pepper •*
*1 hard-boiled egg • 1 tablespoon flour • 1 dessertspoon chopped parsley •*
*pinch of herbs • 3 tablespoons stock or water • ½ lb rough puff pastry*

*Wash rabbit. Dry, and joint it. Mix flour, seasoning and parsley together and dip joints into it. Put a layer of rabbit at the bottom of the piedish, then a layer of bacon cut into small pieces. Add the egg (cut into slices), and the stock. Fill up the dish with the rest of the rabbit and bacon.*

*Roll pastry out to about one-third of an inch in thickness, keeping the pastry about one inch larger than the piedish to be covered. Cut off a strip around the sides of the pastry. Moisten the edges of the dish and place the strip on it. Moisten the edges again and place the remaining piece of pastry over the pie. Trim off the rough edges of the pastry and decorate. Make a hole in the middle of the pie to allow the steam to escape whilst baking. Glaze the pastry with beaten egg. Place the pie in a hot oven until the pastry is risen, then reduce the heat and cook for about 1½ hours.*

## ⬥ BACCHUS CLUB ⬥

For many years, Clive Whitrow, licensee of the Port Noarlunga Hotel, was foodmaster of the McLaren Vale branch of the Bacchus Club. The club would hold its annual general meeting in the hotel, and there would be two or three other dinners (men only) throughout the year, together with a big picnic to which ladies were also invited. Dinners were held at the Port

Noarlunga Hotel and at other hotels in the region, and club lunches were often hosted by wineries. As foodmaster, Clive Whitrow had responsibility for organising the menu (in consultation with the committee) and talking about the food served.

Dinners were mainly held during the winter months when wineries were less busy. They began with savouries, served with a flor fino sherry in front of the hotel's warming fire. Then came soup, usually homemade – pea soup, or consomme, for example – but occasionally canned turtle or toheroa soup. The entree was often whiting, crumbed and served with a tartare sauce, but sometimes devilled kidneys and once, yabbies. At a lunch at Kay's winery, Clive once poached fillets of whiting in sea water and accompanied them with tartare sauce and salad. The main course was typically roast; roast beef was very popular, but roast lamb was seen as 'too ordinary'.

Desserts were very simple – sometimes a homely baked custard, but more often icecream doused with one's choice of liqueur and accompanied by strawberries in season or, one year, by poached cherries. Another dessert served with icecream was pawpaw which had been filled with rum, or port, or some liqueur, and allowed to mature for three days or so. Finally came a selection of four or five different cheeses, local if possible.

In the 1950s the range of ingredients locally procurable was quite limited, but with the resourcefulness of all good gastronomes the Bacchus Club put on some splendid dinners. Quail shot in the nearby paddocks – allowing two per person, eighty were needed for a dinner – were marinated in port for a few days then roasted and served with gravy and vegetables. Wild ducks, both black and teal, were sent up by shooters in the Langhorne Creek area; these were hung (with their feathers on) for a few days then marinated in port before roasting. Also from the Langhorne Creek vineyards came hare; these had two weeks hanging in the coolroom before being skinned, washed in vinegar and again marinated in port.

In those days, according to Clive, there was always plenty of tuna in Gulf waters; he could go fishing off Glenelg for a couple of hours in the afternoon and return with three or four large fish, 10 kg or more. Some of these tuna were once served for a Spanish dinner, which began with an entree of spaghetti with Goolwa cockles. Thick fillets of tuna, about 400–500 g, were laid on a sheet of aluminium foil, and topped with sliced tomatoes and onions, chopped olives and gherkins, pepper and salt and shavings of butter. The sealed parcels were baked for about 45 minutes. No one was allowed to open his parcel until all had been served, so that everyone experienced simultaneously the wonderful aromas.

The Bacchus Club is still active in the McLaren Vale region under current foodmaster Norm Doole and winemaster Mark Maxwell. Its committee still organises five or six functions a year, some at local restaurants and others featuring unusual foods or unusual locations – a lunch of fresh marron and fresh lobster on Kangaroo Island, for example. The male dominance of the early years has disappeared, and in 1996/97 Pip Forrester of the Salopian Inn was not only president of the McLaren Vale Bacchus Club but the first female to preside over a Bacchus Club in Australia.

## ⟶ THE BARN ⟵

The Barn's first cook was Mrs Ruby MacMillan.'Mrs Mac', as 'she was commonly known, often catered for cellar parties in the early years of the McLaren Vale Wine Bushing Festival. In 1974 her suggestions for a 'memorable McLaren Vale meal' included an appetiser of asparagus surprise (a gratin of asparagus and hard-boiled eggs, with plenty of grated cheese) to serve with dry sherry; entree of baked whole snapper in white wine, seasoned with pineapple, breadcrumbs, capsicums and onions, with riesling; main course of roast boned leg of pork, stuffed with prunes and apples, accompanied by dry red wine or moselle; and for sweets, old fashioned apple pie with fresh cream or halved Duchess pears cooked in red wine, with sauvignon blanc to drink.

In its early days the Barn offered a fairly limited menu. In addition to the traditional ploughman's lunch (bread, a wedge of cheese and pickled onions) there would be the 'soup of the day', always served at the table in individual tureens and accompanied by small loaves of bread for diners to slice; the day's roast, pie and casserole; and three desserts – apple pie, apricot pie and Negritas. A rich chocolate mousse, Negritas (which probably took its name from a brand of rum common in France) was enormously popular, one regular customer admitting to being 'a three Negritas person'! The restaurant's recipe clearly takes account of such appetites, but quantities can be reduced for smaller gatherings.

## NEGRITAS

*1.6 kg dark chocolate • 5 dozen eggs, separated • 2 tspns caster sugar •*
*5 caps vanilla essence • ½ flagon brandy (Hardy's Black Bottle) •*
*3 level tblspns gelatine (or 28 leaves gelatine)*

*Roughly chop chocolate, melt in a bowl over boiling water. When melted stir in egg yolks, sugar, vanilla essence and brandy. Dissolve gelatine in a little boiling water and add to chocolate mixture. Whisk egg whites to firm peaks and fold in. Pour into glasses and allow to set in refrigerator. Serve decorated with whipped cream and a fanned strawberry.*

On a domestic scale, proportions are roughly 160 g chocolate, 6 eggs, ½ teaspoon caster sugar, ½ teaspoon vanilla essence, almost ½ cup brandy, and about 3 leaves of gelatine, or about 1½ teaspoons of powdered gelatine.

# PIP FORRESTER, SALOPIAN INN

With the help of chefs Pete Hogg and Justin Harman, Pip Forrester not only runs a successful restaurant and catering business but produces a small range of take-home products, sold under the McLaren Vale Regional Produce label. They include kasundi – a hot Indian relish – dukkah and two olive oils, including the 'Two Groves' made from wild olives harvested from two nearby vineyards. Together with spiced McLaren Vale kalamata olives, dukkah with olive oil is a permanent fixture on the restaurant's seasonally-changed menu, but Pip also combines it with chicken and adds it to pastry to give a light nutty flavour.

## SPICED McLAREN VALE KALAMATA OLIVES

*1 tspn fennel seed • 1 tblspn cumin seed • 1 tblspn ajowan seed (an Indian spice) • ½ tspn caraway seed • 1 kg kalamata olives • 1 small red onion, finely chopped • 1 tblspn parsley, finely chopped • 1 tspn fresh chilli, finely chopped • 2 tblspns olive oil*

*Dry roast all the spices in a heavy pan over low heat until fragrant – this takes only a few minutes. Cool. Add to olives together with remaining ingredients, mix well. Use immediately. Store in refrigerator if necessary, but no longer than 2–3 days.*

## DUKKAH CHICKEN

*6 chicken leg fillets • 3 tblspns olive oil • 100 g McLaren Vale Regional Produce dukkah • freshly ground black pepper*

*In a bowl combine the chicken, oil, dukkah and pepper, allow to stand for 30–60 minutes. Bake or barbecue for about 15 minutes, serve with salad.*

When the Salopian Inn catered for the twilight picnic-cum-cricket match for the Shiraz Ashes on Port Willunga beach, Pip Forrester's menu highlighted Australian ingredients such as yabbies, tuna steaks and kangaroo steaks together with locally-produced olives and olive oil, limes and cherries. The meal began with spiced olives, dukkah with olive oil and miniature goat cheese tarts. From the barbecue hotplate came prawns cooked in their shells and served with preserved lime mayonnaise; yabbies with a whipped lime butter; tuna steaks accompanied by caponata; and kangaroo fillet with a garnish of pickled cherries. Desserts were lemon tart with dukkah pastry and one of the Salopian favourites, chocolate, fig and nut tart.

## TARTLETS OF GOAT CHEESE, TOMATO AND BASIL

PASTRY:

*100 g Brehin's goat cheese • 1½ tblspns freshly grated parmesan cheese • 150 g unsalted butter, softened • scant pinch salt • ¼ tspn cayenne pepper • 175 g plain flour, sifted*

*Blend cheeses, butter, salt and cayenne quickly in a food processor until smooth. Remove to a bowl and fold in flour. Refrigerate pastry for several hours, then roll out thinly and line small tart tins. Bake at 180° for 10 minutes, cool.*

FILLING:

*Brehin's goat cheese, roughly crumbled • firm ripe tomatoes, diced • basil leaves, torn • olive oil • freshly ground black pepper*

*Lightly combine ingredients, put into pastry cases and warm under salamander or oven grill until cheese is slightly melted.*

## PRESERVED LIME MAYONNAISE

*2 egg yolks • ½ tblspn vinegar • 1 tspn Dijon mustard • 75 ml each olive oil and peanut oil, mixed together • finely pureed rind of 1 preserved lime • sugar to taste*

*Lightly beat egg yolks, vinegar, preserved lime puree and mustard, gradually add oil while continuing to beat. Taste, add a little sugar to balance the acidity of the lime.*

*Preserved limes are not available commercially but can be prepared in the same way as preserved lemons.*

## WHIPPED LIME BUTTER WITH OLIVE OIL

*100 g unsalted butter, at room temperature • 50 ml olive oil • 1 tspn chilli jam • 30 ml fresh lime juice • 2 Kaffir lime leaves, very finely shredded*

*Whip butter until pale and fluffy. Gradually add olive oil, as for mayonnaise, then remaining ingredients. Serve at room temperature.*

*This butter can be refrigerated, but bring back to room temperature before using.*

## CAPONATA

This is a slight variant on the recipe in Stephanie Alexander's book *The Cook's Companion* (1996).

*2 eggplants, cut into 2 cm cubes • salt • 1 cup olive oil • 1 onion, sliced • ½ cup well-drained capers • 1½ cups fresh tomato sauce • ½ cup white wine vinegar • 2 tblspns sugar • ¾ cup toasted pinenuts*

*Sprinkle eggplant with salt, leave in a colander to drain for an hour. Rinse well, drain, dry and fry in ⅔ of the oil until golden. Drain on absorbent paper. Saute onion in remaining oil until it begins to colour. Add capers, tomato sauce, vinegar and sugar and simmer for 5 minutes. Stir in eggplant cubes, simmer 10 minutes longer. Check seasoning, cool then refrigerate for 24 hours. Bring back to room temperature before serving, sprinkled with pinenuts.*

*At the Salopian, Caponata often accompanies fish dishes, venison and kangaroo carpaccio.*

## PICKLED CHERRIES

*2 kg cherries • 1.4 kg sugar • 800 ml red wine • 1.2 l Coriole red wine vinegar • 40 g fresh ginger, sliced thinly • 5 g native pepper leaf (optional) • 1 tblspn white peppercorns • 1 cinnamon stick*

*Trim stalks of cherries, pit if desired. In a large pan, dissolve sugar in red wine and vinegar. Add ginger and spices, simmer 10 minutes. Allow pickling liquid to cool then pour over cherries packed into jars. Seal, leave for about 3 weeks before eating.*

## LEMON TART WITH DUKKAH CRUST

### PASTRY

*90 g butter • 2 ½ tblspns icing sugar • 1 egg yolk • 1 scant cup plain flour • 25 g McLaren Vale Regional Produce dukkah, ground very finely • 2 tspns water • 1 egg white, lightly beaten*

*Cream together butter and icing sugar, add egg yolk then fold in flour and dukkah. Add water as necessary to achieve a malleable consistency. Refrigerate for 30 minutes then roll out between two sheets of baking paper. Press into 23 cm flan tin and refrigerate for 30 minutes until firm. Bake blind at 200° for 15–20 minutes, until lightly brown, then brush pastry surface with egg white and return to oven for another 5 minutes longer to seal. Cool.*

### FILLING

*120 g unsalted butter • 200 ml lemon juice • 400 g sugar • 2 egg yolks • 65 g cornflour*

*Melt butter, then combine with remaining ingredients in a heatproof bowl. Cook over hot water, stirring continuously, until custard consistency. Cool to room temperature before filling tart case. Refrigerate for about 6 hours before serving.*

## CHOCOLATE, FIG AND NUT TART

PASTRY

*175 g flour • 110 g unsalted butter, preferably from freezer • 1 tspn sugar • 1 small egg yolk • 1 tblspn milk*

*Place flour, butter and sugar in food processor and pulse to crumble texture (the butter should be well incorporated). Transfer to a bowl, work in egg yolk and milk, knead lightly to form a dough. Refrigerate for 30 minutes then roll out between two sheets of baking paper. Press into 23 cm flan tin and refrigerate for 30 minutes until firm. Line pastry shell with baking paper, fill with dried beans and bake blind at 200° for 5–6 minutes, then remove paper and beans and return to oven for another 2–3 minutes.*

FILLING

*75 g dried figs • 250 g dark chocolate (Haigh's) • 1½ tblspns brandy • 110 ml cream • 30 g unsalted butter • 3 tblspns sugar • 1½ tblspns honey • ¼ tspn ground aniseed (optional) • 60 g pine nuts • 30 g blanched slivered almonds • 90 g whole almonds, roughly chopped*

*Chop dried figs, discard stalks. Roughly chop chocolate. Place all ingredients in a saucepan and cook over gentle heat, stirring until chocolate has melted and mixture is smooth. Pour into prepared pastry case and bake at 180° for 15–20 minutes. Cool before serving.*

## ANDREW DAVIES, D'ARRY'S VERANDAH RESTAURANT

While Andrew Davies certainly does not eschew butter, he also likes to serve interesting variations on traditional 'butter' recipes by substituting extra virgin olive oil. His Olive Oil Potato Purée accompanies many dishes, including whiting, briefly smoked before pan-frying; with the addition of finely chopped dill it is served with steamed or poached Atlantic salmon. The Olive Oil Hollandaise is a component of one of the restaurant's signature dishes, Deep-fried oysters with olive oil hollandaise, courgettes and Old Vine Shiraz sauce. It is also the base for sauces such as mustard mousseline (served with roasted veal loin); mixed with aubergine puree it becomes aubergine hollandaise, an accompaniment to steamed loin of lamb.

## OLIVE OIL POTATO PURÉE

*350 g evenly diced potatoes (peeled) • 2 teaspoons salt • 30 g unsalted butter • 30 ml warm milk • 80 ml (4 tblspns) extra virgin olive oil • salt to taste*

*Cover the diced potatoes with water, add the salt and bring to a boil. Reduce heat and simmer until the potatoes are almost falling apart (25–35 mins). Remove from heat and gently strain out as much of the water as possible. Pass the hot boiled potatoes through a very fine mesh sieve using a spatula (to remove any lumps). Return the potato purée to the pot and over a low heat slowly fold in the butter, the warm milk and finally the olive oil until a very smooth, creamy texture is achieved.*

*NB. Depending on the variety of potato used (Colibans are good for purée) and the amount of excess moisture after straining (the drier the potato, the better the purée), more or less milk plus butter may need to be used.*

*Practice and timing are the two most essential ingredients in making a very smooth, very creamy potato purée.*

## OLIVE OIL HOLLANDAISE

*½ cup white malt vinegar • 1 shallot, chopped • about 30 sprigs thyme • 10 white peppercorns • 4 large egg yolks • 3 tblspns water • pinch of salt • 250 ml extra virgin olive oil*

*Infuse vinegar with shallot, thyme, peppercorns and reduce by half over moderately high heat. Strain.*

*Mix egg yolks, vinegar reduction, water and salt in a stainless steel mixing bowl. Vigorously whisk ingredients together over a double boiler until a ribbon stage is achieved, taking care not to cook the yolks. Once a very light and fluffy texture is achieved remove the bowl from the heat and straight away whisk the olive oil into the egg mixture with a slow, even, pouring motion and a fast, rhythmic, whisking motion, ensuring that the hollandaise does not split.*

*Serve at once or keep at room temperature until ready to serve.*

## ⟜ RUSSELL JEAVONS' ⟞ CATERING

Russell prefers the primordial fire for his cooking. At his Willunga restaurant, most of the dishes are cooked in his wood-fired oven (which also bakes bread and pizza) or directly over the coals of his outside fire; when catering at other venues he often uses gas-fired barbecues. He relies on many local suppliers who provide him with fresh ingredients – organically-grown raspberries, farm-grown marron from Mount Compass, geese in autumn. In addition Russell seeks out wild foods such as rose hips (for jelly) and fennel (for his dukkah). Dukkah is a Middle Eastern blend of nuts and spices which Russell introduced to the McLaren Vale region. Other local restaurants and caterers have since produced and commercialised their own individual blends.

Given the quality of his raw materials and the resources of his kitchen, Russell's cooking is honest and uncontrived. He often likes to add flavour by means of an olive oil marinade for foods to be barbecued or roasted. This is not simply a coating, he maintains; the olive oil enters into and forms a relationship with the food, complementing and enhancing its inherent qualities.

Russell's barbecue or roasting marinade is simply extra virgin olive oil plus his standard seasoning mix (3 or 4 parts salt to one part pepper), together with the appropriate aromatics – which, he stresses, must be dry, not wet;

flavourings such as lemon juice, fresh parsley and fresh basil should be added at the end of cooking. Meat should be lean and trimmed of external fat and marinated overnight or for 2–3 hours as it comes to room temperature. For lamb steaks and cutlets he suggests crushed garlic and fresh rosemary; for fish, grated lemon rind; for prawns, grated lemon rind plus chilli; for quail and chicken, garlic and crushed thyme. Vegetables such as sliced fennel, mushrooms, pieces of pumpkin and halved zucchini also benefit from this treatment. Be generous with the olive oil, advises Russell, but don't waste it; splashing it over the foods on the barbecue is futile and senseless.

## ALMOND TORTE

Russell makes quite a few desserts which take advantage of the sweet almonds from the area. This cake, which gives him the opportunity of using surplus egg whites, is typically served with fresh strawberries or raspberries, or poached fruit, plus thick cream.

*300 g ground blanched almonds (almond meal) • 1 tblspn plain flour • 8 egg whites • 200 g caster sugar*

*Sift almonds and flour through sieve (set aside the ⅓ cup too coarse to pass through sieve). Beat egg whites until stiff, gradually beat in caster sugar to make a soft peak meringue. Gradually sprinkle over the almond-and-flour mixture while at the same time gently and carefully folding it into the meringue. Depending on the size of the eggs, it may not be necessary to use all the almonds; the mixture should not be too dry nor so heavy that folding becomes difficult.*

*Turn into a greased springform tin, the base lined with Gladbake paper, and bake in a fairly slow oven (150°) for about 45–60 minutes until lightly browned on top and shrinking away from sides of tin. Cool briefly in tin then turn on to cake rack. Sift over icing sugar before serving.*

*For variation, add finely grated citrus rind or a little orange flower water to basic mixture.*

# RED HEADS
## FOOD & WINE BAR

Yelka Sever, presently chef at McLaren Vale's newest restaurant, Red Heads Food & Wine Bar, has a long involvement with the McLaren Vale region. She started her cooking career at the Salopian Inn, working with Russell Jeavons, and has since cooked at the Middlebrook winery restaurant, the Victory Hotel and the Star of Greece cafe. In autumn she likes to feature quinces, which are prolific in the McLaren Vale region. The smoked racks of lamb are prepared to order by Willunga butchery Hamlets, where Swiss-born Dominic Betschart cures and smokes his own ham, bacon and sausages.

## SMOKED LAMB RACKS WITH QUINCES AND WHITE PORT GLAZE

SERVES 4

*4 racks of lamb – smoked • 4 quinces • 250 g sugar • 500 ml beef glaze • 100 ml white port*

*Peel, core and quarter the quinces. Poach in a syrup (250 g sugar and 500 ml water) until they are soft and have a nice colour.*

*In a saucepan bring the glaze to a boil, add quince cores and peel. Simmer about 20 minutes. Strain. Place the glaze back on the heat, add the white port and simmer 5 minutes. Slice quince quarters in half and add to the sauce. heat through.*

TO COOK THE LAMB:

*Score the lamb racks and seal in a frying pan for about 5 minutes. Place in 180–200° oven and cook for 15–20 minutes (for medium rare); cooking time depends on size of racks and taste preferences. Remove from oven, cut in half, arrange on a plate with quinces and pour over the glaze.*

## UPSIDE-DOWN QUINCE TART

*5 large quinces – peeled, cored and quartered • 2 l water • 1 kg white sugar • lemon rind • 1 cinnamon stick*

*Place quinces in baking dish and cover with water. Sprinkle over the sugar. Add lemon rind and cinnamon stick. Poach in a moderate oven for about 4 hours until the quinces are soft and a deep red colour.*

FOR THE CARAMEL:

*250 g butter • 250 g sugar*

*In a saucepan melt the butter and sugar and cook until the sugar starts to caramelise to a golden colour. Pour into a shallow 23 cm cake tin and arrange the quince quarters over the caramel nice and firm, filling in any gaps.*

PASTRY:

*250 g puff pastry or shortcrust pastry*

*Roll out the pastry and place on top of the quinces, trimming off any excess, and leaving about a 2 cm overhang for shrinkage. Bake in a moderate oven for 25–30 minutes or until the pastry is golden brown. Remove from the oven and cool for 5–10 minutes. Place a plate over the tin and turn upside down. The caramel will drizzle over the quinces.*

    *Serve with cream or icecream, or crème anglaise.*

# KAY CAZZOLATO, WOODSTOCK COTERIE

Woodstock Coterie is both the restaurant attached to Woodstock Winery and the label for a range of jams and jellies, preserves and pickles, chutneys and relishes made on the premises by Kay Cazzolato, using produce from the winery and its gardens.

## PASSIONFRUIT CURD

*Combine 8 eggs, juice and rind of 4 lemons, 250 g butter, 2 cups passionfruit pulp and ½ cup sugar in heatproof bowl. Cook over simmering water, beating, until thick. Great in tarts, crepes, cakes.*

## PICKLED FIGS

*Make up a very sweet pickling vinegar using 1 litre white wine vinegar, 1 kg sugar, cinnamon stick, bay leaves, whole mustard seeds, cracked black pepper and salt. Add small golden figs, bring to simmering point and simmer until softened. Bottle in warm sterilised jars and seal.*

*Pickled mushrooms are prepared in the same way, with the addition of sliced onion; bring to boiling point then remove from heat. For pickled fennel add fennel seeds to the vinegar.*

## MUSTARD FRUITS

Kay uses peaches, apricots, melons, figs, apples and pears. Cherries and plums are also great but need to be kept separate as their colour tinges all other fruits pink.

*Cook the fruits in a sweet vinegar (as for pickled figs), starting with the firmest such as apples. When all are softened add dry mustard, mixed with water, to taste. Whole chillies may also be included.*

## WINE JELLY

With her kitchen next to a winery, Kay is fortunate enough to be able to collect grape juice – chardonnay and cabernet, for example – straight from the vat. For her jellies, fresh grape juice is strained and cooked with an equal volume of sugar until the jelly sets. It is allowed to cool slightly and then bottled. Kay sometimes adds a dash of rosewater or cinnamon stick for variation.

## OLIVE OIL AND ALMOND CAKE

The McLaren Vale team of Russell Jeavons, Kay Cazzolato, Heidi Bracko and Pip Forrester prepared this cake as part of their menu for the 1997 Australian Regional Culinary Competition, using tangelo as their choice of citrus fruit and accompanying the cake with poached pears, fresh cream and honeycomb. Kay says any citrus fruit can be used – orange, mandarin, grapefruit or lime – or, alternatively, sauterne or sweet white wine, but the grated rind is an essential.

*7 eggs • 140 g caster sugar (about ½ cup plus 1 tblspn) • grated rind of ½ tangelo and ½ lime or equivalent • 1 cup plain flour • 50 g (½ cup) almond meal • ½ cup olive oil • ½ cup citrus juice (or sweet white wine)*

*Preheat oven to 180°. Separate eggs. Beat yolks with half sugar till light and fluffy, add grated citrus rind. Beat egg whites until stiff with remaining sugar. Mix together dry ingredients. Mix olive oil and juice into egg yolk mixture, then fold in dry ingredients and lastly, gently fold in the beaten whites.*

*Turn into a greased springform tin, the base lined with Gladbake paper and bake at 180° for 10 minutes, then reduce temperature to 160° and cook for a further 20 minutes.*

## WOODSTOCK PÂTÉ

*The quantities given below make a commercial volume of pâté which, when sealed with jelly, will keep in the refrigerator for two weeks. Proportions may be adjusted to make smaller quantities if desired.*

*500 g bacon • 2 onions • 3 cloves garlic • 750 g butter • 1½ tspns dried Italian herbs • 2–3 bay leaves • 500 g turkey livers • ½ cup muscat • ¼–½ cup cream • salt and freshly ground black pepper*

*Remove rind from bacon and roughly chop. Peel and chop onions, peel and finely chop garlic. Heat 500 g butter in a large pan, add bacon, onion, garlic, herbs and bay leaves and cook over moderate heat for about 5 minutes until onion is soft and transparent. Meanwhile, trim and clean turkey livers.*

*Add remaining butter to pan, add livers and cook briefly, tossing so that they brown all over but remain pink at the centre. Add muscat, remove bay leaves.*

*Puree mixture in a food processor, adding a little cream to obtain the desired consistency. Season to taste with salt and freshly ground pepper.*

*Turn mixture into a loaf tin lined with plastic wrap and place in refrigerator to set. Remove from refrigerator 30 minutes or so before serving, with crusty bread or thin toast.*

*If desired, the surface of the pâté can be covered with a thin layer of jelly. Kay uses equal quantities of wine and orange juice, set with gelatin leaves.*

## ━ HEIDI BRACKO, ━
## STUMP HILL WINE BAR AT THE
## McLAREN VALE & FLEURIEU
## VISITORS' CENTRE

Adjacent to the wine tasting area, this small cafe serves light lunches together with coffee and tea and an assortment of homemade cakes and pastries. Manager Heidi Bracko counts herself fortunate to receive gifts of local produce – backyard passionfruit in late summer, a glut of pumpkins in autumn. Her Lime and Almond Tart is an adaptation of Jane Grigson's Lemon Tart (*Jane Grigson's Fruit Book*, 1983) which takes advantage of limes supplied by Peter Hoffmann, of Hoffmann's Wines.

## LIME AND ALMOND TART

### PASTRY CASE

*250 g plain flour • ¼ cup caster sugar • pinch of salt • 125 g unsalted butter • 2 egg yolks, beaten*

*Combine flour, sugar and salt. Rub in butter. Add egg yolks until combined. Add a little cold water if the pastry is too crumbly. Roll out, line a 28 cm removable-base flan tin, trim edges and chill for 30 minutes. Preheat oven to 200°. Remove from refrigerator, line with foil and dried beans and bake blind for about 7–8 minutes, then remove foil and beans and return to the oven for 2–3 minutes longer.*

### FILLING

*2 large eggs • 100 g caster sugar • 1¼ cups ground almonds • ½ cup thickened cream • 8–10 limes, depending on size*

*Beat the eggs and sugar together. Add the zest of 5 limes and juice of 8–10 limes (enough for about 4 tablespoons juice). Mix in ground almonds and cream. Pour into pastry case and bake at 180° for about 25 minutes until filling is set and lightly browned. Cool and dust with icing sugar.*

*Serve with fresh berries in season* [Heidi uses local strawberries, blueberries, golden raspberries and whatever comes her way] *and cream, or with a simple syrup of lime juice and sugar.*

## ⟶ McLAREN VALE ⟵
## OLIVE GROVE

The Olive Grove serves snacks and light lunches featuring its various products. For the 'Olive Picker's Lunch', for example, a tray is set with a flask of olive oil, crusty bread and small bowls containing kalamata olives, kalamata olive pesto, dukkah, hard-boiled egg, cheddar cheese, gherkins and pickled onions. Other snacks include a simple bruschetta and warm dukkah bread.

## BRUSCHETTA

*Spread slices of bread with olive oil and finely chopped garlic, toast or lightly bake, top with fresh tomato slices and drizzle with kalamata pesto. Garnish with fresh basil leaves and accompany with a bowl of kalamata olives.*

## DUKKAH BREAD

*Slice a baguette in half lengthwise, brush generously with olive oil, sprinkle with dukkah and heat in oven or under grill.*

# ELIZABETH BAXTER, OLIVER'S COUNTRY CUISINE

Oliver's offers a small menu of simple, homely food prepared by Elizabeth Baxter, who bases her cooking on recipes from her mother, dating back to the 1920s – and quite probably her mother was using recipes of her own grand-mother. Elizabeth's mother was 'a fabulous cook' who excelled at pastry-making and who liked working with yeast. One of the most popular choices at Oliver's is the Ned Kelly pie, a yeast crust filled with savoury mince and shaped 'like little money bags', says Elizabeth. They are served with home-made tomato chutney and vegetables or salad.

## NED KELLY PIES

### YEAST CRUST

*4 cups bread flour • 1 dessertspoon salt • 2 dessertspoons dry yeast • 1 dessertspoon sugar • 1 dessertspoon cooking oil • 2 cups lukewarm water • 1 egg, beaten (to glaze)*

*Sift the dry ingredients, make well in centre, add oil and water and mix to a firm dough. Knead for 5–10 minutes and prove in a warm place until it has doubled in size.*

*Punch down and divide into 12 portions.*

*Roll each portion into a 6 inch (15 cm) circle on a lightly floured board, using a saucer as a guide. Put a heaped tablespoon of filling in the centre of each, bring the edges of the pastry together, pinch a frill across the top.*

*Place on greased baking sheets and glaze with a lightly beaten egg.*

*Bake in a moderate oven (180°) for 20–25 minutes.*

FILLING

*300 g minced steak • 30 g butter • 1 onion, finely chopped • 2 teaspoons curry powder • 1½ cups water • 1 beef stock cube • 3 tablespoons tomato paste • ½ teaspoon mixed herbs • salt and pepper*

*Heat butter in a pan, add meat and brown well, pour off excess fat. Add chopped onion, curry powder, water, crumbled stock cube, tomato paste, mixed herbs, salt and pepper. Stir until all ingredients are combined, bring to the boil, reduce heat and simmer uncovered for 30–40 minutes. Cool before using.*

## MARGARET WALKER, LACEWOOD

Margaret Walker and her husband, Brian, own a mixed fruit orchard at McLaren Flat, growing apricots, peaches, nectarines, plums, apples, pears, quinces, mulberries and passionfruit. She started making jam with the first apricots of the 1994 season, and soon began expanding her range of preserves, often using recipes from her grandmother's 1930s handwritten recipe book. In 1998 she opened a new production kitchen on the property and launched a new range of products using some of the bush foods now being grown locally. Southern Vales Bush Food Inc is promoting the growing in the McLaren Vale region of Australian native food plants which, while not necessarily indigenous to the region, belong to the selection identified as being suitable for commercial cultivation in Australia.

Margaret's bush food range includes a wild lime and apricot spread, marmalade with lemon myrtle, vinegar flavoured with wild lime and lemon myrtle, and olive oil flavoured with bush tomato, lemon myrtle, pepper-corns, pimento, mustard seed, coriander and dried chilli.

Following are two of her recipes.

## BUSH TOMATO BEEF

*1½ tablespoons ground bush tomatoes (available commercially) • 6 pieces braising steak • 2 tbspns olive oil • 1 cup red wine • bush pepper or black pepper • salt • 1 large onion • 1 small tin tomatoes*

*Mix together the ground bush tomatoes, pinch of salt and pepper and press into both sides of the braising steak. Fry for 2 mins each side in a small amount of olive oil until sealed, and place on a warm plate.*

*Chop the onion and gently sweat it in a small amount of olive oil until clear, add the tin of tomatoes together with the red wine, and simmer for 5 mins.*

*Add the steaks and simmer for approx ¾ hour or until the steak is tender.*

*If the sauce requires a little thickening this can be done with a little cornflour.*

*Serve with rice or pasta and vegetables.*

## PASSION JAM

*2 kg ripe tomatoes • pulp of 12 passionfruit • 2.5 kg sugar • juice of a lemon or lime*

*Peel and chop the tomatoes and place them in a jam pan to simmer for approx 30 mins, when the liquid should be reduced by about ¼. Add the passionfruit pulp, lemon juice and sugar and cook for approx 30 mins or until a setting point has been reached.*

*The jam is a rich golden colour with the passionfruit seeds showing through the clear preserve.*

*Heat jars for 15 mins in a 180° oven and fill while still warm. Seal when cold.*

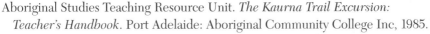

# SELECT BIBLIOGRAPHY

Aboriginal Studies Teaching Resource Unit. *The Kaurna Trail Excursion: Teacher's Handbook*. Port Adelaide: Aboriginal Community College Inc, 1985.

Amery, Rob, ed. *Warra Kaurna: A Resource for Kaurna Language Programs*. First publ. 1995. Revised ed. Adelaide: Warra Kaurna Language Project, Inbarendi College, 1997.

Angas, George French. *South Australia Illustrated*. London: Thomas M'Lean, 1847. Facs. rpt. Sydney: Reed, 1967.

Archives Committee, Willunga Branch of the National Trust of South Australia. *Willunga Courthouse and Police Station*. Revised ed. Willunga, 1976.

Baxendale, Ruth & Lush, Faye. *Willunga Walks*. Fourth ed. Willunga, 1995.

Bleasdale, John. *On Colonial Wines*. Melbourne: Mason, Firth, & McCutcheon, 1873.

Boehm, E.W. *Deep in My Vineyard*. McLaren Vale: Seaview Winery, 1987.

Boomsma, C.D. *Native Trees of South Australia*. Adelaide: Department of Woods and Forests, 1972.

Brunato, Madeleine. *McLaren Flat Methodist Church: a brief history*. McLaren Flat, 1966.

Bull, John Wrathall. *Early Experiences of Life in South Australia and An Extended Colonial History*. Adelaide: E.S. Wigg & Son; London: Sampson Low, Marston, Searle & Rivington, 1884.

Burden, Rosemary. *Wines & Wineries of the Southern Vales.* Adelaide: Rigby, 1976.

Burgess, H.T., ed. *Cyclopaedia of South Australia in two volumes: An historical and commercial review*. Adelaide: Cyclopaedia Co, 1907–09. Facs. rpt. Adelaide: Austaprint, 1978.

Campbell, Jean. *James Cant 1911–87, Dora Chapman 1911–95*. Sydney: The Beagle Press, 1995.

Colwell, Max. *The History of the Noarlunga District*. Noarlunga: Noarlunga District Council, 1972.

Conigrave, J.F. *South Australian Manufactures & Industries: a paper read at a meeting of the Chamber of Manufactures, Nov. 1875*. Adelaide: W.K. Thomas & Co, 1875.

de Castella, Hubert. *John Bull's Vineyard: Australian sketches*. Melbourne: Sands & McDougall, 1886. Facs. rpt. Burwood: Overseas Press Service, 1981.

Department of Primary Industry. *Report of the Inquiry into the Grape and Wine Industries*. Canberra: AGPS, 1985.

Dunstan, Martin. *Willunga, town and district 1837–1950*. 4 vols. Adelaide: Lynton Publications/Investigator Press, 1977, 1978, 1979, 1987.

Education Department of South Australia. *The Kaurna People: Aboriginal People of the Adelaide Plains*. Adelaide: Education Dept of SA, 1989.

Edwards, Robert. *The Kaurna People of the Adelaide Plains*. Adelaide: South Australian Museum, 1972.

Ewens, L.J. *Willunga, a pioneer district*. Adelaide: Pioneers' Association of South Australia, 1957.

Franek Savarton & Associates. *Greening of the South: Executive Summary*. Adelaide, 1990.

Gara, Tom. The life of Ivaritji ('Princess Amelia') of the Adelaide tribe. *Journal of the Anthropological Society of South Australia* 1990; 28 (1): 64–104.

Gerner, Sanderson, Faggetter, Cheesman. *Willunga Post Office & Telegraph Station (62 High Street) Heritage Study & Restoration Report*. Adelaide, 1978.

Groome, Howard & Irvine, Jan. *The Kaurna, First People in Adelaide*. Adelaide: Tjintu Books, 1981.

Hall, R.H. *The Story of the Southern Districts War Memorial Hospital Incorporated 1945–69*. McLaren Vale, 1969.

Hallack, E.H. *Our Townships, Farms and Homesteads: Southern District of South Australia*. Adelaide: WK Thomas & Co, 1892.

Harcus, William, ed. *South Australia: its history, resources and productions*. London: Sampson Low, Marston, Searle & Rivington/Adelaide: W.C. Cox, Government Printer, 1876.

Hart, Deborah. *John Olsen*. Sydney: Craftsman House, 1991.

Hassell & Moana Landcare with Kaurna Heritage Group. *Ochre Point Management Plan*. Adelaide, 1995.

Hassell, Kathleen. *The Relations between the Settlers and the Aborigines in South Australia, 1836–1860*. Adelaide: Libraries Board of South Australia, 1966.

Hawker, James. *Early Experiences in South Australia*. Adelaide/Perth/London: E.S. Wigg & Son, 1899. Facs. ed. Adelaide: Libraries Board of South Australia, 1975.

Hemming, Steve. Aborigines at Port Willunga: Reminiscences of Thomas Martin. *Journal of the Anthropological Society of South Australia* 1985; 23 (9): 24–28.

Norman, Peter L., comp. *Four Hewetts venture north: A History of Charles Thomas Hewett and Four of his Children*. Adelaide, 1986.

Peters, Audrey M., comp. *History of Charles Thomas Hewett and his second son Onesimus Hewett*. Adelaide, 1983.

Hoad, J.L. *Hotels and Publicans in South Australia 1836–1984*. Adelaide: Australian Hotels Association and Gould Books, 1986.

Hylton, Jane. *Adelaide Angries: South Australian painting of the 1940s*. Adelaide: Art Gallery Board of South Australia, 1989.

Hylton, Jane. *The Painted Coast: Views of the Fleurieu Peninsula south of Adelaide from 1836*. Adelaide: Art Gallery Board of South Australia, 1998.

Kelly, A.C. *The Vine in Australia*. Melbourne/Sydney: Sands & Kenny, 1861. Facs. rpt, with introduction by Dennis Hall and Valmai Hankel. Sydney: David Ell Press, 1980.

Klepac, Lou. *Horace Trenerry*. Adelaide: Art Gallery of South Australia, 1970.

Laffer, H.E. *The Wine Industry of Australia*. Adelaide: Australian Wine Board, 1949.

Lake, Max. *Classic Wines of Australia*. Brisbane: Jacaranda Press, 1966.

Lawrence, Susan & Jackman, Greg. *Historical Archeological survey of Port Willunga Linear Park*. Report on behalf of Archeology Department, Flinders University, to the District Council of Willunga, 1995.

Leigh, W.H. *Travels and Adventures in South Australia, 1836–38*. First publ. 1839. Sydney: Currawong Press, 1982.

Light, William. *A Brief Journal*. First publ. Adelaide, 1839. Facs. rpt. Adelaide: Public Library of South Australia, 1962.

Linn, Rob. *Cradle of Adversity: A history of the Willunga District*. Adelaide: Historical Consultants, 1991.

Manning, Geoffrey H. *Hope Farm Chronicle: Pioneering Tales of South Australia*. Adelaide, 1984.

Manning, Geoffrey H. *Hope Farm, Cradle of the McLaren Vale Wine Industry*. Adelaide, 1980.

Manning, Geoffrey H. *The Tragic Shore*. Willunga: National Trust of South Australia, Willunga Branch, 1988.

McDougall, Kate & Vines, Elizabeth. *Willunga District Heritage Survey*. Adelaide, 1997.

McDougall, Katrina. *Winery Buildings in South Australia 1836 to 1936: The Southern Districts*. Working Paper 7, Department of Architecture, University of Adelaide, May 1993.

McMurtrie, Audrey. *McMurtrie History*. McLaren Vale, 1977.

Meyer, H.A.E. *Manners & Customs of the Aborigines of the Encounter Bay Tribe, SA*. Adelaide: George Dehane, 1846.

Moody, Clarence. *South Australian Cricket: Reminiscences of Fifty Years*. Adelaide: W.K. Thomas & Co, 1898.

Morphett, Sir John. *South Australia: latest information from this colony, contained in a letter written by Mr. Morphett, dated Nov. 25th, 1836*. London: John Gliddon, 1837. Facs. rpt. Adelaide: Public Library of South Australia, 1962.

Murphy, Dan. *The Australian Wine Guide*. Melbourne: Sun Books, 1966.

Newman, Lareen. *Environmental History of the Willunga Basin 1830s to 1990s*. Honours thesis, Department of Geography, University of Adelaide, 1994.

Olliver J.G., Scott D.C. & Young D.A. *Willunga Slate Deposits: A Review of the History, Geology and Mining of the Roofing Slate Industry of South Australia*. Report Book 76/23, South Australian Department of Mines and Energy.

Parkinson, Tony. *Historic Willunga: from original pencil drawings*. Willunga, 1971.

Pike, Douglas. *Paradise of Dissent: South Australia 1829–1857*. Second ed. Melbourne: Melbourne University Press, 1967.

Planning Branch, City of Noarlunga. *Noarlunga Local Heritage Inventory*. Noarlunga, 1996.

Pointon, Rev. J. Harrold. *Methodism in the Willunga Circuit*. Reprinted from *The South Australian Methodist*. Adelaide: Gillingham & Co, 1957.

Pridmore, Adele. *The Rich Valley: An Account of the Early Life of McLaren Vale*. McLaren Vale Institute Committee, 1949.

Richards, Eric, ed. *The Flinders History of South Australia: Social History*. Adelaide: Wakefield Press, 1986.

Ross, Betty, ed. *Aboriginal and Historic Places around Metropolitan Adelaide and the South Coast*. Moana Sub-Committee of the Anthropological Society of South Australia Incorporated, 1985.

*South Australia in 1842, by one who lived there nearly four years*. London: J.C. Hailes, 1843. Facs. rpt. Adelaide: Libraries Board of South Australia, 1971.

*South Australia: its history, progress, resources, and present position*. Adelaide: W.K. Thomas & Co, 1880.

South Australian Department of Fisheries. *Aldinga Reef Aquatic Reserve*. Adelaide, 1992.

South Australian State Planning Authority. *Metropolitan Development Plan: Supplementary Development Plan, Part Willunga Rural Area*. Adelaide, 1978.

Stephens, John. *The Land of Promise; being an authentic and impartial history . . . of South Australia . . . embracing a full account of the South Australian Company, with . . . numerous letters from settlers . . . By One Who is Going*. London: Smith Elder, 1839. Facs. rpt. with intro by Rob Linn, Adelaide, 1988.

Stow, J.P. *South Australia: its history, productions and natural resources*. Adelaide, E. Spiller, Government Printer, 1883.

Talbot, M.R. *A Chance to Read: A History of the Institutes Movement in South Australia*. Adelaide: Libraries Board of South Australia, 1992.

Taplin, G., ed. *The folklore, manners, customs and languages of the South Australian Aborigines*. First publ. 1879. Facs. rpt. Adelaide, 1989.

*The Art of Ivor Hele*. Preface by Sir Will Ashton. Adelaide, Rigby, 1966.

*The Hardy Tradition: tracing the growth and development of a great wine-making family through its first hundred years*. Adelaide: Thomas Hardy & Sons, 1953.

Tindale, Norman B. *Aboriginal Tribes of Australia*. Berkeley: University of California Press, 1974.

Tolmer, Alexander. *Reminiscences of an adventurous and chequered career at home and at the antipodes*. London: Sampson, Low, Marston, Searle, & Rivington: 1882. Facs. rpt. Adelaide: Libraries Board of South Australia, 1972.

Towler, David J. *A Fortunate Locality: A history of Noarlunga and district*. Adelaide: Peacock Publications, 1986.

Twidale C.R., Tyler M.J., Webb B.P., eds. *Natural History of the Adelaide Region*. Adelaide: Royal Society of South Australia Inc, 1976.

Vaughan, Malcolm. *The Development of Agriculture and the Slate Industry in the Willunga area in the Nineteenth Century*. Advanced Diploma of Teaching thesis, Salisbury CAE, 1973.

Vine Hall, Nick. *Buxton Forbes Laurie of Southcote*. Sydney, 1976.

Vivienne, May. *Sunny South Australia*. Adelaide: Hussey & Gillingham, 1908.

Ward, Ebenezer. *The vineyards and orchards of South Australia*. Adelaide: The Advertiser, 1862. Facs. rpt. Adelaide, 1979.

Whitington, Ernest. *The South Australian vintage 1903*. Adelaide: WK Thomas & Co, 1903. Facs. rpt. Friends of the State Library of South Australia, 1997.

Wilkinson, George Blakiston. *The working man's handbook to South Australia*. London: Murray, 1849.

Williams, Michael. *The Making of the South Australian Landscape*. London/New York: Academic Press, 1974.

Willington, Joan Kyffin, ed. *Maisie: her life, her loves, her letters, 1898 to 1902*. Adelaide: Wakefield Press, 1992.

Willunga Basin Planning Strategy Steering Committee. *Economic Study of the Willunga Basin*. Adelaide, 1994.

*Willunga, 'place of green trees': A brief history*. Willunga Progress Association, 1952.

*Willunga, Aldinga, McLaren Vale & Noarlunga Agricultural & Horticultural Society Inc. A Souvenir History, 1856–1961*. Adelaide: Show Society, 1961.

Wilson, Shirley Cameron. *From Shadows into Light: South Australian Women Artists since Colonisation*. Adelaide: Delmont, 1988.

Wollaston E.M., ed. *The Aldinga Scrub Conservation Park: A report on its history and natural values*. Adelaide: Nature Conservation Board of South Australia Inc, n.d.

Wood, Vivienne. *Aboriginal heritage desktop study for the proposed re-establishment of the Washpool Lagoon and wetlands, Aldinga*. Report to Kinhill Engineers Pty Ltd, 1996.

Wyatt, William. The Adelaide Tribe. In *The Native Tribes of South Australia*. Adelaide: E.S. Wigg, 1879.

# LOCAL HISTORY COLLECTIONS

**National Trust of South Australia**. Archives

**Aldinga Library.** Local history files including oral histories from:
Mrs Constance Martin, Tom Strout.
Eatts, R.T. *As I remember Aldinga & Sellicks.*
Fisher, Helen. *Memories of Aldinga Beach: First and lasting impressions in 1934 – aged 4 years – and on.*
Kangarilla Progress Association Inc. *Kangarilla Historical Records: A tribute to the Early Pioneers.* First publ. 1955. Facs. rpt, 1975.
Hay, Nancy E. *Aldinga Christmas Holidays diary 1946–51.*
Pretty, W.A. *Almond Growing in South Australia (at Willunga).* 1976
Sparrow, Jack. *The Life of Jack Connor Sparrow of McLaren Vale*
Thomason, Eric. *A History of Maslin Beach, South Australia.*
Vaudrey, D.P., Vaudrey G.C. *Facts, Facets and Phases: A Potpouri of Items.* Four parts, 1991–93.
Vaudrey, G.C. *Samuel White of White's Valley 1840–1868.* Willunga, 1989.
Vaudrey, G.C., Vaudrey, D.P. *Philip Hollins of the Horseshoe Inn.* Willunga, 1993.
Weisbrodt, Nancy, in conjunction with her father, Kenneth William Hay.
   *Memories of Aldinga Beach 1942–1951 – The Boat Harbour.*
*South Australian Company Records 1839–1949.* Mortlock Library, BRG 42.
   Selected records relating to Willunga District.

**Noarlunga Library**. Local history files including oral histories from: May Amos, Colin Clements, Geo. C. Davies, Chrystabel Duell, Eric and Kathleen Dungey, Cliff England, Lilian Gawley, Reg Hyde, 'Cud' Kay, Bess McKay, Gwen Rayner.
Gadd, Fae. *Goin' to Christies.* n.d.

**Willunga Courthouse and Police Station Museum**
Scrapbooks and newspaper cuttings, including those collections maintained by the Willunga branch of the National Trust and the Aldinga library, together with the memoirs of Mary Maud Aldam, Fred Low and Mrs Ethel Martin of Nene Farm, McLaren Vale and Fred Low.

# ACKNOWLEDGMENTS

Many individuals and institutions have contributed to the making of this book, which was initially made possible by a Commission grant to Wakefield Press from the Literature Fund of the Australia Council. The support of the City of Onkaparinga is also gratefully acknowledged.

The resources of the State Library of South Australia, and in particular the Mortlock Library, were extremely useful, and the assistance of the Library and of its staff is greatly appreciated. The State Library of South Australia holds extensive wine literature, menu collections, and over 70,000 photographs depicting life in South Australia.

The Local Studies Collections of the Noarlunga, Aldinga and Willunga libraries were also valuable, and I would like to acknowledge the generosity of Faye Lush, Team Leader, Collection Management, City of Onkaparinga Library Service.

The Art Gallery of South Australia allowed access to its research library and, through Jane Hylton, Curator of Australian Art, authorised reproduction of images from the Gallery's collection.

Robert Hannaford graciously allowed reproduction of his painting , Maslin Beach; and John Perkins, Art Curator at the University of Adelaide, gave permission to reproduce H.P. Gill's painting Evening, Mouth of the Onkaparinga.

The Aboriginal Education Unit of the Department of Education, Training and Employment authorised reproduction of the map, Adelaide Plains prior to European Settlement.

Both the National Trust of South Australia and the State Heritage Commission made available their documentary resources for consultation.

Val Power A.M., representing Garnet Wilson, Chairperson of the South Australian Aboriginal Heritage Committee, advised me on Kaurna history and legend.

Bill Hardy arranged for me to use the scrapbook of Thomas Hardy and other Hardy family records.

The staff of McLaren Vale Winemakers, and in particular Heather Budich, have been particularly helpful throughout the whole project.

Local historian Ruth Baxendale guided me through the mazes of local history and always came up with the right information; Vanessa Caterall set me straight for the Noarlunga area; and Russell Jeavons helped me to see the region through his eyes.

Among the many individuals who offered information and advice, I would like to mention the following: Rob Amery, Elizabeth Baxter, Sophie Bickford, Sue Bridle, Tony Brooks, Zar Brooks, Kay Cazzolato, Philip Clark, Tony Cole, Ian Collett, David and Joan Dallwitz, Andrew Davies, David Dean, David Dridan, Elva Dyer, Zannie Flanagan, Kerry Flanagan, Pip Forrester, Rosemary Gartelmann, Emmanuel Giakoumis, Simon Gladewright, David Hardy, Valmai Hankel, Ross Haynes, Jeff

How, Iris Iwanicki, Alex Johnston, Philip Jones, Kaurna Aboriginal Heritage Committee and 'Cud' Kay, Colin Kay, Margo Kellett, Heidi Lacis, Ann Lavis, John Lawrie, Kate McDougall, Mark Lloyd, Ken Maxwell, Andrew Oliver, Sue Oliver, d'Arry Osborn, Anne Pollard, Lesley Redgate, Sue Reggione, Ben Riggs, Murray Roberts, Henry Rymill, Vince Scarfo, Dom Scarpantoni, Yelka Sever, Hugo Shaw, Tracy Siviour, Mark Staniforth, Brian Swanston, Greg Trott, Andy Tyler, Margaret Walker, Ruth Wallace, Paul Watson, Gerry Wedd, Nancy Weisbrodt, Clive Whitrow, Geoff Wilson.

Without these people and others, past and present, the stories could not have been written; but they were my fingers that flew over the keyboard, and I accept responsibility for any discrepancies of fact or interpretation.

Finally, I express my heartfelt thanks to Christo Reid for his superbly evocative photographs, and to both Wakefield Press and Liz Nicholson of Design Bite, for making this book happen.

Publisher's note
Every attempt has been made to ascertain and procure the copyright owners' permission to use the chosen artistic work. In the event of outstanding claims please contact the publishers.

# PHOTOGRAPHS
## AND ILLUSTRATIONS

All colour illustrations are the work of Christo Reid, together with the black-and-white images on pages 45, 59, 70–71, 72, 91, 92–93, 105, 121, 166, 185, 186, 199, 268 and 297.

The plan of the harbourmaster's cottage at Port Willunga on page 116 is reproduced courtesy of Susan Lawrence and the Archeology Department, Flinders University, from their Historical Archeological Survey of Port Willunga.

Ruth Baxendale supplied the photograph on page 81; Tony Brooks the photographs on pages 87, 168, 190, 195 and 287, together with the one of McLaren Vale winemakers and Cuthbert Burgoyne, 1903, on page 140; Russell Jeavons supplied the photograph of slate on page 102; Bill Hardy the photograph of Thomas Hardy on page 129, together with the Wine Week photographs on pages 148 and 149; David Hardy the André Simon photograph, page 153; McLaren Vale Winemakers the photograph of auction wines, page 154; Bushing King and Queen, page 193; and beach cricket, page 220; Zar Brooks the award reproduced on page 170; Paul Watson the photograph of the Willunga Almond Blossom Festival parade on page 186; Jill Reeves and the McLaren Flat Show Society its badge, page 182; Mark Lloyd the photograph on page 206 and the Coriole label, page 294; Christine Lawrence the photograph of artists at work, page 284; and Glenn Howlett the photograph of his stained glass window on page 292.

The pruning certificate on page 143 is reproduced by courtesy of Ruth and Alec Baxendale. The wine selection (page 151) for the wine-and-cheese party came from The Australian Hostess Cookbook (c. 1969).

The author and publishers gratefully acknowledge the following institutions and individuals who have supplied photographs or given permission for illustrations to be published.

## ART GALLERY OF SOUTH AUSTRALIA

**page 8:**   E.C. Frome (Australia 1802–1890)
Sand-bar at the mouth of the Onkaparinga
1840 Port Noarlunga, South Australia
Watercolour on paper, 15.5 x 22.7 cm
Art Gallery of South Australia, Australia
South Australian Government Grant, Adelaide City Council &
Public Donations 1970

# INDEX

## H

## I

## J

## K

*Also by Wakefield Press*

## SOUTH AUSTRALIA: HORIZONS BEYOND

Tony Baker, Megan Lloyd and David Gibb
with a foreword by Peter Goldsworthy

*South Australia: Horizons Beyond* displays a place where the good life is still possible – where the joys of the grape and the table, consumed under clear skies in a clean environment and accompanied by lively debate, move many to declare that they would not live anywhere else.

The book is a bold photographic portrait of a community moving into the twenty-first century. Evocative images celebrate the state's variety, from its natural wonders to its modern industries. Photographs by South Australia's leading photographers are complemented by contemporary design.

ISBN 1 86254 422 0    RRP $49.95

*Also by Wakefield Press*

# ➤ THE ORIGINAL ➤
# MEDITERRANEAN CUISINE

## MEDIEVAL RECIPES FOR TODAY

### Barbara Santich

'*The Original Mediterranean Cuisine* is a fascinating and intelligent book on a riveting subject. It is packed with gems of information and also provides delicious eating.'
Claudia Roden

'A book to be placed both on the history shelves and on the kitchen table.'
Maggie Beer

'One of the most uncommon cookbooks to reach shelves groaning under the weight of cookbooks.'
Tony Baker

Here is a book that brings authentic medieval food to today's table, with seventy recipes translated and adapted from fourteenth and fifteenth century Italian and Catalan manuscripts.

ISBN 1 86254 331 3   RRP $19.95

*Also by Wakefield Press*

# ⟶ SHE'S A BEAUTY! ⟵

## THE STORY OF THE FIRST HOLDENS

### Don Loffler

This book is a loving history of the first model Holden, the 48-315, known popularly as the FX, and its famous successor, the FJ. These two models have become among the most loved Holdens ever made.

The exciting period between 1945 and 1948, from the building of the first experimental cars to the launch of the Holden, is fully described. Entertaining memories of GMH employees and remarkable survival stories of the earliest Holdens illuminate the book.

Don Loffler has spent sixteen years researching *She's a Beauty!*, corresponding with people all over Australia as well as in the United States, England and Germany. The book includes stories never told before, photographs never published and a wealth of technical information.

ISBN 1 86254 440 9   RRP $29.95

## ～ LOOKING FOR FLAVOUR ～

### Barbara Santich

In *Looking for Flavour* Barbara Santich teases out intriguing issues including regionalism and food culture, the mystique of markets, banquets ancient and modern, the 'language' of food, debates over vegetarianism, and the fascination of the Mediterranean.

She also asks the important questions – can we claim all-Australian dishes, and how do they rate in the culinary world scheme? Whatever happened to the kangaroo steamer, she asks, and may we still eat and enjoy crumbed cutlets?

Above all else Barbara Santich promotes and argues for 'flavour first!'

ISBN 1 86254 385 2    RRP $19.95

Wakefield Press has been publishing good Australian books
for over fifty years. For a catalogue of current and
forthcoming titles, or to add your name to our mailing list,
send your name and address to

Wakefield Press, Box 2266, Kent Town, South Australia 5071.

TELEPHONE (08) 8362 8800  FAX (08) 8362 7592
WEB www.wakefieldpress.com.au

Wakefield Press thanks Wirra Wirra Vineyards and
Arts South Australia for their continued support.